DAUGHTER DETOX

DAUGHTER DETOX

RECOVERING FROM
AN UNLOVING MOTHER
AND
RECLAIMING YOUR LIFE

Peg Streep

Île D'Éspoir Press

New York, New York

ISBN-13: 978-0692973974 (Custom Universal)
ISBN-10: 0692973974

This book was designed by Claudia Karabaic Sargent, and is typeset in the Bodoni URW font family, available through Adobe Typekit.

*For my readers and daughters everywhere
who seek validation of their experiences and need the
support they so sorely lacked in childhood.*

A special thank-you to my own daughter, once again.

TABLE OF CONTENTS

INTRODUCTION

Every week I get messages from women—left as comments on my blog posts, on my Facebook page, and in email—that say the same thing: "I always thought I was the only one with a mother who didn't love her. I feel better knowing that I'm not alone." They usually add, "I'm so relieved to discover that I'm not crazy or imagining that this happened. You have no idea how long I've worried."

Actually, I do. I was an unloved daughter myself.

These women are all ages—from early thirties to mid eighties—and from all walks of life. They are stay-at-home moms, cashiers, doctors, hairdressers, lawyers, professors, secretaries, salespeople, and even therapists. In almost every case, their outward achievements belie how they really feel about themselves; they are still made unhappy by their childhoods, despite the work they do and the families they've raised. They are women who have become devoted mothers but who are still hobbled and hurt. They are women who recognize that they've never reached their full potential, who have hurtled from one relationship disaster to another, unable to get off the merry-go-round. Some have had children while others deliberately chose not to, afraid of repeating history. Some have battled depression, disordered eating, or addictive behaviors and are only now beginning to see how their behaviors connect to their childhoods. They are women who still want their mothers' love and struggle with setting boundaries, wanting to attend family celebrations but still needing to protect themselves. They are women who have chosen to divorce their mothers, opting for peace along with self-orphaning over the status quo.

If you are reading these words, you are most likely one of these daughters—and, no, you are *not* alone. In fact, you have more company than either you or I would ever have imagined. You believed and perhaps still believe, as did my younger self, that you were to blame for your mommy's not loving you. You were afraid—just as I was for many years—to tell anyone because you wanted to be like all the other daughters, the ones who were hugged by their mothers and whose moms smiled when they came into the room. You discovered, when you did confide, that people thought you were being dramatic, because your mom seemed perfectly nice to them, and you were fed and clothed, weren't you? You were probably hopeful—and you might even be now—that somehow, you'd still get your mother to love you. Somehow, maybe tomorrow, or the next day, or the next.

Ours is a story no one wants to hear. Everyone wants desperately to believe that, in a world where love is so hard to find and even harder to hang on to, one kind of love is inviolable—a mother's love.

The truth of the unloving mother who actively wounds, dismisses, or disparages her child in words and actions is a cultural secret no one wants to acknowledge. We suffer alone and in silence in a sea of pastel-tinted sentiments plastered on T-shirts and mugs that say, "Home Is Where Mom Is" and "World's Best Mom." Over the last few years, I've come to see that the sense of isolation—of being singled out in this way, of being labeled as damaged or less than, of being afraid that there is something terribly wrong with you—is just as wounding as the lack of mother love itself. The hole left in our hearts fills with shame, self-doubt, and sometimes, self-loathing. But the discovery that there are others like us—that this is actually a shared experience for count-less numbers of girls and women—is liberating. *Daughter Detox* offers a route to the way out.

That's why I wrote this book. It's filled with stories told to me over the years by daughters whose experiences, while they differ in the details, hurt and changed them just as ours did. But even more important, *Daughter Detox* lays out strategies drawn from science to get out from under the influence of the past so that you can finally become *you*, not just your mother's daughter.

I've written it so that you can come to recognize and understand your childhood experiences, see how they have shaped the person you are in the moment, and take action to help yourself heal and grow into the very best version of you. It's the book I wish I'd had when my mother's voice still played on an endless tape loop in my head.

I'm sure you, too, have struggled with that tape—the one that says you're inadequate, unlovable, stupid, difficult, worthless, fat, or any other variation on the theme. The pages of this book will help you understand the process that internalized that voice and help you locate an off button once and for all and, more important, find another tape, one composed by you, to play.

HOW TO USE THIS BOOK

Each chapter of *Daughter Detox* focuses on a step-by-step process to guide you through the seven stages of reclaiming your life and recovering from childhood. The process includes expanding your understanding of the circumstances of your life, reading stories shared by other daughters, and then using strategies and techniques that are meant to help you move forward. You are working on undoing damage done over the course of many years so you may find yourself needing to go back to a previous chapter even if you've already read it. *That's to be expected: Recovery isn't a linear process.*

Because I'm neither a therapist nor a psychologist, I've drawn on strategies suggested by psychological and other research and, in some cases, steps that have worked for me as an unloved daughter who had to reclaim herself. This book isn't a substitute for therapy, of course, since nothing works quite as well or effectively as one-on-one work with a gifted counselor.

Here are the seven steps and what each of them entails. Journaling exercises for helping you heal organized by chapter and stage can be found beginning on page 235 in Chapter Ten.

Discovery: For many daughters, though not all, the first problem is recognizing the mother wound. There are many reasons—some complicated, some simple—that understanding the connection between the pain and unhappiness you feel and your mother's treatment of you is very hard for many daughters. Even for those who recognize at a young age that their mothers don't love them as a mother should (I was one of them), the full understanding of what this means and how it shapes you in every meaningful way is a slow revelation. The first two chapters of the book are devoted to discovery.

Discernment: Understanding the relational patterns in your family of origin is the goal of this next step. Recognizing how the other people in your early and later life contributed or detracted from your mother's treatment of you is part of your growth; this includes how your father behaved and the attitudes of siblings and other people who formed a part of your childhood world. This step moves past discovery into the path of fully understanding the emotional connections you were exposed to and how they shaped your personality, your view of yourself, and your thoughts and emotions. Teasing out how your own behaviors were formed in response to your treatment by your mother and others is the second stage of discernment. Figuring out your own patterns of attachment—whether you are anxious or avoidant—is part of this step, as are beginning to recognize triggers and starting to work on coping mechanisms to thwart them. Chapters Three and Four focus on discernment.

Distinguish: You're not in your childhood room anymore but the chances are good that you are bringing the relational patterns of the past into the present, and not just with your mother. Getting to the root of your own unhappiness in the present—whether that's an inability to maintain friendships or intimate connections, a sense of isolation, being unable to connect to anyone, constantly fighting with someone you know you love, or a series of relationships that make you feel marginalized or "less than"—is part of being able to distinguish older patterns, which are covered in Chapter Five.

Disarm: This is the heart of *Daughter Detox*: figuring out how not to be the little girl in your childhood home. All of the previous steps lead to this path but it isn't a slam-dunk. Why? It is about both her and you, and you have to bring the unconscious patterns in your behavior, formed in response to your mother's behaviors, into conscious awareness. Specific strategies to deal with ruminative patterns of thought, recognizing emotional triggers, learning to identify and process emotions more productively, and more are the focus of Chapter Six.

Reclaim: This step tackles how to go about changing your thinking and reactions so that you can move on to a new phase of your life. Learning how to harness your motivation so that you can achieve new goals, practical steps for achieving earned secure attachment, and using techniques that help you to reframe your thoughts to stay on track are all part of Chapter Seven.

Redirect: One of the key decisions you'll make as you move forward is redefining your relationship to your mother and most probably other members of your original family. Chapter Eight specifically focuses on helping you decide whether or not you should or can continue to be in contact or not. It details the pros and cons of continuing the relationship and what obstacles and barriers you're likely to face as you put boundaries in place. The decision to go no-contact—its perils and rewards—is also explored in depth. One of the main goals of the redirect step is to enhance your ability to feel self-compassion and, indeed, to mother yourself.

Recover: The final stage involves seeing the healing process as one that is ongoing, and that really incorporating self-acceptance and self-compassion into your life remains a daily task. Using the Japanese art of *kintsugi* as its primary metaphor, this step requires you to understand healing in a different way and to make peace with the pace of the process.

Chapter Ten is devoted to exercises keyed to each of the stages of recovery. You can do them after reading each chapter or at any other time.

ABOUT THE EXERCISES IN DAUGHTER DETOX

Most of the work involved in reclaiming your life from the effects of a toxic childhood is about bringing unconscious patterns of thinking and feeling to the surface so that they can be changed through consciousness. It's all about connecting the dots. A great deal of research attests to the fact that much of what we think is, in fact, not governed by rational and conscious deliberation but by automatic, unconscious thought processes that the brain uses as shortcuts. (To use psychologist Daniel Kahneman's terms, slow thinking versus fast thinking.) Thought processes are also affected by what are called "primes" in the environment, as research by John A. Bargh and Tanya L. Chartrand showed. So the environment in which you do these exercises, including journaling, matters.

Choose a place to sit that makes you feel calm and focused. If a pile of unpaid bills or a sink full of dirty dishes is part of your visual landscape, you're not going to be fully focused. Being in a well-lit space is important. Carve out enough time to do the exercises without interruption. If you are in therapy, do not do these exercises without discussing them with your counselor first.

JOURNALING

Research by James Pennebaker and others has shown that writing helps us not just to make sense of our experiences but also permits us to create a coherent narrative of them. Creating a coherent narrative—connecting the dots between cause and effect—is an important part of healing from a toxic, abusive, or chaotic childhood. Writing has been shown to be a therapeutic tool, provided you follow some simple rules.

Pick a notebook or a blank book for journaling, rather than using single sheets of paper. You should write by hand, rather than using a tablet or computer, because writing longhand uses a different brain circuitry. There's scientific research, too, that shows we remember and think more clearly when we write by hand, rather than type. Remember that this isn't a test, and if writing makes you anxious, start by writing down phrases or words instead of full sentences.

What to Do When You Are Journaling (and What to Avoid)

When you are writing about the past, make sure you are recalling *why* you felt as you did, not *what* you felt. Focusing on why you felt as you did is done best by recalling an event or experience as if from a great distance or as if it happened to someone else. This is called "cool processing." The problem with remembering what you felt—which is called "hot processing"—is that if the feelings are vivid enough, they can actually put you emotionally back in the moment, act as a trigger for rumination, and effectively set you back a step or two. If you find yourself hot processing—remembering the pain you felt as a child when your mother taunted you or ignored you, or recalling a moment when you felt hopelessly alone and adrift—stop writing immediately. You need to be able to recall in the cool way.

The first stop is *discovery*. It's the first baby step in the direction of understanding and, ultimately, healing.

Chapter One
The Truth About Maternal Power

I've spent the last 25 years trying to get my mother's voice out of my head—the voice that tells me it's just a matter of time until everyone realizes I'm not who I seem. The tape still plays when I get anxious, but, most days, I can muddle through and ignore it.

~Alexis, 40

The baby girl, just one month past her first birthday, is perched on the long Plexiglas table, her hands and chubby knees touching its cool, smooth surface. She's round-faced and smiling at her mother, who's on the other side, out of reach. Even though she's not walking yet, this baby in her pink coveralls is a confident crawler; she's calm and more curious than anything else about her unfamiliar surroundings.

The Plexiglas she's on is part of a very famous experiment called the "Visual Cliff," originally designed and conceived of by scientist Eleanor Gibson to test whether depth perception was innate or learned. The idea came to this mother of two as her young children played near the edge of the Grand Canyon on a family vacation while she fretted about their safety. In the experiment, a checkerboard pattern lies flush under the Plexiglas for half of its length, but then the fabric slants some four feet, creating the illusion of a sheer drop beneath the solid surface. Gibson and her colleague Richard Walker tested rats, kittens, puppies, and baby goats, as well as human infants, and discovered that once an animal or infant was old enough to locomote, depth perception had kicked in, causing them to screech to a halt at the sight of the drop. Babies crawled readily across the "shallow" end, but only a very few dared to take on the "deep" end. Even when there was a toy placed at the end to lure them, babies typically stopped their crawling at the point of the illusion of a drop-off.

James Sorce and his colleagues took the cliff experiment one step further, exploring what a one-year-old does when her eyes are telling her one thing—Yikes! There's a drop ahead!—while her palms and knees, solid against the plastic, are telling her another. When her sensory perceptions contradict each other, how does she resolve the ambiguity? She looks to her mother for guidance.

The researchers had the babies' mothers stand on the deep end and assume various facial expressions. It's in this experiment, among others, that the extent of maternal power becomes crystalline. When the researchers had the mothers look happy and smiling, they discovered that an astonishing 74 percent of the babies began crawling and kept going, even over the deep end. The signals conveyed by their cheery mothers' faces—All is well! You're safe!—caused the babies to ignore the danger of a drop ahead that their own senses registered. In contrast, an angry face from their mothers on the other side was enough to stop every baby in his or her tracks. Some babies actually retreated, crawling backward, at the sight of their mothers' disapproving expressions.

What's extraordinary about the results of the "Visual Cliff" isn't just that one-year-olds seek out and react to the emotions their mothers express, but that they rely on them sufficiently to override their own sensory perceptions about what is safe and what is dangerous. That's called total trust; after all, the baby doesn't know the drop isn't real.

This and other experiments revealed that an infant is hardwired to use her mother's expressions, tones of voice, and behaviors as her lodestar for navigating life, long before she understands words or the complexity of the world. It's a process that appears to begin even before birth: One study showed that the heart rates of near-term babies in utero increased when tapes of their mothers reading poems were played and slowed when they were played a tape of a stranger's voice. Babies are born recognizing their mothers' voices, can distinguish them from other female voices, and can identify their mothers by smell. Infants as young as five days old undergoing a neonatal heel pinprick can even derive comfort from smelling the scent of their mothers' breast milk. They have been shown to self-soothe faster and cry less than babies exposed to the scent of a stranger's breast milk or formula undergoing the same pinprick. Another experiment showed that a mother's voice calmed and stopped agitated motor movements in babies one to four days old.

Because it takes a human infant so long to reach maturity and take care of herself—compared to a newt or duckling or fawn, say—evolution has assured that she is exquisitely sensitive to her mother, adept at "reading" her cues in the most subtle ways. That is not, as we'll see, always a bonus, since evolutionary adaptation is focused on aiding survival in times of stress, not necessarily on fostering psychological wellbeing. Adaptation, it turns out, is a yin/yang thing.

Notably, there's no parallel evolutionary development of responsiveness in human mothers; there's only the reproductive equipment to bear a child and produce breast milk, a mix of hormones, but not an innate ability to nurture or love. In truth, elephants are more instinctually suited to mother well than humans. This is perhaps unnerving news for most people, who like to believe that being a "good mother" is something that comes naturally and automatically.

In fact, some infant and toddler behaviors appear to have evolved with the absence of hardwiring of mothers' love taken into account. To make sure that mothers don't forget their babies—either in the fields during hunter-gatherer times or at the mall or in a car seat today—the infant's cry is pitched in such a way to get the attention of the adult brain. That's why you can't sleep through that baby's wail on a crowded plane—even though it's not yours and you may not even be a parent. A study by Katie Young and Christine Parsons showed that the more primitive parts of the brain were activated by the sound of an infant's cry within 100 milliseconds—yes, that's one tenth of a second. Basically, that means that your brain is on high alert before you've even consciously registered the cry. And if you're wondering, none of that happens when adults sob, dogs bark, or cats meow.

And it gets even more interesting. Consider whining, for example. Why whine, scientists asked? Why not grunt or wheeze or yell? Like that high-pitched infant cry, the pitch and modulation of the whine are much more effective than other sounds in terms of intruding into and penetrating a mother's consciousness. In fact, the whine—as shown in a study by Rosemarie Sokol Chang and Nicholas S. Thompson—was the most effective way of distracting participants so that they couldn't even perform the simplest of subtraction tasks.

So babies are not just hardwired to need their mothers' attention and love but also come equipped with behaviors that make it hard for their mothers to ignore them; you can think of infants as heat-seeking missiles, in search of love, protection, and attunement. This is why, if your connection to your mother has been fraught, difficult, or downright damaging, a very big part of you still wants and needs her love, no matter what. There doesn't appear to be an expiration date on that need either.

More than half of the time, children get what they need to thrive and to explore the world with a reliable person—their mother—as a safe home base. This is called "secure attachment," a psychological construct first proposed by John Bowlby and later expanded by his student Mary Ainsworth. It was Ainsworth's experiment, the "Strange Situation," that shed new light on the mother's power and influence, and her ability to shape how her child connected to the world at large, not just in childhood but also throughout life.

APPRECIATING THE "STRANGE SITUATION"

Ainsworth's line of inquiry went beyond the automatic responses supplied by evolutionary hardwiring and looked at how the infant's experiences with her mother shaped her innate responses. What she discovered would revolutionize not just the understanding of the extraordinary and lasting influence a mother has on her offspring but would also shine a bright light on why some individuals are able to forge close and sustaining emotional connections and others aren't.

The "Strange Situation" was a series of staged encounters, beginning with the mother and child coming into the unfamiliar lab room. The mother would sit back as the child played and explored the room. Then a stranger would enter, speak to the mother, and approach the infant; while the baby was distracted, the mother would leave the room. The child would realize her mother was gone, and the stranger would interact with the child. Afterward, the mother would return and comfort the child, while the stranger left. The mother would again exit, and the child would be alone in the room. The stranger would enter and respond to the child. Finally, the mother would return, pick up the infant, and the stranger would exit inconspicuously.

Ainsworth hypothesized that, deprived of her mother, the child would go through reliable stages of response—that her mother's presence would make her feel safe enough to explore an unfamiliar place, that distress and protest would be the response to her mother's disappearance, that she'd show predictable wariness of the stranger when she was alone with her, and that she'd be calmed by her mother's return. And that's precisely what happened with more than half of the babies.

But significant numbers of children—more than 30 to 40 percent of them—behaved in ways that were highly unexpected. Some of the babies derived no comfort from their mothers' presence in the unfamiliar room and didn't try to explore. Some didn't react when left alone with the stranger and displayed little affect when their mothers returned. Others showed distress when their mothers left, but then either ignored their mothers when they came back or actively pushed them away. Still others cried and fussed even after their mother came back, wailing as they clung to her.

What made the quality of these connections so different? What, if anything, had taken place between mother and child in the past so that the behaviors typical of the securely attached were supplanted by other patterns? What happens when a baby doesn't get what she needs?

If you're reading this book because you are an unloved daughter (and the odds are good that you believe you are), you already have emotional knowledge of what not getting what you need from your mother feels like. But few of us understand the full impact an unloving mother has. To recover from the wounds of childhood, we have to be able to see them first. To start, let's look at the science that explains, in part, how you were affected by your experiences in infancy and early childhood.

NAMING THE PROBLEM

I spent my childhood and most of my early adulthood trying to get my mother's attention. I was an only child, but you can forget that coddled, fussed-over thing. My mom ignored me literally. I tried everything I could to please her and get her to see me, but she never did. She still doesn't.

—Lydia, 37

Ainsworth began to see consistent patterns in maternal behavior that produced relatively reliable responses in their infants, and called these children "insecurely attached." Within that grouping, she distinguished between those who were "avoidantly attached" and those who were "ambivalently attached"; her student Mary Main later added a third category, "disorganized attachment," which results from physical abuse and extreme neglect. These categories aren't the result of hardwiring but of experience, and they influence the child's development in profound and lasting ways.

The interactions between the infant and her mother shape the infant's developing brain and her ability to self-regulate and calm herself; it's a dyadic dance as the responsive mother reads her child's cues—her facial expressions, her vocalizations, her movements—and gives her what she needs in the moment. The securely attached child has her needs reliably and regularly answered; she is comforted when she's afraid, held when she feels lonely, fed when she's hungry, soothed when she's overtired, given space when she needs to calm down, and feels safe enough to explore a room away from her mother's side. She seeks proximity when she needs it, but as she gets older, she also becomes confident in herself. Her mother is attuned to her and she, in turn, will become attuned to the changes in her mother's expressions and gestures.

This interaction shapes behavior and the development of the infant's brain. The latest neuroscience confirms that brain development is both a function of programming and of environmental influence, the most important of which is the mother/caregiver relationship to the infant. When a mother is attuned and the child is securely attached, development proceeds in an optimal fashion.

But insecure attachment produces different results in infant behaviors, the brain, and the ability to self-regulate. Unless the mother's early behaviors are caused by something temporary—she initially suffers from postpartum depression from which she recovers, she has an illness that affects her behavior, which is then treated—they are likely to remain consistent. What begins in her daughter's infancy continues through her early and middle childhood, adolescence, young adulthood, and adulthood, unless there is some kind of therapeutic intervention or change in awareness.

Remember that the child comes with the heightened ability to sense her mother's reactivity; we can thank evolution for that, since the baby's survival depends in a very literal way on this one person. Avoidant and ambivalent attachments are the baby's way of dealing with a mother who is either never emotionally present or attuned, or sometimes there and sometimes not, but never in the right balance. Rather than experience stress every time her mother doesn't respond to her or overresponds to her, the baby distances herself by either avoiding contact with her mother (this is avoidant attachment) or responds ambivalently because her mother's responses have, in the past, been unreliable.

Do babies experience stress? You bet. Another famous experiment—this one called the "Still Face"—demonstrates not only how desperately a baby needs her mother's love and attunement but also the cascade of emotions and efforts released in the baby when her needs aren't met. Originally conducted more than 40 years ago by Edward Z. Tronick and his colleagues, the results have been successfully replicated many times over by different experimenters and make it clear how truly stressful it is for a baby not to get a response from her mother.

When it was first published in 1978— accompanied by a then novel video of the interaction—this experiment made quite a splash, demonstrating that an infant, even as young as four or five months, could be an active participant in interactions, instead of existing solely as a small being on whom the mother projected feelings and responses. In the video, the experimenters first have the mother interact with the child, making eye contact, smiling, and talking; the child responds with smiles, vocalizations, wiggling in her seat, and pointing her finger at various things in the room. She is thoroughly and deliciously engaged. Then the mother turns away and the baby looks up to see a frozen, impassive, unsmiling face. At this point, the baby is still game, and she starts doing all the things Mommy normally reacts to—smiling, waving her arms, pointing, vocalizing—but the face stays the same.

What happens next is both amazing and heartbreaking in its own way: The infant starts to fret, turning away from the still face, protesting with her arms, and finally beginning to wail. If you watch the video, you witness a meltdown in progress, as the baby literally slumps in her chair. Only at the end, when the smiling mommy reappears—this is an experiment, after all—does the infant begin to calm down. She doesn't return to her earlier level of connection, though, so it appears she hasn't forgotten. If she were able to talk, she might say, "Yay, my mommy's back! Boy, that was scary. I don't know if it will happen again, but I hope it doesn't."

But imagine if this were the baby's daily experience, a pattern of either a mother with a consistently still face, one who ignored her baby's cues consistently, or one who switched back and forth from lack of response to intrusive responses. (Yes, one pattern yields avoidant attachment and the other ambivalent.)

In one of his articles, Edward Tronick has us imagine a game of peek-a-boo as played by an attuned and loving mother who is watching her child's responses. She'll understand when the play gets too intense and the baby pulls back—averting her gaze and sucking on her thumb—that she's trying to self-regulate. That mother pauses for a moment, allowing the baby space, looking at and talking to her, and then, when the baby's ready, continuing their play. On the surface, this is just a game of peek-a-boo, but in fact, this is an ongoing conversation and a teaching moment in which the mother enables her child to begin to regulate emotion. "Too wound up?" her gestures ask, and then she provides the solution: "That's okay. Just take a moment." These inter-actions, as we'll see, provide the lay-down for neural patterns in the infant's brain and are the building blocks for what will, over time, become mental models of how relationships work, as well as the first seeds for the growth of emotional intelligence.

In contrast, there's the unattuned mother who initiates the game and then, seeing the baby withdraw, moves her face closer to the baby's face and starts clucking her tongue, trying to get the baby's attention even as she is turning away. The baby starts fussing, and may even push the mother away with her hands, but the mother doesn't stop; she's not paying attention to the infant's cues. The more the mother intrudes, the more the baby retreats, physically and emotionally, and by the end, the baby is staring out into space. This isn't just a failed game of peek-a-boo but a failure of communication that, if it is a consistent pattern of interaction, will have a real impact on how the daughter develops.

The "Still Face" experiment, in all of its variations, gives us insight into how both the mother and her baby participate in these early communications, and how formative they are in terms of the baby's development. Of course, only one person in the dyad has the power to change the interaction and, yes, that's the mother, not the so-called "cranky" or "unresponsive" baby.

Most important, the "Still Face" experiment permits us to see why some children become avoidant or ambivalent in their attachments. Of course, it's not possible for a mother to be "on" and attuned all the time, no matter how loving she is. These interactions aren't scripted, humans are decidedly imperfect, and yes, exchanges can get messy at times. But as Tronick and others assert, it's the mother's ability to repair mistakes in the interactive process that matters.

Here's an example, adapted from Tronick, which has special resonance for me because my own daughter was an inveterate hair-puller and, boy, it not only hurt but it was a true test of my own ability to manage my emotions. Imagine me on the floor playing with my baby. Suddenly, my daughter leans forward, grabs a hunk of my hair, and pulls hard. My reaction is swift and reactive: I scream, "Ow," my face contorts in pain and anger, signaling a threat to my little girl, and I unthinkingly swat her hand away. My daughter lets go and puts her hands in front of her face, as if ducking a blow. I rub my scalp, then look back at my baby, and start the work of repair—reaching out to her, making soothing sounds, coaxing her to reconnect. It takes a few minutes—there's been a breach in communication, after all—but my daughter begins to smile and move back toward me.

But what I took pains to do isn't the only possible scenario, of course. Imagine the mother totally losing it—growling and screaming at the baby or, even worse, hitting her or pulling her hair "to teach her a lesson." The mother gets up off the floor, still angry, and pays no attention at all to the baby's reactions. There's no effort at repair.

In the course of a day, a week, or a month, there are many opportunities for mother-child interactions to go slightly awry or totally off track and, equally as many opportunities for reunion and reattunement.

The power to fix things, though, remains totally in the mother's hands. Lest you think that there's a certain amount of reading-in on Tronick and his colleagues' part—infants can't tell us what they're thinking or feeling, after all—it's useful to look at another experiment involving the "Still Face," this time conducted with toddlers who were two and a half. Developmentally, these children were light years ahead of the babies, aged two to twelve months, originally studied; not only did they speak but they knew about standards of behavior—how they and other people are supposed to act.

The responses of toddlers to the "Still Face" were variations on the theme seen with much younger infants, validating the earlier findings and quelling criticisms that the researchers were projecting emotions onto infants. Confronted with their mothers' unresponsive faces, these toddlers tried various strategies—addressing Mom in a louder and louder voice (maybe she isn't answering because she didn't hear me?), waving a toy or object in her face (Mom, are you awake?), even tugging at her in frustration. And like the infants, when all of their efforts to get things back on track failed, the toddlers turned their backs on their mothers, choosing to avoid contact rather than experience the cascade of negative feelings that ensues from being shut out. It's in this way that avoidant behavior becomes the default setting when a mother is unresponsive.

These scenarios demonstrate the effect on infants and toddlers when a mother is emotionally unavailable; what they don't address is the dynamic when the conversation between mother and child becomes orally driven. It's at this juncture—when the child herself speaks and is old enough to understand—that the unloving mother has another weapon at her disposal: words. How she uses her words—by withholding praise and support or by actively undermining, criticizing, or dismissing her daughter—will determine the kind of damage she does to her daughter's sense of self.

From her first moments on the planet, the baby is busy making sense of the world around her. If she is responded to regularly and consistently, she begins to understand the world as a fundamentally reliable place, where she can count on love and security and responsiveness. As she grows, what her mother says about her will become the foundation of her sense of self. But if she and her needs are ignored or unmet, the interactions with her mother will diminish her.

Each of these moments of mother-child synergy alone is feather light but, repeated again and again, these interactions have enough force to transform a child's inner landscape in ways that are more literal than not. Like a steady stream of single drops of water on soil, they create grooves and channels through which daily events flow, are interpreted, and reacted to. These channels or mental models are unconscious processes that lie below the surface of conscious thought. The words that are said to a daughter—whether they're supportive and caring or hurtful and critical—are internalized as truths about herself and how connections between humans work.

Because these mental models form unconscious patterns that motivate and direct a daughter's behaviors in childhood and later, they cannot be altered without first recognizing them and bringing them to the surface of consciousness. This is why the wounds of childhood are so difficult to repair and why healing from them is complicated. Paradoxically, while the daughter feels unloved, she often can't see the ways in which she is wounded; additionally, the hardwired need for her mother's love never abates, even as she seeks to protect herself by withdrawing, just as she did as an infant.

This is the predicament all unloved daughters face.

BAD IS STRONGER THAN GOOD

I do remember that I was three or four, and she dressed me like a doll. I have the photos and she's holding me like a doll, too—away from her body like an object, not cradling me affectionately. The attention is on how well she's doing with me, her DIY project. I also remember being punished if I played in those clothes or got them dirty or got my undies wet. Every photo shows her beaming with her prize in hand. And the little girl, me, isn't smiling. Pictures don't lie. Now I can see the truth.

-Abigail, 52

It's a psychological truism that "bad is stronger than good," meaning that negative events have a much more significant and lasting impact on us than good ones, despite the fact that we have many more days and years that are basically good than bad over the course of a lifetime. Think about how detailed your recall is of a bad encounter or traumatic event, and then compare it to a memory of a day when nothing went wrong; it's the bad times that stand out. Long after our memories of our beach vacation fade, we still remember the absolute nightmare of the plane ride back and the loud, drunken idiot sitting in front of us, capped by the loss of our luggage when we landed.

We can thank evolution for our sensitivity to negative experiences, since the most reactive of our forebears were more likely to survive than those who didn't register possible dangers, as were those who committed untoward events to memory with as much detail as possible. Remembering how someone standing under a tree was struck by lightning and died, for example, or that a certain cave flooded when it rained, could mean the difference between survival and death. Having those specific bad experiences easily retrievable from memory was beneficial; indeed, bad and painful events are stored in a different place in the brain than good ones. This is our evolutionary legacy, and it remains true for all of us, all these millennia later.

This means that a child's *not* getting what she needs has a greater impact on her than actually getting it. While getting love and attention will allow her to thrive, it will not change her. In contrast, deprivation, neglect, and stress all leave their marks on personality, sense of self, the working models of relationships, and the ability to self-regulate.

As the song goes, if you're happy and you know it, you clap your hands. That's pretty much that; happiness or feeling good doesn't require emotional process. But because bad things have a greater impact, they release negative emotions, which do require processing. Remember the game of peek-a-boo I described or the hair-pulling incident? In both of those cases, an attuned mother works to help the baby regulate her negative emotions—learning to self-soothe when overstimulated, recovering from feeling sad or scared, being able to calm down and to derive comfort from someone else. Anxious and avoidant children of unattuned mothers don't learn how to deal with their negative feelings. This, as much as anything else, shapes all of their behaviors from childhood through adulthood and is, in many cases, hobbling.

The fact that bad is stronger than good shows up in research pertaining to family dynamics in many different ways, and should be kept in mind as you read these pages and begin to process your own experience of childhood. Even in healthy and loving families, for example, seeing a brother or sister treated differentially by a parent —getting more attention or love, being treated as special in some way—influences a child's development and perception more than the love she actually receives from that parent. Poignantly, one group of researchers wondered whether the presence of a reasonably attentive and affectionate parent could offset the damage done by a verbally aggressive one and discovered that, alas, it couldn't. In fact, the effects of parental verbal aggression and parental verbal affection seem to operate independently of each other. More tellingly, while verbal affection on its own appeared to support healthy development, it didn't appear to offer any buffer against the ill effects of verbal aggression. So if a father is kind and loving and a mother is verbally abusive to a daughter, Dad's kindnesses won't mitigate the damage done by Mom one bit. It turned out, too, that a parent's showing verbal affection after a display of verbal aggression did nothing to mitigate the damage done or the effect of such aggression.

That early mother-child interactions create the working models of relationship each of us unconsciously stores in memory is made clear by psychological research. It's been the contribution of brain science to show that these interactions shape the very structure of the brain and all of its connections.

THE DEVELOPING BRAIN AND MATERNAL BEHAVIOR

The last two decades have shone extraordinary new light on the workings and growth of the brain, which, science now knows, doesn't fully mature until long after childhood has officially ended, somewhere between the ages of 25 and 30. (It was long thought that the maturity of the brain coincided with the end of growth in the skeleton and skull during late adolescence. Nothing could be further from the truth.)

The human brain develops from the bottom up; infants come into the world with the primitive parts of the brain—those that control the autonomic functions such as breathing—fully developed. It's the higher brain—the parts that govern emotions, language, and abstract thought—that's developed over the course of the first three years of life. By the time a child is three, her brain will have achieved 90 percent of its adult size. The growth of synapses is exponential during these years, creating far more connections than the brain actually needs, and therefore "pruning" these connections is part of later childhood.

There is startling evidence that the brain of a child literally adapts to the environment in which the child finds herself. Yes, that's what the work of Martin Teicher and his colleagues discovered and the implications are very profound indeed. While our genes provide the foundation and structure of the brain, all of its connections—both neural and how the separate parts of the brain function alone and together—are shaped by experience. The truth is that the brain reacts as readily to a negative environment as a positive one and, as psychologist Allan Schore writes, both positive and negative experiences shape the brain's structure equally, either enabling its optimal growth or inhibiting it. Once again, this is not a metaphor but a literal statement. We can "thank" evolution for this adaptability (yes, that's irony) since, under stress, the brain goes into survival mode, retooling so as to deal with that stress.

We've already seen how a child's development is shaped by the absence of attuned and consistent maternal behavior, but we also need to turn to the presence of negative behaviors and their effects, especially verbal abuse. Verbal abuse has an especially powerful and lasting effect on the brain. Studies have identified the areas of the brain most affected as the corpus callosum (responsible for transferring motor, sensory, and cognitive information between the two brain hemispheres), the hippocampus (part of the limbic system, which regulates emotions), and the frontal cortex (which controls thought and decision-making). Psychiatrist Akemi Tomoda and others showed correlation between verbal abuse and changes to the gray matter of the brain.

What this means is that these early interactions can either produce a regulatory system—the brain—that can process emotions, handle stress optimally, and enable close emotional connections, or one that doesn't. Daughters with insecure attachments generally have trouble regulating emotion, may exhibit maladaptive behaviors, and are more at risk for anxiety, depression, and poorer mental and physical health. If you experienced verbal abuse, there's no reason to despair. The saving grace is that the brain retains its plasticity—its ability to grow and make new neural connections—throughout the lifespan. We will look at the effect of verbal abuse more closely in the following chapter.

So while maternal treatment and verbal abuse can change the brain, the effects can be reversed. That's very good news indeed.

ATTACHMENT IN ADOLESCENCE AND BEYOND

Those early childhood attachments—secure or insecure—continue to be unconscious scripts that govern how girls in adolescence and women in adulthood behave in relationships, whether romantic or friendly in nature. In order to better understand the distinct patterns, psychologists have expanded the original types of insecure attachment proposed by Bowlby and Ainsworth through a variety of studies. First, Phillip Shaver and Cindy Hazan proposed a three-part model of insecure attachment that was then expanded by Kim Bartholomew into four.

As you read the descriptions below, see where you would locate yourself *most* of the time. (Because these are descriptions of behavior, and behavior may shift according to the situation, they are not as mutually exclusive as they seem. Your goal is to identify how you *most often* act in situations that are close and intimate.)

Securely attached: Secure adults have a positive view of themselves and of other people. They have strong feelings of self-worth and they are comfortable expressing closeness. They enjoy knowing others and being known, and feel good when they are connected in love or friendship with others. They're good at identifying their feelings accurately and manage negative emotion well. They're flexible in their responses and have a variety of coping mechanisms at their disposal. They are resilient and can handle setbacks, large and small.

Anxious-preoccupied: These are daughters who were anxious ambivalent in childhood, and their behaviors carry forward. Even though they may be high achieving, they have deep wells of self-doubt and low self-esteem. They seek validation in relationships because they have a positive view of others but they are also volatile, clingy, and then demanding and reactive, by turns. They are on a constant state of high alert, searching for signs that the people they're intimate with, whether lovers or friends, will leave or reject them and can be triggered by the smallest of slights as a result. Generally, these women are always in one relationship or another, characterized by swings in behavior and highs and lows. Not surprisingly, these daughters often have trouble holding on to lasting friendships with other women.

Dismissive-avoidant: These daughters think well of themselves and have a low opinion of others, which Bartholomew attributes to coping mechanisms adopted during a childhood with a rejecting mother. On a conscious level, they're likely to consider themselves independent and self-contained, and not in need of intimate relationships for sustenance. They may come across as aloof or arrogant to others, as well as fiercely independent. Even though avoidants have relationships, they remain shallow because these daughters, deep-down, don't want close connections or intimacy. Their romantic relationships remain superficial; these women look as though they are involved, but they always maintain their emotional distance from the supposed objects of their affection.

In a similar way, their friendships tend to be organized around shared interests or hobbies, rather than confidences, closeness, and disclosure. Unlike the anxious-preoccupied daughters, whose volatility guarantees conflicts, these daughters steer away from conflicts, perhaps because they might reveal their true vulnerability.

Fearful-avoidant: The dominant word here is "fear." Even though these daughters actually crave intimacy, they don't trust anyone enough to let them get close. The experiences of childhood have taught these daughters that people are uncaring and unavailable, and that they themselves are unlovable as well. All of this plays out close to the surface, since these women come across as intensely vulnerable, openly worried, insecure, and self-conscious.

All three of these insecure styles can be seen as defensive postures adopted in childhood in an effort to both self-protect and reduce stress from maternal interactions. Remember how infants and toddlers turned away from their mothers in the "Still Face" experiments? These ways of responding are really no different, but unfortunately, they are unsuccessful strategies to deal with stress and negative emotion.

How happy we are largely depends on how well or badly we handle stress and the emotions that accompany it, and much of the unloved daughter's unhappiness in adulthood has to do with her difficulty in handling negative feelings. She has trouble sustaining happiness because it's so easily interrupted. Under stress, the secure daughter brings up mental representations and conscious thoughts of emotional support and positive experiences that help her manage negative emotions in the moment; she's inclined to look forward and to realize that resolutions to her problems exist. She's able to get angry without getting hostile and, even in the midst of an argument, is able to shift her thoughts to how to repair the rift.

In response to stress, the anxiously attached daughter, in contrast, is more likely to remember dispiriting or painful experiences as well as those times that she needed help and only encountered rejection. These memories arouse more anxiety, which, in turn, amps up whatever stress she is feeling, effectively flooding her with negative emotions. Unable to process them, she'll end up replaying those bad moments on an endless loop, making her feel hopeless and powerless. Her so-called coping mechanisms only serve to exaggerate her distress. While she may turn to others for support, she's too anxious to listen and, likely as not, will feel abandoned or unsupported. Her neediness is enormous, and she's likely to get demanding and then angry that her needs aren't met by her partner or friends. Additionally, her anxiety prevents her from drawing on positive connections when she needs to keep them in mind.

The avoidant daughter turns inward and off, denying the stress she's feeling and effectively walling off her emotions; of course, denying feelings is very different from recognizing and coping with them. By cutting off access to all of her emotions, the avoidant daughter effectively blocks all the positive emotions and experiences that actually would help her manage the stress. By isolating herself in this way, the avoidant daughter prolongs her emotional turmoil with no way out, unable to access her own positive thoughts and to reach out to others for support. In many ways, it is the worst of all possible worlds.

The inability to manage stressful situations and to effectively regulate negative emotions is among the most lasting legacies of an unloving mother. Recognizing the myriad ways that *then* influences *now* can be a bitter pill to swallow since it seems so unfair. But until you do, the past will govern your future.

In the chapters that follow, we'll be looking closely at maternal behaviors and seeing which behaviors spark different kinds of defenses. Please keep in mind that not only can secure attachment be earned—something we'll address in full later in the book—but also that we can transform these attachment styles when we become conscious of them and the triggers that activate our defenses.

Conscious awareness is the ultimate weapon at the unloved daughter's disposal.

MATERNAL POWER AND A DAUGHTER'S PERSONALITY

Among the various theories about personality, there's one that brings real understanding to the effect of the mother-daughter relationship on an individual. Set forth by Andrew J. Elliott and Todd M. Thrash, it posited that individuals could be characterized as being largely motivated by "approach" or "avoidance." These two tendencies are hardwired into humans as well as every other species; generally, we approach things that are potentially beneficial to us and will make us happy, and we avoid those that might harm us or bring us pain. This is a general trait we have in common with earthworms, elephants, and amoebas. But Elliott and Thrash's theory goes well beyond the basic hardwiring; it focuses on how people differ in whether they are largely motivated by approach or avoidance. The difference is attributed to childhood experience.

What motivates one girl to set her sights high, to prepare herself for possible setbacks, and go for it, while another contemplates a challenge and sees nothing but possible failure and humiliation? Why is that some women hear a voice in their heads cheering them on to go for it *(approach)* while another just hears a repetitive tape that tells her she is lacking, not good enough, and better not even try because she'll be humiliated and laughed at *(avoidance)*?

The answer is, once again, attachment; the girl who emerges from childhood securely attached will be motivated by approach goals, while the insecurely attached daughter will focus largely on avoiding negative outcomes. Keep in mind that everyone—depending on the situation—will shift focus from approach to avoidance from time to time; the difference here is that these are broad underlying tendencies and ways of responding that affect every decision and thought process in every area of life, including work and relationship.

Here's what we know about daughters who are largely motivated by avoidance: Fear of failure—or rather, the shame associated with failure itself—is a driver of this behavior. Often, this simply means that the daughter rejects challenges as too difficult, and change as impossible to effect, so she stays where she is, regardless of whether it makes her happy or not. One study by Elliott and Thrash showed that fear of failure was actually closely connected in college students to mothers' withdrawal of love when the child had transgressed some rule or had performed in such a way as to displease the mother. (It's important to note that this study relied on students' self-reports on what their relationships were like, along with the administration of an attachment scale.) The withdrawal of love on the parent's part when a child makes a mistake, breaks a rule, or somehow disappoints the parent can take many forms, among them looking at the child coldly; refusing to speak to or look at the child; expressing dislike of the child; moving away from the child or isolating her in another room, thereby symbolically banishing her; or even worse, threatening to send her away. These scenarios are ones that may resonate with many unloved daughters. It's interesting to note that in this study, fathers did not practice love withdrawal.

In the pages that follow, you and I will be looking at the maternal behaviors most likely to produce a daughter who is largely motivated by avoidance and what that means in practical terms. But there's one experiment in particular, conducted by Heather C. Lench and Linda J. Levine, that can act as a metaphor for the effect avoidance can have on a daughter's life. The researchers had the participants identify themselves as either approach- or avoidance-oriented and then gave them three sets of seven anagrams that they had to solve within a specified time period. What the participants didn't know was that the first set was unsolvable. The approach-oriented people were able to give up on the first set and move on, while those who were focused on avoiding failure kept working away at them, futilely, guaranteeing that they'd fail the test overall.

In a second study, rather than rely on self-reporting on approach and avoidance, Lench and Levine divided the participants into two groups, telling one that this timed test was a measure of verbal intelligence and that they should focus on attaining success, and instructing the other that this was a test of verbal weaknesses and that they should avoid failure at all costs. Once again, it was those who were told to avoid failure who kept at that first set of anagrams, feeling more frustrated and angry by the moment, and ultimately failing as a result.

Daughters motivated by avoidance often find themselves stymied in life situations, so focused on not failing that they end up dooming themselves to failure. Not only do they miss opportunities, but they become complicit in staying in situations that make them unhappy long past the expiration date. That applies to all the relationships they have, including those with their mothers and perhaps other family members.

If this is you or a pretty close-to-true description of you, the good news is that there are solutions at hand. We can all be thankful for the plasticity of the brain and ability of all dogs, young and old, to learn new tricks. Most important, the past need not dictate the future. Being unloved by your mother doesn't mean that no one will ever love you or, for that matter, that you can't learn to love yourself. There's a road out of the past that can be taken with work, time, and effort, and the pages ahead will help you on your way. Really.

CHAPTER TWO
THE POWER SHE HAD OVER YOU

I had no idea that there were other women whose mothers didn't love them. Can you imagine discovering this at the age of 40?

-Cecile

Having seen the extraordinary power a mother has in shaping her daughter as science understands it, the second stage of discovery is more personal: seeing how your mother shaped you. It's true enough that in sharing our stories, we discover deep commonalities, understanding that what happened in my childhood home happened in yours and in Carla's, in Annie's and Charlotte's. We'll look at those shared experiences first.

That said, there are also meaningful differences in individual experiences, and understanding them is also part of the task at hand.

Let's begin with the common ground so you can start to reconstruct the effects of your childhood experiences with the broadest of brushstrokes.

CHILDHOOD: COMMON GROUND

During childhood, a daughter usually draws the following conclusions, all of them incorrect, but they affect her sense of herself and her experiences in ways that are complicated, and may—in and of themselves—shape her almost as much as the love that's withheld or lacking. As you read, you will want to note how many of these thoughts and feelings were yours during childhood and beyond.

That she is unlovable: Because maternal love is so essential to a daughter's ability to thrive, even the love and care shown by others don't assuage her belief that there's something about her that stops her mother from loving her. The child tries unsuccessfully to come up with strategies to win her mother's love, on the one hand, and to explain its absence, on the other. The first explanation that comes into most children's minds—that they are unlovable—is both terrifying and disheartening. Dislodging this thought is one of the primary tasks of healing since it is deeply internalized and lies at the heart of the daughter's fears and insecurities even in adulthood.

That she is isolated and alone: Virtually all daughters believe they are the only unloved girls on the planet when they are children and much later in life. In childhood, an unloved daughter is likely to be too scared to tell anyone and, besides, she's worried that she *is* maimed or awful and that the fewer people who know, the better. In adolescence, the need to fit in usually trumps the daughter's need to talk; she wants to be taken for one of those lucky girls whose moms take them shopping and blow kisses at them from the car. In adulthood, few people will understand her story because of the cultural myths about maternal love; she'll hear people say, "You're fine now," or "It couldn't have been so bad," which only underscores her aloneness. The size of the family doesn't seem to matter; an only child is no more isolated than a child with siblings who are treated differently by their mother.

The feeling of being the only unloved child in the world inflicts a kind of wounding almost as devastating as the lack of maternal love itself.

That it's her fault: Blame-shifting is part of the abuse of power, and some unloving mothers, through their criticism and hostility, will actually do exactly that ("You are impossible and difficult. It's no wonder I can't stand looking at you") so it's easy for the daughter to internalize the blame as self-criticism. Children as young as toddlers are often treated this way, and they assume, given how little they understand of the dynamic, that they must be lacking somehow or deserving of their mother's treatment. Internalizing either things said ("You're a bad little girl and no one will ever be your friend") or extrapolating from actions and gestures ("My mommy yells at me because I'm a bad child") are heavy burdens for the young self and become, for most, a wellspring for self-doubt and even self-loathing. In other households, assigning blame may be more subtle and less articulated, but the burden is still on the daughter to *disprove* why she's unloved.

That she might be "crazy": In later childhood and adolescence, a daughter's perception and understanding of the relationship may sometimes become clearer. But any effort to question her mother will be batted down, denied, or ridiculed, and often, she will—as I did by the age of seven or eight—come to the conclusion that her point of view and her mother's are incompatible and that one person of the two has to be wrong—or even worse, "crazy." Many daughters are gaslighted by their mothers—in other words, they're manipulated into believing that their vision of reality is skewed—a subject we'll return to in the pages that follow.

That she belongs nowhere and to no one: An unloving mother robs her daughter of a sense of belonging because if you aren't loved by the person who put you on the planet and you don't feel as if you're part of your family in a very real way, to whom or where will you ever belong or fit in? That sense of being the odd girl out or some kind of outcast dogs many daughters in both obvious and subtle ways, especially if they've been scapegoated or bullied by their siblings. Those daughters brought up by mothers who are aggressive in their treatment—combative or hypercritical—often see the cost of belonging as high and perhaps not worth it. Those raised by dismissive or unreliable mothers may despair of ever feeling secure anywhere. For many unloved daughters, the quest for belonging is lifelong.

COMMON WOUNDS

Again, while the behaviors learned in childhood depend on the variations in maternal behavior and treatment, there are nonetheless generalizations to be made about the psychological damage done. As you read, you will want to think about which of these you exhibit and, additionally, which plague your interactions in the present most forcefully.

Lack of confidence: The unloved daughter doesn't know that she is lovable or worthy of attention; she may have grown up feeling ignored or unheard or criticized at every turn. The voice in her head is that of her mother, telling her what she isn't—smart, beautiful, kind, loving, worthy. That internalized maternal voice will continue to undermine her accomplishments and talents, unless there is some kind of intervention. Daughters sometimes talk about feeling that they are "fooling people" and express fear that they'll be "found out" when they enjoy success in the world; this feeling of fraudulence can absolutely coexist with high achievement and often does. Alternatively, some daughters are so beaten down by the barrage of criticism or the effects of being constantly marginalized or dismissed that they become chronic underachievers. Ironically, underachievement or, even worse, self-destructive behaviors only help to convince these daughters that their mothers are right about them after all.

Lack of trust: The attuned and loving mother teaches her child that the world is a safe place where her needs will be tended to, her questions answered, and someone will have her back if there's trouble or difficulty; the securely attached daughter doesn't find it hard to depend on people and doesn't feel vulnerable trusting others because of her vision of the world and her confidence in her own judgment. For the unloved daughter, the world presents itself very differently—as a potentially hostile place filled with people who can either hurt you or be unreliable. "I always wonder," one woman confides, "why someone wants to be my friend. I can't help myself from thinking whether there's some kind of hidden agenda, you know, and I've learned in therapy that that has everything to do with my mother." These trust issues emanate from that sense that relationships are fundamentally unreliable, and flow over into both friendships and romantic relationships.

All insecurely attached daughters have trust issues, although they present in different ways. The anxiously attached woman scans the horizon for potential breaches of trust, reading into every conversation, gesture, and facial expression so as to be on guard. She needs constant reassurance that trusting is the right thing to do, and, ironically, her vigilance often creates relationships that are marked by extreme emotional turbulence, which, of course, tends only to trigger her anxiety even more.

The avoidantly attached daughter assumes that fully trusting someone and making herself vulnerable are terrible mistakes. If she's dismissive-avoidant, she adopts a stance of "trust no one" as a maxim to live by to keep the upper hand; if she's fearful-avoidant, she does it because she needs to self-protect.

Difficulty setting boundaries: Starting in infancy, attuned mothers teach their daughters about healthy dependence and independence, respecting their children's emotional and physical spaces rather than intruding on them. These behaviors affirm both the child's independent self ("You are you, and that's a good thing") and a strong sense of connection at once ("If you fall, Mommy is here to help you"). In contrast, the unloved daughter who's ignored may have trouble seeing her independent self because she's too focused on getting her mother's attention; these daughters often replay the same role in their adult relationships, becoming inveterate "pleasers" and plagued by the inability to say "no." They tend to over-immerse themselves in relationships because they don't really understand how boundaries work, which, ironically, may end up assuring their worst-case scenario, being left.

The daughters of combative and enmeshed mothers—mothers who don't respect their daughters' boundaries at all—may end up confusing a coat of armor or a fortified wall with what constitutes a healthy boundary.

The larger problem is that the inability to manage and understand the importance of boundaries makes it virtually impossible for the daughter to forge and maintain healthy ties until she brings the unconscious lessons learned in her childhood into consciousness and begins to change how she acts.

Difficulty seeing the self accurately: We learn who we are by seeing ourselves reflected in the faces of other people—especially our mothers—and how they respond to us, our words, and our actions. These cues—beginning early in childhood—build the self-concept, one experience at a time. A loving and attuned mother not only helps a child build a positive self-concept but also allows her to develop self-acceptance. Self-acceptance permits you to see yourself with both strengths and weaknesses as part of the whole. The bottom line: You can deal with not being perfect because you know you'll be loved and accepted anyway.

That does not happen, alas, with the unloving mother.

While, again, the specific maternal behaviors directly affect the daughter's self-concept, all unloved daughters have problems seeing themselves clearly. Many have internalized their mothers' belittlement or disparagement as self-criticism—the habit of attributing every failure or setback not to circumstances but to fixed personality and character traits which define her as worthless or a failure.

Being overly sensitive: Words and gestures act as emotional triggers that recall childhood treatment for many daughters, making life in the present hard to navigate because of the weight of the unconscious and unexamined past. These daughters' sensitivity to slights—both real and imagined—and the reactions that often accompany any kind of criticism complicate their lives in highly unproductive ways. A daughter may mistake banter for critique and overanalyze and even obsess about an offhand remark. She's likely both to read meaningfulness into situations where there is none and to misread intentions and motivations because of her experiences in childhood.

Her sensitivity is further complicated by the difficulty she has managing her emotions, what I call "The Goldilocks Problem." I'll turn to that momentarily.

Replicating the mother bond in relationships: Unconscious patterns—those mental models of relationship—draw us to what we know, like a moth to a flame. If you are securely attached, this is actually very good news since you're likely to be attracted to friends and romantic partners who are themselves secure, are able to open themselves up to others, and actually need and enjoy intimate connections. Insecurely attached people, alas, are also drawn to what they know; they end up in relationships that make them unhappy in the end but that are nonetheless "comfortable" because they are familiar.

These are comfort zones that offer no comfort, and doom the daughter to seek out connections that make her feel as she did in childhood. "I married my mother, for sure," one woman says. "He was, on the surface, completely different from my mother, but, in the end, he treated me much the same way, the same seesaw of not knowing how he would be with me. Like my mother, he was indifferent and attentive by turns, horribly critical or vaguely supportive." As many of you will attest, she is not alone in having chosen a partner who treats her as her mother did.

THE GOLDILOCKS PROBLEM

The most significant effect an unattuned and unloving mother has is that her daughter doesn't learn how to manage her emotions in infancy and childhood. What does this mean precisely, and why does it matter?

The interactions of the mother and infant teach the child not just that it's safe and okay to express happy feelings—having your smiles and coos and gestures answered in kind—but also that negative feelings—being afraid, lonely, sad, or in pain—can be dealt with, too. With comfort offered by the responsive mother—by soothing her child when she's distressed—over time, she'll also teach her to self-soothe in times of need and stress. The child learns to bring up mental images of connection that reassure her that she's not alone, that she's loved, and that things will be okay. Research shows that securely attached children grow up to be adults who are reasonably adept at managing negative feelings when they're stressed. Why? Just as working models of relationships are stored unconsciously in the brain, so are instances of beneficial interactions with caring others and memories of coping successfully in bad times. These memories help the securely attached person not only to weather whatever storms life hands her more easily but also remind her to seek out the support of others in times of crisis. Like Goldilocks in the three bears' house—trying to navigate between too big and too small, too hot and too cold—they have the capacity to live "just right," finding the balance between an integrated, whole, and independent self and depending on others when they need to.

The unloved daughter learns none of that. She's Goldilocks, always finding herself in a place that's either too hot or too cold and without the tools to make it just right. When bad stuff happens, the memories that her brain offers up are negative and dispiriting—recollections of being rejected and alone— and will probably make her even more frantic and worried than she is or, in fact, needs to be. She doesn't know how to regulate negative emotion and so will either flood with feeling or cut herself off from what she's feeling entirely. The anxious Goldilocks won't be able to stop talking or thinking about what she's going through, and will even unconsciously exaggerate her feelings and fears to get attention. The avoidant Goldilocks puts her emotions in lockdown, convinced that there's no one out there to help her anyway and that the only person she can depend on is herself. The problem is that, deep-down, she really doesn't believe it.

Positive emotions don't need regulation or management. But your degree of happiness—at least the roughly 40 percent of happiness that science thinks we're actually in control of—has to do with how well you manage your feelings of unhappiness.

That's exactly where her childhood experiences have damaged the unloved daughter the most: her inability to self-regulate emotion and self-soothe. Her inability to self-soothe productively, alas, can lead her to fill the hole in her heart in other, destructive, ways. Often, she doesn't understand the connection between these behaviors and her childhood experiences.

BEHAVIORAL RESPONSES TO THE LACK OF A MOTHER'S LOVE

In her groundbreaking book, *The Hungry Self*, Kim Chernin detailed and explored the primal connections between food and female identity, as well as between mothering and emotional hunger. These connections are both subtle and obvious. In response, a daughter may seize on eating or not eating as something she can control, as a way of countermanding her mother's vision of the world or her place in it. Some daughters will develop clinically disordered eating while others will simply carry their complicated relationships with food and its connection to self-image into adulthood.

Food is often a freighted issue for daughters, and not just those who have emotionally unavailable mothers. In most households, the mother prepares the food, and what she serves and to whom she allocates the best or most favored portions can be part of both favoritism and scapegoating. In her book, *When Food Is Love*, Geneen Roth (the daughter of a physically abusive mother and an emotionally distant father) explains that disordered eating may be an act of self-protection, a way of armoring the self against pain. It may also be a way for the daughter to locate a small piece of her intimate universe she can actually control. Recent studies more closely exploring the connection between insecure childhood attachment and disordered eating have made some interesting discoveries. For example, Jenna Elgin and Mary Pritchard found that while it was true enough that secure attachment was negatively correlated with disordered eating, not every type of insecure attachment was positively correlated. Only the fearful attachment style (which includes both a negative view of self and a negative view of others) was positively correlated with bulimia, but neither the dismissive or preoccupied styles were associated with disordered eating.

Self-harming may be another way of bringing emotional pain to the surface, to a place where it feels more manageable. Many emotionally neglected daughters often comment that they wish the maltreatment had been physical because, as one woman put it, "then, at least, the scars would show and I wouldn't have to prove their existence to anyone." It's been hypothesized that self-harm or cutting is intimately connected to lack of love, another effort both to fill the emptiness and to feel pain that you are able to control. In their book *Bodily Harm*, Karen Conterio and Wendy Lader write, "self-injury represents a frantic attempt by someone with low coping skills to 'mother herself.' . . . Bodily care has been transformed into bodily harm: the razor blade becomes the wounding caregiver, a cold but available substitute for the embrace, kiss, or loving touch she truly desires." Following up on previous lines of research, Jean-François Bureau and his coauthors looked at specific dimensions of parenting and their relationship to NSSI (nonsuicidal self-injury) in young adults. What they found was that among those engaging in self-injury, their descriptions of childhood included portraits of parents who failed to protect them and abdicated their roles as parents, of parents from whom they felt alienated, and of parents who were overly controlling. These parents were generally seen as less caring, untrustworthy, and more difficult to communicate with. Generally, research has confirmed the link between self-harm and emotionally distant or abusive parenting and insecure attachment.

Substance abuse, compulsive shopping, and even sexual promiscuity have been understood as ways of filling the hole in the heart. Unloved daughters may turn to the instantaneous self-soothing and oblivion offered up by alcohol or drugs. In her book *Mothering Ourselves*, psychotherapist Evelyn S. Bassoff writes that, "For some, alcohol—which warms, fills, and anesthetizes the inner emptiness or aching—becomes the soothing mother . . . the alcoholic stupor replaces the sensations of being wafted to a sound sleep in mother's arms." Writer Hope Edelman describes the "emotional hoarding" of the unloved daughter and writes, "Back-to-back relationships, overeating, overspending, alcoholism, drug abuse, shoplifting, overachieving—all are her attempts to fill that empty space, to mother herself, to suppress feelings of grief or loneliness, and to get the nurturing she feels she lost or never had."

As Andrea, age 39, confided, "I remember throwing myself onto my mother's lap when I was three or four, and she would swat me away. I would try again and she would get angry, telling me I was mussing her clothes. I became a promiscuous teenager—desperate for love and attention. I grew up to be a desperate adult, always, inevitably, finding the wrong partners. It took a long time for me to realize that every guy was a stand-in for Mom and the love I never got in the beginning."

UNDERSTANDING THE CORE CONFLICT

One of the significant differences among individual daughters is the timing of two events: when they first recognize the lack of maternal love and attunement and when they begin to glimpse the degree to which they are wounded. These two perceptions are not necessarily simultaneous; in fact, they may be separated by years or even decades for some daughters. This seems counterintuitive but is explicable when you consider what I call the "core conflict."

The core conflict is between the hardwired need for a mother's love, attunement, and support and a daughter's own perceptions of her pain, her unfulfilled needs, and her continuing struggle to give voice to herself. Because the world of a child is small and the interactions that go on in it are familiar, most daughters begin by accepting their mothers' treatment as "normal." That's reinforced by the fact that the mother doesn't just rule that little world but also dictates how actions and interactions in it are to be understood. For example, a mother often labels her harsh words and castigation as "discipline" that is "necessary" for correcting flawed behavior or character. Even if her mother treats other children in the house differently, the daughter subjected to this kind of labeling is likely to believe that it must be *her* fault that she's treated one way and her siblings another—and besides, she remains hopeful that, somehow, she'll be able to change things. The effort to make sense of things—especially for adolescents and young adults who don't seek counsel from either friends or a therapist—is emotionally turbulent and confusing, and can keep a daughter locked into the patterns for years.

There are other factors, too, that contribute to what I call the daughter's "dance of denial." Her own ability to trust her perceptions has been eroded by her mother's treatment so entertaining the possibility that her mother is right about her—and that it's some innate character flaw that keeps her mother from loving her—keeps floating to the top. (That's another example of what psychologists call "self-criticism.") Few daughters ever discuss the problem with anyone—they keep the code of silence because of feelings of shame and fear—so that there's little chance of getting support for those perceptions. Gaslighting by her mother or other family members such as siblings—manipulative comments meant to make the daughter doubt her perceptions and thoughts—also may get in the way. Then there's hopefulness that somehow she'll be able to wrest that love from her mother in the end— by pleasing her, by saying or doing the right thing, or by making her proud.

Caught in the conflict, the daughter continues to deny or rationalize her mother's behavior as she desperately tries to come up with a reason—a fixable, answerable reason—that her mother doesn't love her. This can go on for years until there's a moment of crisis—the daughter becomes sufficiently unhappy that she has to change the status quo— or revelation, sometimes provided by a therapist, spouse, or friend who confirms her perceptions.

The real problem is that until you can see the wounds—which entails not just jettisoning denial and rationalization but also giving up on the hopefulness inspired by the need for maternal love—you *cannot* begin the process of healing. That's the bottom line.

IDENTIFYING THE EIGHT TOXIC MATERNAL BEHAVIORS

What follows aren't, of course, scientific descriptions but ones gathered from all the interviews I've had with daughters over the last decade or so, and they're an effort to categorize how unloving mothers act and how, in turn, their specific behaviors affect their daughters. These categories aren't mutually exclusive; mothers may be combative, self-involved, and dismissive by turns (mine was) or may shift behavior as the daughter gets older (a dismissive mother may become much more aggressive and combative, for example). Her mother's treatment directly shapes her sense of self—her mother's face is a daughter's first mirror—and molds both her reactions and behaviors.

Use these descriptions as a way of organizing your own thoughts about your childhood experiences as you read, and consider which you found personally hardest to take or most hurtful. At the end of each description of maternal behavior is a brief summary of the ways in which each maternal pattern of relating potentially affects the daughter's own development.

THE DISMISSIVE MOTHER

What does it mean to have a dismissive mother? Some daughters describe their mothers as simply ignoring them in very literal ways. One daughter, now in her forties and married with a child of her own, remarked, "The pattern has always been the same. My mother asks me what I want to do and then proceeds to make other plans as though I haven't said a word. This extends to every realm of life. When I was a kid, she'd ask if I was hungry, and if I said I wasn't, she'd pile food on a plate and get angry if I didn't eat it." Daughters of dismissive mothers describe themselves as feeling invisible—unseen and unheard—as did Barbara, 43: "I grew up this quiet, interiorized little girl with practically no social skills at all. I couldn't make friends because I didn't understand how exchanges work—you know, deciding what game you want to play or what you want to do. I was used to saying nothing, the way I did at home."

Dismissive mothers marginalize their daughters' thoughts and feelings by not assigning them importance or not paying attention to them. As Ruby, 39, explained, "I would tell my mother I was unhappy and explain why, and she'd keep doing whatever she was doing as if I'd said nothing. Then I'd ask her if she heard me and she'd nod her head and say something like, 'Well, you'll get over it. It's not a big deal.' By the time I was a teenager, I didn't even bother talking to her about anything." Other dismissive mothers may actually voice contempt for their daughters and engage in subtle or not-so-subtle put-downs.

It's what a dismissive mother doesn't give her daughter that does the most damage. By ignoring her daughter's presence, along with her feelings and needs, the dismissive mother's message is: "You're not important to me, and neither is what you feel and think." It's a crushing blow to the developing self and a subtle form of emotional abuse.

As the daughter gets older, her mother's consistent lack of attention—ignoring requests, not listening to her, acting as though she's said nothing worth answering—often ramps up into a cycle of protest behaviors initiated by the daughter. She'll engage her mother in any way she can, both productively and unproductively, to get her attention. As a young child, she may act out or even do things that she knows are forbidden just to get her mother to respond. When she's older, she may go much further than that, as Jenna describes: "By the time I was nine or ten, I was pretty sure that no one would ever like me or want to be my friend. It was made worse by the fact that while my mother ignored me, she heaped attention on my older sister who could do no wrong. By the time I was an adolescent, I was willing to do anything—and I mean anything—to get attention. I was a hot mess, and I count myself lucky that nothing bad happened to me during those years."

Some daughters embark on proving themselves worthy by becoming high-achievers, only to be put down and marginalized by their mothers, no matter what, as Adele recounted: "I decided that I'd have to be a star to get my mother's attention, and so I became one at school. I got every honor in grade school, junior high, and high school, and then went on to a prestigious college. My mother's response was always the same: She'd say things like, 'Well, the competition must not have been too tough,' or, 'Being good at school doesn't do much for anyone in the real world.' And I believed her. I felt like nothing, no matter what I did."

Even high-achieving daughters often feel deeply insecure, worthless, or not good enough. A dismissive mother robs a child of her sense of belonging, whether she's an only child or has siblings. But the effects can be different. Patti, age 40, was a singleton and says, "I didn't realize until I was in my twenties that how my mother marginalized me wasn't normal. It was my very caring mother-in-law who pointed it out. It was only then that I began to understand why I was always anxious, worrying about failing or disappointing people. It took therapy to stop me from being the world's doormat, the girl who could never say 'no.'"

It's true enough that many daughters of dismissive mothers become habitual pleasers, always putting their own needs last, in part because they've absorbed their mothers' words and gestures and don't believe that what they want matters. Ironically, the combination of needing desperately to please and feeling that they are invisible to everyone may cause them to be drawn to those, both in friendship and romantic relationships, who treat them just as their mothers did. And the daughter who is dismissed by her mother may be further damaged by the constant comparisons to her siblings, who, she is told, outshine her in every way, as well as the differential treatment and affection given to them. Her unmet needs for validation and approval may become even more poignant if she is also the "odd girl out."

There's a further irony in being the daughter of a dismissive mother: Often, these daughters find it hard or impossible to break free of their mothers' influence as adults. Without conscious awareness, even though she knows intellectually that the well is dry, this daughter may keep going back, hoping for the validation she never got in the first place and staying on the merry-go-round, to her own detriment.

Common Effects of Maternal Dismissiveness
- Difficulty identifying and articulating her own needs and wants
- Avoidance of conflict and argument with others even when she's been wronged
- Tendency to please or mollify by default
- Social awkwardness and trouble making and maintaining intimate connections
- Being interiorized and unable to assert herself even when she's angry or upset
- Low self-esteem

THE CONTROLLING MOTHER

While the dismissive mother makes her daughter feel invisible by withholding the validation and attention essential to her child's inner growth, the controlling mother does much the same thing, although it looks very different on the surface. Here's what Ella, now 48, had to say about her childhood: "My mother was widely admired in our community for how perfect her life looked: a tended-to house, gorgeous garden, and an outwardly successful child. That would be me: the all-A student, the cheerleader, the beautifully turned out little girl. But I wasn't allowed to make a single decision growing up. Not one. Not my clothes, not my friends, not even the college I went to. And you know what? I didn't realize I was being controlled until I fell apart at the age of 30 when my marriage imploded and I looked inside and there was nothing there."

The controlling mother deprives her daughter of her own voice, her ability to choose for herself and to learn from her mistakes, and most important, to be seen for who she is, instead of as a projection of her mother's needs and wants. While the dismissive mother has little involvement in her daughter's life, the controlling mother throws herself into every aspect of it, and the messages she communicates are always the same: "Without me, you are nothing." "If I weren't here to do for you, you would fail at every step." "It's my way or the highway."

While she may be a perfectionist—needing everything in her life, including her children, to be "just so"—the controlling mother is often deeply insecure, afraid of making mistakes and looking "less than" in the eyes of others. She sees her children as an extension of herself, not as individuals in their own right, and is determined that they reflect well on her. And when they don't, she takes immediate action. "If you didn't fall into line, you got scapegoated," Marnie, 44, tells me in an email. "My mother encouraged us to tattle on each other as a way of gaining favor with her because the more you pleased her, the better she treated you. My older sister dared to rebel against her and, boy, did she ever pay for it! I didn't have the courage to but I wish I had. My sister left at 18 and never looked back. She is a personal success, and I'm still struggling."

It's a pity that "helicopter" parenting has crept into the

contemporary discussion because I think it sounds more benign than the word "controlling," and it really isn't.

The controlling mother—no matter what you call her—actually believes that she's doing the right thing by her child, and she usually has a host of rationalizations (aka "explanations," from her point of view) to justify her behavior; in that way, she's like the hypercritical or combative mother who also believes she's disciplining or inspiring her wayward child.

The controlling mother teaches a child that love comes with strings attached and that if you fail or disappoint, no one will love you.

Common Effects of Maternal Control

Whether the daughter goes with the program—doing what she can to fulfill her mother's expectations and working overtime at pleasing—or rebels, there is real damage to the self. The daughter of a controlling mother:

• Defines herself by how others see her and is detached from her inner self

• Attributes her successes to luck and her failures to character flaws

• Is drawn to other controlling people because she's afraid of failing or choosing

• Is intolerant of hesitation in others because she believes life has "rules"

• Lacks emotional resilience

• Has no sense of herself as independent. Whether she plays by the rules or rebels, she is always defined by her reactivity.

THE EMOTIONALLY UNAVAILABLE MOTHER

Of all the patterns of maternal behavior, among the most wounding is that of the emotionally unavailable mother. These women are emotionally distant and withdraw from their children on both a literal and symbolic level and, as a result, don't fulfill many of the basic needs we know children need to thrive. These mothers aren't necessarily outwardly neglectful—they may walk through the paces of what society expects of them as mothers and often do very well on the surface—but they are unresponsive and uncaring on a fundamental level. They also ignore and dismiss their children's emotional selves, don't work at maintaining close bonds, and are more comfortable when there's physical and emotional distance between themselves and their daughters. Natalie, 46, recounts what it felt like: "I think I literally craved love and attention as a child. The more my mother withdrew, the more frantic I became. I became a troublemaker because I knew she would pay attention to me, even if it meant punishment. It sounds weird, but that's what I did. Since I couldn't get her love, I settled for her anger. At least in those moments, she was there."

Although these mothers aren't necessarily verbally abusive and don't put their daughters down the way a dismissive mother can, the withholding of affection and attention is another form of emotional abuse. While some mothers are, by nature, cold and unresponsive—they are themselves avoidantly attached—others use unavailability with intention and malice, as a way of feeling powerful in their own right. Either way, their behavior tells the daughter that she's unworthy, that she's insignificant in the scheme of things, and that she doesn't matter. None of that necessarily tamps down the daughter's efforts to somehow get her needs answered. Lily, 48, wrote that, "I loved being sick because that was the only time I felt mothered. Granted, she didn't tolerate whining or crying and she didn't cuddle me, but she did bring me tea and toast or soup and crackers. It doesn't sound like much, but they are my happiest childhood memories. It's sad, really."

Many emotionally unavailable mothers are much more comfortable with children who require specific kinds of caretaking and permit her to mother by *doing* instead of connecting emotionally. That was what Jane, now 60, experienced: "What was really confusing was that my mother was stone-cold to me but responsive to my older sister and younger brother. My sister had learning issues, and I think my mother felt needed by her in a way that was comfortable. My brother had severe allergies, and Mom fit nicely into the role of his caretaker. But I didn't need her to do things for me. I needed her to connect to me. And she couldn't." Even more confounding is the fact that emotionally unavailable mothers may be deemed highly successful at nurturing by others; they usually have organized households, seem attentive to their daughters' external needs, and may even be involved in the community.

The confusion is real for the daughter who feels emotionally starved and neglected, invalidated and lonely, despite all the pretty things in her room and closet or even the family photos hung up on the wall. She's apt to doubt her own perceptions and worry that, somehow, her own neediness or some other flaw is to blame for the lack of love and emotional connection she feels in her mother's presence. It may take her a long time not just to recognize the problem but also to act on it.

"Being constantly rebuffed in childhood made me armored," one daughter writes me in an email, "and I don't like being dependent on anyone." Her voice is that of the avoidant variety of insecure attachment: These daughters keep their distance even when they're in a relationship and pride themselves on their independence. But having an unavailable mother—physically present in the household but maddeningly out of reach— may also create an anxious working model of relationship, filled with longing, fraught with difficulty and frustration, and animated by rejection and pain.

Common Effects of Having an Emotionally Unavailable Mother

• Turning to unhealthy substitutes or addictions in lieu of maternal love
• Lack of trust in others
• Extreme emotional neediness and problems with boundaries or being walled off and self-isolating
• Trouble making friends and other intimate connections
• Difficulty identifying and acting on her feelings
• Heightening of the core conflict because the need for mother love is so amped up

THE UNRELIABLE MOTHER

Perhaps the most difficult pattern of maternal behavior to deal with and to recover from is that of the unreliable mother. These mothers don't regulate their own emotions and vacillate wildly between being unbearably present—intrusive, invasive, utterly without respect for the child's boundaries—and being absent and withdrawn. Remember the story about playing peek-a-boo I described in the first chapter, in which the infant momentarily withdraws in order to collect and

regulate herself and the mother impinges on the baby, literally crowd-
ing her? That's one aspect of the unreliable mother. These mothers
aren't capable of consistent attunement and pay no attention to
the cues their infants and, later, their children communicate; they
swing between overinvolvement and withdrawal. It's like being in a
Goldilocks world where everything is either too hot or too cold all the
time.

And it puts the child in a fearful and emotionally paralyzing mode
because she never knows whether the good mommy or the bad one
will show up; in children, this type of attachment is called "disorganized" for a reason. The dynamic within the child is one of conflict:
The need for her mother causes her to approach and seek her out, but
the fear of that "other" mommy causes her to push off and disconnect. This kind of emotional confusion—an interiorized tug-of-war—
affects an unloved daughter in myriad ways. This is how Caroline, 41,
described her experience: "I trace my own lack of self-confidence back
to my mother. She was horribly critical of me one day, ignored me the
next, and then was smiley and smothering the day after that. It took
me years to realize that the lovey-dovey in-my-face stuff only happened
when there was an audience. I'm still armored, and really sensitive to
rejection, have trouble with friendships, you name it. These wounds
run deep."

These daughters can demonstrate anxious behavior and avoidant
behavior by turns in adulthood. They both desperately need love and
affection and are also fearful of the consequences of that need. One
daughter wrote me that, in retrospect, she realized that, "My mother
could be loving (seeming) in one moment, but it could turn on a dime.
There came a time when I no longer trusted her good behavior. I'd
seen such intense cruelty that those tender moments seemed like a
lie."

These daughters are Goldilocks in exile—never finding anything
quite right—and have terrific trouble managing emotions as well as
knowing what they're feeling. They feel that same tug to try to make
their mothers love them, but as they do, it fills them with fear and
hopelessness. For them, the core conflict—between still wanting their
mothers' love and recognizing the need to save themselves—is even

more intense and complicated than in other unloved daughters.

Common Effects of the Unreliable Maternal Style

* Heightened and even extreme lack of trust
* Emotional volatility and inability to self-regulate
* Replication of the mother bond by being attracted to abusive people
* Being drawn to controlling friends and lovers because she mistakes control for consistency and reliability
* Impaired emotional intelligence and ability to identify and process emotions
* An intensified version of the core conflict with heightened emotional confusion

THE SELF-INVOLVED MOTHER

In recent years, this type of unloving mother, the one high in narcissistic traits, has garnered the most press and even spawned acronyms in the world of self-help: the NM (Narcissistic Mother) and DONM (Daughter of NM). This mother is the sun of her own universe and her children, revolving planets; her treatment of them is completely self-referential and superficial and, not surprisingly, she's incapable of real attunement because she's low on empathy. This mother exerts control over her children but in much more subtle, less overt ways than her controlling counterpart: She favors the children who reflect well on her and ostracizes those who don't by belittling them. Like a combative mother, she is a mistress of the put-down when necessary and enjoys pitting one family member against another. People high in narcissistic traits are also game-players; they glow in the light of adulation—they need it to thrive—but they also need to feel the rush of power. They play games setting one child against another, giving extra points and gold stars to those who make her feel completely in control. They are verbally abusive, specialize in scapegoating, and cover their tracks with charm and a perfectly maintained façade.

Perhaps one reason labeling unloving mothers as narcissists has had so much popular appeal is that they take total advantage of the imbalance of power implicit in motherhood discussed in the first chapter. Given the taboos about criticizing mothers, the self-involved one is easy to target once you've figured out who she is.

The story shared by Laura, now 41, brilliantly captures what life is like with this kind of mother. It appears to have all begun when this seemingly ordinary child was deemed extraordinary by others: "There was definitely a clear delineation between the years before I got slapped with the 'gifted' label by my teachers and after. Before, she couldn't have cared less about me. I was just this nuisance she had to tend to all day when she'd rather be watching her soap operas. After I was labeled, I think she saw me as having potential value she could exploit."

The irony here is that Laura also confides that this turning point—seized upon by her mother—was actually unwelcome for her. She didn't like the attention, hated being singled out, and wanted nothing more than to blend in at school. That was not going to happen with her mother around: "Suddenly, she became very interested in being a parental helper in my classes at school when she never wanted to be involved before. (She did *not* show this same interest in my brother or his classes.) My mother took it upon herself to swoop in and make sure everyone was focused on me. She was also hypercritical of my teachers and my school, often acting like she knew more than they did. She was in the habit of criticizing assigned reading material and lesson plans, for instance, saying things like, 'This isn't *challenging* enough for my daughter. She is exceptional and needs to be *challenged*.'"

And, needless to say, it became totally about her, as Laura recounts: "She also became hypercritical of me, my interests, my friends, how I spent my free time . . . everything. My feelings and actual interests were not considered important, when their existence was acknowledged at all. Often I'd try to communicate what I liked or didn't like the way any kid would. ('Mom, I like mashed potatoes, but I don't like yogurt.') She'd come back at me with 'information' about my own feelings. ('Don't be silly. You *love* yogurt. You don't want mashed potatoes. Mashed potatoes are fattening, and you don't want to grow up to be fat.') If something about me or my personality wasn't perfectly in line with what she wanted it to be, she'd do everything she could to convince me to change it, often berating interests and emerging values I had that didn't fit the mold, while encouraging substitutes of her choosing." This is a form of psychological control.

In many ways, Laura's story functions as a summary of what it's like to be the daughter of a mother high in narcissistic traits. First, there's the mother seizing an opportunity to aggrandize herself through her child, both literally and symbolically. Once again, what matters most is the outside world's perception, not what the daughter is feeling or what she actually wants. Second, her marginalization of her daughter's thoughts and feelings—especially if they don't coincide with her own— often leaves this daughter feeling fraudulent and ignored, despite her achievements.

No child really wins or gets what she or he needs in this household, but one child's success with the Queen Bee and another's failure may not make that obvious. Laura's brother, for example, grew up on a steady diet of "Why can't you be more like your sister?" With a self-involved mother, you're either on Team Mom or rejected from it, and if you find yourself in the off position, the chances are good that you'll be scapegoated and picked on. These mothers care deeply about how they look to the outside world so there's lots of pressure on the children in the household to succeed and to shine since they are essentially ambassadors for how terrific Mom is.

Perhaps the most dangerous—and psychologically important— lesson the self-involved mother imparts is that attention is earned, never given freely or without condition. And whatever attention's available is sparingly doled out and substitutes for love. It's as though saplings under the canopy in the rainforest are duking it out for a glimmer of sunlight; is it any wonder that the sorties, skirmishes, and battles orchestrated by the Queen among and between siblings endure through childhood and all of adulthood?

Not surprisingly, since all the attention is focused on external success—no use talking to this particular mother about someone's soulfulness or character—many daughters become high achievers because that's what it takes to have a favored position in Mom's orbit. Their achievements, though, don't fill the void in their hearts left by their mothers' lack of attunement or by the recognition of how tenuous the emotional connection is. Perhaps the most poisonous part of a self-involved mother's legacy is the idea that love has to be earned: This puts the daughter in a position where she's always trying to figure out what she can do to wrest her mother's love from her. It is a thankless task and impossible to fulfill.

And then, of course, there's the Odd Girl Out: the girl who either can't ever win her mother's approval or who is necessary to the mother's gamesmanship in the family. We'll look at gaslighting and scapegoating and other manipulative tactics later in the chapter in depth, but for the daughter of the self-involved mother, whether she's the Trophy Child who can do no wrong or the Odd Girl Out, she has been indelibly shaped by her mother's behaviors.

How a Daughter is Affected by the Self-involved Mother
• Detached from her own feelings and thoughts and has trouble identifying them
• Lacking in real self-esteem and dependent on others for superficial validation
• Unhappy but doesn't see the source because she accepts her situation as normal
• Trouble with intimacy and closeness
• Feels lonely and adrift without knowing why
• Attracted to others high in narcissistic traits
• Deeply immersed in the core conflict if she's the Odd Girl Out. The Trophy Child is unlikely to recognize the conflict at all.

THE COMBATIVE MOTHER
This mother takes winning and absolute control of the household and the children in it very seriously, and she can get angry at the drop of a hat. She considers herself feisty and outspoken, not tyrannical and repressive, and she's often proud of how tough she is because she thinks it gives her authority and agency. The truth is that sometimes she's a bully who's bullied by a hot-tempered and tightly-wound husband, but not always. In other households, the father may simply be an appeaser, absenting himself from parenting and permitting his wife to run the ship as she sees fit. In addition to being highly combative, these mothers are often hypercritical, determined that life look "perfect," at least from the outside; they don't tolerate any deviation from the rules they've set, and they're not shy about voicing their displeasure. Woe to the child who ignores her.

Like a narcissistic or self-involved mother, the combative mother largely sees her child or children as an extension of herself, and she has high standards that have to be met. Once again, there's a great disconnect between what is seen by the outside world and what goes on in private, as Geri's story makes clear: "My mother's public self was carefully cultivated. She was always beautifully groomed and careful to appear 'thoughtful' to others. She was the first to volunteer for a bake sale or charity drives. But at home, she was a tyrant and a screamer. It was horribly confusing to try to figure out who my mother was. The one who berated me for being too fat and lazy or the woman the neighbors all admired for her gardening skills and her baked goods? No wonder I didn't tell anyone. Who would have believed me?" My own mother was highly combative, and I, too, was confused by the switches between her public self and the private one. The world thought my mother was charming and beautiful. The other thing that was confusing was I could see that she liked being angry and yelling at me. I knew that, even as a little girl, and it scared me.

Of course, the idea that a mother would actually enjoy berating her child runs counter to every cultural trope we hold dear about motherhood. That's why these daughters keep their silence long past childhood and mothers rationalize and justify their combative behaviors. As one daughter recounted, "I thought my mother was doing it for our own good—those constant fights to make us tougher, the lectures about how only the strong survive. I believed that until I was in my early thirties when I finally noticed the way I'd been damaged and my siblings had been hurt. I wasn't tough; I was a fearful person with armor against the world. My mother liked the power her anger gave her, I think. She still does. She thrives on drama, trying to set me against my siblings or my siblings against me. But when I finally realized that about her and said so, my three siblings turned on me like a united front."

This mother's brand of aggression is largely verbal, although she may resort to physical aggression from time to time. She rationalizes her hypercriticality and verbal abuse, insisting that her words are a necessary corrective given her child's flaws, or she justifies words and actions by saying she was "provoked." The denial is another layer of abuse. The constant pattern of shifting the blame for her own behavior onto her child's shoulders is, in and of itself, abusive.

The combative mother guards her territory fiercely, and while she wants her children to validate her, she's also competitive. That can yield even more confusion, as Karen, now 42, related: "My mother had been a beauty queen, and she was very proud of her looks. I was the only girl and super-cute as a small child. The photos of me look as if I'm a china doll, dressed to the nines. She looks proud and beaming. But as I got older, how pretty I was bothered her. She criticized everything I did. She screamed my inadequacies and mocked my failures. It was horrible. I didn't get it, and I just kept trying to please her. Strangely, it was my grandmother—her mother—who explained it to me, right before I left for college, in two words: 'She's jealous.' That was the first inkling I had that I had done nothing to deserve her wrath."

The combative mother shapes a daughter in specific ways. Imagine a seedling planted too close to the gutters of a house, pelted to the ground every time it rains, and you have an accurate picture of what it's like to be a child in these circumstances. Many daughters, not surprisingly, go down for the count as children. They become fearful and guarded, terrified of making a mistake. They hide in plain sight.

Others report that they just muzzled themselves out of fear during their adolescent years. One daughter wrote to ask, "Is it true that teenage girls actually challenge their mothers?" I answered by saying it was normal, and weird if they didn't, and then she and ten others chimed in with pretty much the same response: "I would have been cut to ribbons if I'd done that."

The Roles the Daughters of Combative Mothers Take On

The home as battleground spawns different ways of coping, each damaging to daughters in different ways. Based on interviews with many women, I've given them wholly unscientific names because my evidence is anecdotal, but they capture what happens in broad strokes.

The appeaser: This daughter becomes a peacemaker or a pleaser, doing what she can to turn down the volume and velocity of fights. She's often timid and so focused on stopping potential conflict that she forgets her own needs and wants, if she can even recognize them.

Unfortunately, these girls often end up in relationships with people who take advantage of their need to please, a pattern that usually persists into and through adulthood.

The scrapper: This daughter takes on her mother in many ways but can get tripped up by both fighting her mother and wanting her love at the same time. (It's a specific variation on the core conflict.) Management of emotion is often a problem for these daughters, most specifically anger because it's aroused by old triggers very quickly. These daughters also have difficulty distinguishing among emotions, confusing hurt with anger.

The avoidant: This daughter will do anything to dodge conflict of any kind; she's learned to armor herself living with a combative mother and she's distrustful of people. The problem is that in her effort to live conflict free, she's also missing out on the possibility of close connection, which is something she actually wants. Because she doesn't really trust anyone deep-down, she's more likely to fold her tents and flee than try to work out difficulties with anyone. In many senses, she is the most wounded of the daughters who came of age in the combat zone.

The combative mother is the easiest to spot on the surface but she leaves behind a complicated legacy of fear.

Common Effects of the Combative Mother
◆ Daughter's impaired ability to identify and manage her feelings
◆ High reactivity to even the hint of conflict
◆ Difficulty with intimacy and closeness
◆ Maladaptive behaviors when there's any kind of interpersonal tension
◆ Problems regulating emotions

THE ENMESHED MOTHER
Maxie, 69, was 14 and her brother was 10 when her mother came home to discover that her husband and their father had left them: "The apartment looked as if it'd been robbed: he'd taken the furniture, the linens, the art on the walls, the dishes and cookware. Only our clothes remained. My mother was a salesgirl at a store, and there was no way we could live on her salary. My father didn't want to pay her

much in alimony or child support so he dragged things out so she'd cave in and accept whatever crumbs he offered. Instead, she borrowed money and merchandise and started a business, and my brother and I worked in it. It became very successful. I lived at home until I was 29—my mother needed me—and moved into an apartment she picked out for me that was five minutes away. She hired the interior designer and had keys to my place. I was in therapy for years, and my therapists urged me to live my own life, but my mother couldn't let me go. I think the first decision I made totally alone was when I was 54 and planning her funeral. She loved me but not enough to let me go and stand on her own. That's not really mother love, is it?"

The enmeshed daughter disappears in the hot glare of her mother's attention. This daughter lacks a sense of self because her mother only sees her daughter as an extension of herself and observes no boundaries. The way out of this especially tangled relationship is very difficult and singular because even though the daughter may feel as though she's choked by the connection, she may also feel loved. It's a thorny paradox. These mothers actually do love their daughters, but the degree to which they engulf them is wounding nonetheless. It's the mother's own neediness that trumps all.

The classic example of the enmeshed mother is the stage mother—Gypsy Rose Lee, Frances Farmer, and some contemporary stars had them—or those who hope to live off of, be enriched by, or aggrandized by their daughters' achievements or status. Still others—such as the mother of Vivian Gornick as portrayed in her memoir *Fierce Attachments*—look to live through their daughters vicariously. These mothers are usually single—widowed or divorced—and deprived of other social connections; they experience the world through their daughters and use guilt and other forms of emotional manipulation to keep their daughters tied to them.

It's the mother's own unfulfilled needs that drive and define how she connects with her daughter. The enmeshed daughter is often an only child, but she may also be the last-born of a number of children who are separated by many years. Not knowing where she begins and Mom ends, this daughter looks to her mother for everything from advice to company, unconsciously subjugating her own needs and wants—if she can even recognize them—to her mother's. During childhood and adolescence, the daughter may chafe at her mother's intrusiveness but, often, she simply gives in and settles into the routines dictated by the person who says she always knows best. Young adulthood often presents a crisis for the daughter as she tries to find her own voice—and her mother pushes back. Some enmeshed daughters make it to college and may manage to live on their own, but others fail, moving back to the safety and oxygen-deprived atmosphere of their childhood rooms. Enmeshed daughters have great difficulty resolving the problem until they seek professional help, and even then, it can be an uphill battle.

Patterns of enmeshment may also emerge from relationships with self-absorbed or narcissistic mothers, who also see their daughters as extensions of themselves. These patterns are a bit different since the enmeshment is one sided and driven by the daughter's need to please her mother and stay within her orbit. The mother, in fact, is not enmeshed but a solitary star dictating her daughter's path.

Enmeshed daughters are sometimes able to salvage their relationships to their mothers by enforcing strict boundaries. These mothers aren't actually unloving; they just lack the ability to allow their daughters to breathe and be.

Common Effects of the Enmeshed Style
- Alternating feelings of anger, guilt, and emotional confusion
- Impaired sense of self
- Difficulties being independent and articulating and acting on her own needs
- Unhealthy coping mechanisms
- Inability to see the core conflict clearly

THE ROLE-REVERSED MOTHER
Anecdotally at least, this is the least reported pattern and usually happens when a mother is young or overburdened (she has too many responsibilities or children and not enough resources), is physically or mentally ill, or has experienced some other kind of life-altering crisis. The child, usually the oldest but sometimes the most capable, is thrust into the role of caretaker, no matter her age, and effectively becomes the "mother" in the family. These mothers aren't necessarily

unloving—in fact, many of them love their children deeply—but are rendered incapable for one reason or another. That said, there's no denying the damage they wreak: They rob their daughters of their childhoods and girlhoods, put burdens on them that they're not ready to take on, and force them to take on inappropriate adult roles.

Amy, a 32-year-old, shared her story: "My father died suddenly and unexpectedly when I was 13 and my little brother was 10. My mother fell apart and became very depressed, spending most of her time in bed. My dad's parents lived too far away to help. My mom's parents didn't really have time and had issues of their own. Everyone chalked it up to mourning and thought it would stop. It didn't. I was the mom for five years, cooking, cleaning, taking care of my brother. I didn't have time to see friends or date. I did poorly in school. I got married at 18 just to escape. That marriage fell apart, and when my brother turned 18 and I refused to come home to care for her, she finally got help. We still talk, but I am scarred and guarded."

Sometimes the daughter is pushed into the role of best friend or confidante to a lonely mother, which prevents her from being a child, burdens her with too much adult information, and blurs all the important boundaries. This relationship inflicts its own kind of damage as Grace, 39, told me: "My father divorced my mother, moved away, and remarried when I was six. Did you see that movie *Anywhere but Here?* That was my life. My mother wanted me to mother her, listen to her, support her. She wouldn't let me be a kid and, you know, she's the same now that I'm an adult. Being with her is like being in a room without air. I don't exist."

This pattern of relationship is different from the others and there is often reconciliation between these mothers and daughters as whatever obstacles that stood in the way of the mother's functioning are addressed or improved. This isn't to say that the relationship doesn't affect the daughter's development—it does—but it is also always clear that what's happening has nothing to do with the daughter herself. She never feels at fault or blamed or somehow responsible. She may also have compassion for her mother's predicament even as she chafes at the role she's been forced to take on. All of that makes a huge difference.

Common Effects of Role-Reversed Mothering

* Experience of a "lost" childhood; being forced into maturity the daughter isn't ready for
* Often, poor social skills and a feeling of isolation
* Feeling conflicted: Daughter loves her mother but also resents her
* Great difficulty with forming close and intimate relationships

USING THE EIGHT BEHAVIORS FOR UNDERSTANDING

Very few women report just a single behavior dominating their childhoods and young adulthoods; almost everyone says that their mothers displayed one or more at various times. You'll note that I've used unscientific descriptions, and I've done that deliberately, even in the case of the self-involved mother whom I've declined to call a narcissist. One reason is that I'm not a therapist or psychologist, but even if I were, I couldn't "diagnose" someone I hadn't talked to. The second is that, while there's a reassurance and aha! moment in realizing that your mother's a narcissist or maybe borderline, it doesn't focus you on what happened to you. *Daughter Detox* is about you, not her. Her behavior is only important as an aid in seeing how you were shaped and affected.

The point of these categories is for you to start understanding *how* you were treated with some specificity. There's a lot of unconscious process that prevents you from really seeing how you were affected; that's why seeing your wounds is so hard. The more experience is brought into the light, out of the murk of unconsciousness, the better equipped you'll be to stop the past from leaking into and directing the flow of the present.

THE ARSENAL: VERBAL ABUSE IN ALL OF ITS FORMS

Verbal aggression and abuse are usually part of the daughter's emotional landscape, although she may not recognize either except in hindsight. Some of that has to do with the child accepting that what goes on at her house is normal because she has nothing to compare it to; remember that her world is tiny and the interpretation of that world is controlled by her parents. Harsh words are often justified by mothers as disciplinary in nature or a necessary corrective ("I wouldn't have to get angry if you didn't mess up all the time"). Additionally, abusive mothers marginalize or deny the pain of verbal abuse, which adds to the child's confusion and shame ("They're just words. Stop being a crybaby and grow a spine"). One daughter, now 47 and a mother herself, described what it was like: "My mother filled the house with her rage and yelling but told me I had no right to be sad or to be angry, that I should be glad I was being fed and clothed. She shamed me for reacting. She sabotaged and mocked me when something made me happy or feel proud and I felt myself get smaller and smaller. I tried very hard to disappear, you know?"

But not all abuse is loud or even articulated. In fact, counterintuitively enough, some of the worst kinds of verbal abuse are quiet; silence in answer to a question asked or a comment made can pack a mightier wallop than a loud rant. Silence effectively ridicules and shames. The child subjected to quiet abuse often experiences more emotional confusion than one who's being yelled at or insulted, precisely because the absence of rage sends mixed signals, and the motivation behind willful silence or a refusal to answer is impossible for a child to read. There's a special kind of hurt in being treated as though you're invisible or that you are so unimportant in the scheme of things that you're not even worth answering. Is there anything more chilling and hurtful than seeing your mother act as though she can't see you, her face calm?

Everything science knows about the effects of verbal abuse applies to the quiet variety, too. Following are the different kinds of subtle verbal abuse you might have experienced.

Being ignored: Because much of the information children have about the world and relationships comes to them secondhand, the child with a mother who ignores her learns that her place in the world is precarious, even though she doesn't know why, and even worse, generalizes that most relationships make you feel bad about yourself. Remember the effect that Edward Tronick's "Still Face" experiments had on babies and toddlers? How those children had to self-protect? Well, being ignored 24/7 effectively disappears a child's sense of self instead of validating it, and she learns that avoidance doesn't hurt but expectation of engagement does. That, too, is abusive.

Stonewalling: From a child's perspective, being stonewalled may seem very much like being ignored, but it has different emotional consequences, especially as she matures. She's likely to recognize this abuse by the time she's an adolescent, which will increase volatility in the household, depending on whether she fights back or folds her tents. It's the younger child who's especially vulnerable. The child's lack of developed and effective defense mechanisms is precisely what researchers in Israel homed in on when they examined the long-term effects of childhood emotional abuse. They concluded that the damage done to individuals' self-esteem had much to do with their inability to protect and defend themselves and to internalizing the thought that they weren't good enough to warrant their parents' attention when parents were uncaring or harshly controlling.

Contempt and derision: Shaming a child can be accomplished sotto voce or even with physical gestures like eye-rolling or laughing at her to convey contempt or making her the butt of jokes. This particular variety of bullying can become a team sport in some households, if siblings are asked to join the fray and make the child a scapegoat. Controlling parents or those who need to be the center of attention often use these techniques to maintain the dynamics of the household as they want them. Once again, damage can be done without a raised voice.

Gaslighting: This tool of manipulation is aimed at having the child doubt her perceptions. (The term derives from a play, *Gas Light*, which was then made into a movie, about a man who tries to convince a woman she's losing her mind.) Gaslighting doesn't require shouting or yelling; all it takes is a simple statement that something that actually happened didn't. Given the imbalance of power in the parent-child relationship—and the fact that a young child accepts the adult as the last word and authority on most things until she gets old enough to begin questioning her mother's judgment—gaslighting is relatively easy. Gaslighting not only makes a child worry about being "crazy" but also erodes her confidence in her own thoughts and feelings in a profound and lasting way. Again, keep in mind that children don't have conscious defense mechanisms.

Hypercriticality: In many households, both the loud and the quiet kinds of verbal abuse are rationalized by the need to correct perceived flaws in the child's character or behavior. Hypercriticality—nitpicking and then magnifying every misstep or mistake—may be "justified" or "explained" by having to make sure the child "isn't too full of herself," "doesn't let her successes go to her head," "learns humility," "knows who's boss," and other self-serving statements that are just excuses for cruel adult behavior. Delivered in a quiet tone, the barrage of criticism makes a child believe she's unworthy of attention and support because she's worthless.

The absence of praise, support, and love: The power of what isn't said cannot be overstated because the void it leaves in the child's psyche and heart is enormous and, yes, it's emotionally abusive. Children are hardwired to need all the things that the unloving mother neither voices nor demonstrates in order to thrive and develop normally. In truth, words that articulate why a child is worthy of love and attention are as essential as food, water, clothing, and shelter.

Normalizing or excusing the abuse: As I've already mentioned, it's a sad truth that a child's world is so small that she thinks that what goes on in it goes on everywhere. Most children attribute verbal abuse to their flaws and "badness"; as Rachel Goldsmith and Jennifer Freyd note, this attribution may actually be less scary than "the scarier prospect that the caregiver can't be trusted and may help create an illusion of control." Even as adults, those verbally abused in the quiet manner during childhood may rationalize or normalize their parents' behaviors for many different reasons.

Maternal power—that ability to dictate how things that happen in the household are interpreted—and the daughter's acceptance of what happens at home as "normal" stand in the way of her seeing how she's being emotionally abused. Then, too, her continuing need for her mother's love also keeps her more focused on somehow turning things around than analyzing the real dynamics. She's more apt to look for reasons why her mother treats her as she does and make excuses for the behavior rather than confront the terrible and painful truth. This is what I call "the dance of denial." It's little wonder that so many daughters struggle for decades long after their childhoods are officially over.

MOVING FROM DISCOVERY TO DISCERNMENT

You may be feeling a sense of relief at this moment, seeing the ways in which your mother behaved expressed in words on the page in black-and-white, along with the recognition that other girls had experiences similar to yours. As one woman wrote after being on my Facebook page, "It's strange how knowing that I have company in this awful situation, that others have gone through what I did, and felt some of the same feelings of isolation and hurt, has made me feel better and less daunted." The list of the toxic patterns of maternal behavior is meant to be used as a tool for you to begin seeing how her actions and inactions, what she said and what she didn't say, affected your own reactions and behavior in the past and continue to do so in the present. Recognizing your own mental models of relationship—your predominant attachment style—is a necessary step in the process. These first two chapters have sketched the terrain the unloved daughter finds herself in; the following two will begin the process of untangling the threads that form the tapestry of your personal experiences. It's what I call "discernment," and the first stop is taking a close look at the family of origin and its dynamics.

Chapter Three
All in the Family: Understanding Ripple Effects

There were four of us, growing up—two boys and two girls.
My brothers got all the attention, which I resented when I was
young but I now see that wasn't necessarily a good thing. Our
mother was enmeshed and controlling in the boys' lives, and
dismissive of my sister and me. My sister is the youngest, and
she simply went her own way. I was the needy one, desperate
to please my mother and get my father's attention. Nothing
worked. I married the first guy I dated at 18 and that set me
on a path for a life of underachieving. I divorced him and
married another. Now I'm 45 and trying to reroute my life.
I don't speak to anyone in my family other than my sister.
~Clarice, 45

A mother's treatment of her daughter doesn't take place in a vacuum, of course; the drama plays out in a household, each of which has its own unique aspects. This chapter marks the first step toward discernment: being able to see and then fully understand both the ways in which your childhood experiences were similar to those of others and the ways in which they were different and unique. Each pathway to healing is, in the details, singular because we are all individuals with our signature quirks and ways of seeing the world. Once again, we will begin with the broadest of brushstrokes so that you can locate your experiences in the common threads and then begin to see the differences.

As small children, the world of the family is the only one we know. We may feel its undercurrents—the arguments between our parents, shifts in routine that may signal larger changes of which we're unaware—but we have no way of knowing whether this family is like the other families we see out in the greater world. Everything that happens in this little world affects us in small ways and large even though we don't know that as children. One of the largest obstacles to our healing as adults is the young self still inside each of us who, in the hope of feeling at one with that family and belonging to it, still believes that what happened was "normal." Or that if it wasn't quite normal, the dynamic can somehow be fixed or altered, even now.

Family dynamics—the interactions among the individuals within the group—are defined by both presences and absences: the presence of siblings or the absence of them, the presence of a father or the absence of one, the presence of extended family or its absence, the presence of addiction or its absence, the presence of stability in all of its forms and its absence.

And then, too, there is the presence or absence of love and attunement. The presence or absence of aggression, anger, manipulation, and chaos. The presence or absence of mutual support, respect, and caring.

Each family is different, although there are discernible patterns that aid our understanding. While this book focuses on a specific lack—maternal support and love—the losses suffered by a daughter usually involve other relationships as well. Depending on the dynamic, wresting love from her father may be as hopeless a task as trying to get it from her mother. Then there is the sibling connection, the relationship that can potentially span more decades of life than any other. For many daughters, sibling relationships become the locus of more pain and loss.

All of these experiences—fallout out from the maternal relationship—also mark the daughter in specific ways.

FORGETTING THE IMAGE OF THE SCALES

Colloquially, when we talk about relationships and their pluses and minuses, we often use images that summon up scales, employing words like "balance out" when we're focused on the pros of staying in or, when we're not, referencing the thing or things that "tipped the scales" and made us bail. There's only one problem with the imagery and the vocabulary, especially as we move toward understanding how the dynamics of our family worked and affected us: They're not accurate. You may remember that, in the first chapter, I wrote about how "bad is stronger than good," and how bad events and negative emotions affect us much more quickly and deeply than positive ones. And how they're stored in the brain for easy retrieval. And how the verbal expression of caring by one parent doesn't do anything to mitigate or buffer the effect of verbal aggression by the other. A study of some 2,000 adults in their sixties showed that, when it came to telling their life stories, painful events were recalled quite differently even when there'd been a long interval of time since they occurred, with the exception of childhood trauma. The researchers concluded that older adults perceived positive events as central to their lives largely because of cultural norms, but that negative events were perceived as central or a turning point because of coping skills and emotional distress.

Well, all of that is part of a larger psychological truth: The systems that process good events and experiences and bad ones are separate and run parallel to each other. So there's no weighing, no balance, no tipping, no offset.

As you approach the task of discerning the patterns of interaction in your family of origin, you need to make an effort to see them objectively and separately, and not in concert. Being treated well by your father may have helped build your sense of self, but it did little to assuage the wounding your mother's disparagement inflicted.

THE UNSEEN PLAYER: THE MARRIAGE BETWEEN YOUR PARENTS

The roles mothers and fathers play in their children's lives—whether they are essentially loving and caring parents or not—are usually closely tied to the relationship the two adults have to each other. Small children aren't really in a position to understand the relationship except in the most obvious of ways; you may have parents who are usually laughing and hugging or grow up in a place where slammed doors and yelling are the norm. But the dynamic of that central relationship—is it one in which each partner listens to the other and compromises are made to benefit the couple, or is it one that is all about power?—inevitably spills over onto how both mother and father parent. How happy your mother and father are in the relationship matters, too, of course, and shapes all of the family's interactions, as does whether his or her individual expectations are being met by the other partner. It's very easy for marital dissatisfaction to become anger directed at a child. And, of course, the breakdown of that relationship (if it occurs)—whether it ends in an amicable divorce, a prolonged battle lasting years, or a literal disappearing act—spills out and over onto each child in the family in a very personal way.

As adults, we can finally begin to see the subterranean currents in our parents' marriages we felt washing up against us as children but couldn't identify.

THE OTHER GROWN-UP: YOUR FATHER

Research shows that in healthy families, fathers contribute to a child's development in significant ways, through actions, words, modeling of behavior, and displays of affection. Paternal influence may be key in teaching a child to regulate emotions—through the roughhouse style of play that fathers tend to favor—as well as helping a child form a cognitive perspective on empathy in childhood and adolescence. In a healthy family, the dyad of husband and wife is actually strengthened by the expansion to include the child in a new triad, even though it may take conscientious effort. A few studies make it clear that the father's influence isn't insubstantial. For example, one by Jennifer Byrd-Craven, Brandon J. Auer, and others showed that a daughter's relationship to her father plays a significant role in her management of stress. Measuring for cortisol, a hormone released by stress, researchers noted that cortisol levels went down with warm and caring connections between father and daughter. Daughters in relationships that were more negative and not close showed both higher levels of cortisol and increased sensitivity to emotional changes and an inability to inhibit reactivity.

Something else happens when a mother is unloving or rejecting.

When we become parents, each of us—whether it's the role of mother or father we're about to take on—brings to the table not just our own childhood experiences but also our ideas, all of them untested and many of them not totally articulated, about how best to rise to the challenges of parenting and the desirable or "proper" role each parent should play. The childhoods of daughters (and sons) raised from the 1940s to the 1970s were shaped by traditional views of the father as the breadwinner, rule setter, and disciplinarian and the mother as in charge of raising children and running the home. For most of these daughters of unloving mothers, the role of the father was culturally and socially marginalized, which had real-life consequences.

But recent research reveals that, even now, the involvement of fathers continues to be limited since, even in these more enlightened times, mothering is seen as more important than fathering, and raising children continues to be a woman's turf, as does the care of the home, even in households with two wage earners. It turns out that mothers end up deciding whether or not and to what degree fathers are involved in childrearing, a phenomenon called "maternal gatekeeping." When a mother gate-keeps, she criticizes, disparages, or discourages her husband's efforts at childrearing; as a result, fathers are likely to withdraw from active roles.

Almost 20 years ago, Mary DeLuccie's work revealed that both the stability of the marriage and the wife's support were strong predictors of paternal involvement with their children. Interestingly, the more negative the mother's experience had been with her own father, the more eager she was for her husband to be an active parent. Daughters of rejecting fathers were also more likely to be supportive and happy with their husbands' efforts. More recent research, including that of Sarah Schoppe-Sullivan, sees maternal gatekeeping as a significant factor when coparenting fails. Unloving, rejecting, and controlling mothers tend to be described by their daughters as expert gatekeepers; they want control of what has traditionally been a woman's turf.

For some daughters of unloving mothers, the father's mere presence at home helps to de-escalate the criticism and hostility; for other daughters, though, their closeness to their fathers will heighten the conflict with a jealous or competitive mother, or a highly self-involved one who wants the attention of the man of the house all to herself. A father who is emotionally withdrawn from the household—present in fact but essentially absent by choice—can increase the confusion the unloved daughter feels and add to her feelings of abandonment and betrayal. The truly absentee father—either through divorce or because he's simply skipped out—affects the unloved daughter in yet another way.

Again, I've given thoroughly unscientific descriptions of some of the roles fathers can play in the dynamic of the mother-daughter relationship and in the one-on-one relationship with their daughters. Sometimes, behaviors will overlap or change over time. Keep in mind that these patterns are meant only as tools to help you sort out and understand the role your own father played in your childhood and later.

The Yes Man: Whether he does it consciously or unconsciously, this father becomes a co-conspirator with the mother. In some cases, the mother makes sure that she doesn't say or do anything hurtful to her daughter in her husband's presence; in others, where the behavior is witnessed, the mother quickly shifts the blame onto the daughter. No matter what rationale is offered—the child needed correction, was disobedient or disrespectful, is too "sensitive"—the father buys into it. Dad's joining Team Mom makes it easy for the daughter to consider herself responsible for her mother's lack of love. With Mom and Dad teamed up, the daughter may be wary of all relationships with both women and men.

Some Yes Men don't team up with their wives but end up playing the appeaser role, which is a variation on the theme. Their commitment to the marriage and their own acceptance of how their spouses act ("That's just who she is" or "She means well—she's doing it for your own good") trump all and lead them to actively encourage their daughters to feel the same. Unfortunately, by acting as appeasers, they further marginalize and deny their daughters' perceptions and feelings. These men may have some measure of love and affection for their daughters but ignore or look away from maternal treatment and its consequences since their first allegiance is to Team Spouse and Marriage. Their consistent lack of support results in emotional confusion and more complicated issues of trust.

The Chorus: It's sad but true that some unloved daughters report growing up with two emotionally abusive parents—each for his or her own reasons—who take their grievances out on a single child or a number of them. Yes, fathers can be unloving, too, and sometimes— horribly enough—an unloved daughter finds herself in a situation where the messages, even if different, are all negative, all the time, separate from the dynamics of the marriage.

The King of the Castle: As counterintuitive as it sounds, the presence of a loving and involved father can actually complicate the dynamic in the household in destructive ways. His closeness to his daughter can quickly become a catalyst for escalated conflict, especially as the daughter gets older, since the mother perceives the attention her daughter's getting as rightfully hers. Jealous, competitive, or self-involved mothers will often see the daughter as a potential rival for what she thinks of as her throne by the King's side. Mothers who competed for their fathers' attention as daughters—my mother was one—are especially susceptible to feeling threatened. These mothers will escalate the warfare by amplifying their criticism of their daughters and doing what they can to turn their husbands into Yes Men.

The more unstable the marriage is, the more the father's affection for his daughter looks like a threat to the safety of her mother's world. Sometimes, the daughter becomes a stand-in for the "other woman," real or imagined. As daughters tell it, the King of the Castle scenario is very toxic and impossible to resolve. Jealousy heats up a mother's behaviors, no matter what form they take, and spurs on her vindictiveness and meanness. The daughter effectively doesn't have a chance.

The Absentee: Sometimes, daughters discover that both parents are equally emotionally unavailable, even if their parenting styles are very different; some daughters report that their controlling mothers controlled their husbands as well, and these fathers tended to disappear into the woodwork. While the Yes Man joins Team Mom, the Absentee simply stays out of the fray as much as he can. This is what Sarah recounted: "I have practically no memory of my father that doesn't involve television or his shop in the basement. He ate dinner in silence, never asked about my day, and disappeared once he put down his fork. Until I was an adult, he was a cipher to me."

In troubled marriages, fathers often emotionally vacate the premises long before they leave (and some of them don't ever leave), and spend more time at work, out of the house, and attending to hobbies and sports outside of the familial circle. Extramarital affairs remove them even farther from the emotional center of the family and, of course, their daughters. The emotional pain inflicted on daughters by the lack of maternal love is compounded by the sense that their fathers have abandoned them and failed to protect them, leaving them alone and at their mothers' mercy. Daughters report a great deal of emotional confusion when fathers are absent, and if their mothers end up abandoned by their fathers, they may actually align themselves with their mothers, creating another kind of inner conflict. The need for mother love rises to the surface, and loyalty to the mother in these circumstances sometimes outweighs the need for self-protection.

Parental divorce creates a special conundrum for daughters of unloving mothers, who usually end up living with their mothers; daughters of enmeshed mothers will find the going very rough as whatever slight boundaries once existed disappear under stress. An older daughter may be able to recognize that her father has left because he's been treated the way she has, and that can lift the burden of feeling responsible for the failure of the maternal relationship and create an enduring alliance with the father, even if the time spent with him is scanty. Even though these fathers are physically absent from their daughters' lives, they are nonetheless emotionally present and caring. When the daughters reach adulthood and begin to set boundaries with their mothers, their bonds to their fathers may remain strong.

The Rescuer: While few daughters report feeling totally protected by their fathers from their mothers' treatment—there doesn't seem to be a White Knight—many do feel that their fathers' presence rescued or saved them in important ways. As Jackie, 61, put it, "I didn't spend all that much time with my father—he spent a lot of time hiding behind his newspaper, avoiding the conflict, or puttering with some home improvement project that couldn't be interrupted—but when I did, I was actually able to breathe. I could see myself, the good stuff, reflected in his face, and that gave me the courage not to quit on myself and fall into the trap of believing everything she said. It helped. It didn't fix me up all spic and span, but he saved me nonetheless."

Jackie is like many daughters of dismissive or combative mothers whose fathers' encouragement of pursuits and acknowledgment of their talents and abilities acted to counterbalance their mothers' focus on failures and shortcomings. Daughters of rejecting or emotionally distant mothers often find a safe haven in their fathers' company and affection, even when it's relatively limited in scope because of maternal gatekeeping. Many daughters—and I count myself in that number—received validation from their fathers that permitted them to begin to understand, even at a relatively young age, that they had done nothing to provoke or deserve their mothers' treatment. In some families, especially if the unloved daughter is the eldest or the only child, the father can become a gateway to the outside world as he encourages her to try new things or persist in pursuits he considers valuable.

Unlike the Yes Man, the Appeaser, or the Absentee, the Rescuer tends to act more like a free agent, navigating between his love and loyalty to his wife and daughter. Many daughters with Rescuer fathers often end up walking in paternal footsteps when it comes to work and career. Others report that their fathers were the voice of encouragement when it came to cultivating an interest or talent such as music, a sport, or a creative endeavor. Studies show that while women build closeness by talking, men usually build bonds through shared activity, and that's true, too, of the father-daughter relationship. This is what Jenny, 37, recounted: "My father never took my side when my mother picked on me or mocked me for not being popular like my brother. But he cheered me on quietly when it came to my schoolwork and then, when I started writing stories, he would read everything I wrote. I don't think he said a word to my mother about them. I got a scholarship to a college writing program, and he drove me there alone. She had other things to do. He wasn't a protector, and I was hurt in childhood but still, he helped me in his own small way."

It's important to realize that even having a Rescuer father isn't a version of the "out of jail" card in a board game. Remember the point about the negative and positive experiences being processed and stored in the brain differently? Yes, the Rescuer helps, but the daughter is still left with a boatload of emotional baggage and a journey of healing ahead of her. I am living proof.

THE ONLY CHILD

The singleton faces some challenges that are unique and others that aren't. The little world all children live in is even smaller when it's made up of three people and, sometimes, just two. And it's not just the mother myths that this daughter must contend with but those pertaining to children without siblings. Having been an only child for the first nine years of my life, I know firsthand what this feels like. In the 1950s—when the Baby Boomers came of age—10 percent of the population were onlies, a relative rarity in a sea of 3.6 siblings; today, 20 percent are singletons. But the myths of the only as bratty, spoiled, coddled, unsocialized, and somehow maimed still remain part of the cultural consciousness. After all, the so-called father of psychology, G. Stanley Hall, wrote that "being an only child is a disease in itself," while Alfred Adler, in the next century, declared, "The only child has difficulties with every independent activity and sooner or later, they become useless in life." The truth? Study after study has shown that singletons actually fare no worse, and sometimes better, than their siblinged counterparts.

So is the stereotype of the "lonely only" wrong? Well, again, it depends on how that only daughter is attached to her mother and father and whether the triangle that is the family is stable or not. And if it isn't and her mother falls into any one of the eight toxic patterns, she is likely to have a very hard time of it, although recognition of the pattern may actually come earlier to her. Only children spend more time with adults than other children and are exposed to more adult conversations and activities than children with siblings; they are used to listening or even eavesdropping on what adults say. (This is all anecdotal, but I was one growing up and I am the mother of one and have interviewed many.) But recognizing the pattern for what it is doesn't help the only child manage the negative emotions she feels, or soothe the pain of being unloved. Because outsiders are likely to believe that the singleton is more coddled than other children, this may impose a special kind of isolation, upping the ante on keeping the silence.

The spotlight shone on the only child is unwelcome when a mother is combative, enmeshed, or self-involved; there's no one else to take the heat or provide a momentary respite.

While it seems counterintuitive, only children can also be scapegoated even in the absence of a herd. The scapegoated only child is sometimes blamed for something that has gone wrong in her mother's life; it could be the thwarting of her ambitions or success ("If I hadn't had you, I would have had a brilliant career in dance"), choices she made ("I'd have finished college if it weren't for you"), the state of her health or looks ("I never was able to lose the weight I gained when I was pregnant with you"), or the failure of her marriage. The latter is the charge most frequently raised, especially if the daughter looks like her father, reminds her mother of him, or is sufficiently "disloyal" to want a relationship with him and his relatives. That was 35-year-old Jody's story: "My dad left when I was six and remarried days after the divorce became final. My mother blamed me for his leaving. She said that if I hadn't needed so much of her attention, he wouldn't have felt neglected and cheated. I believed her for years and years and felt guilty and terrible. Even worse, she made me feel awful for loving my dad and wanting to see him. You have no idea how torn I was. I was saved by going away to college, where my unhappiness finally landed me in a therapist's office. It was a lifesaver."

The mythology pertaining to only children assumes they aren't capable of individuating and are to some degree enmeshed, and while that's not true in a healthy family, it can be true in an unhealthy one, as Ariel Leve's harrowing memoir, *An Abbreviated Life*, demonstrates. The only child of an extremely self-centered mother and a loving father who literally lived on the other side of the globe, Leve could only live her own life by cutting her mother off completely. Enmeshed, engulfed, manipulated, and gaslighted by turns, she appeared to have no other way to move forward.

THE COMPLICATED TRUTH ABOUT SIBLINGS

As an only child for the first nine years of my life, I had two major fantasies. The first involved a hospital mix-up on the day I was born and it included my "real" mother ringing the doorbell and coming to reclaim me. The second was of a wise, protective, loving older sister—think Jo in *Little Women*—who would be my best friend, tell me I wasn't to blame for how our mother treated me, and would even run away with me if need be, just like Hansel and Gretel but with two girls.

My fantasies notwithstanding, the truth is that sibling relationships are complicated under the best of circumstances, even in loving families. Despite the mythology of all mothers treating and caring for each child equally, favoritism occurs in almost every family, as a large body of research and an acronym (PDT, for Parental Differential Treatment) attest. Because mothering isn't biologically driven in our species but learned behavior, personality and other factors shape a woman's ability to mother a specific child, which can result in differential treatment. Personality or "goodness of fit," as it's called, may make one child easier to raise than another.

Imagine a relatively introverted mother who needs quiet with a highly expressive, rambunctious child, and then imagine her with a calmer child who is much more like her. Which of the two will she feel closest to? Who will frustrate her less? How much more stress will she feel parenting one rather than the other? External factors such as the mother's age and emotional maturity, the economic status of the family, the amount of stress the mother is under, and the stability of the marriage also shape how and why children are treated differentially. In a loving family, differential treatment can even be motivated by good intentions, such as a mother's perception that one child needs more support and attention than another. So sibling rivalry, even with a loving mother, has a basis in reality.

Most importantly, research shows that the impact of a child's perception of differential treatment ("Mom loves Timmy/Molly more than she loves me") is greater than the impact of the love and attention she receives directly from her mother. For example, Judy Dunn and Robert Plomin demonstrated that observing differential treatment of a sister or brother had a greater effect on a child than the actual love received from a parent. (Again, this proves the psychological truism that "bad is stronger than good" or that negative experiences affect us more than positive ones.) Other studies show that children who are given more support and affection by their mothers—having the favored status—have greater self-esteem and better adjustment skills than their discounted siblings who are likely to be at a greater risk for depression. A study of young adult children confirmed these findings, along with diminished sibling relationships, when PDT was part of the family dynamic. Needless to say, the effect of differential treatment was greater when the favored sibling was the same gender.

The belief that having more than one child is beneficial to children and parents alike has pervaded thinking about family dynamics for so long that the term "sibling rivalry" passed into the popular lexicon as a relatively benign, if sometimes unpleasant, side effect of the larger family. That's not always true since more recent studies show that sibling rivalry and competition can be highly destructive to the individual and that bullying, alas, is learned at home.

Keep in mind that these observations are drawn from healthy families in which the basic emotional needs of the children *are*, in fact, met. When you add an unloving mother into the mix, there are many variations on the theme, most decidedly not pretty. When a mother is unloving to or hypercritical of one child but not another, patterns of relationship emerge that vaguely resemble patterns in relatively healthy families but that differ in kind because they are cruel, deliberate, and conscious.

Some mothers actively orchestrate their children's behavior by pitting them against each other or by co-opting the siblings so that the daughter becomes the odd girl out (called "triangulation" by Murray Bowen). Sometimes, the behavior is aimed at keeping the family's attention on the mother or making sure that the mother's vision of what's happening becomes the family truth. One adult daughter, now estranged from her mother, recounted that when her brother confessed that he'd had coffee with his sister, their mother hung up the phone. She then sent him an email, demanding that he never do that again because "your sister always has been difficult and crazy, and it's painful and insulting to me that you are taking her side. Do not ever contact her again if you want to stay in contact with me." The controlling, combative, or self-absorbed mother will usually do what she can to make sure that sibling relationships are neither close nor intimate unless she is in control of them.

Thus, the lack of maternal love is often not the only emotional loss sustained; sibling relationships, a sense of belonging to a family, and connectedness are among the others, all of which affect the daughter's sense of self in myriad ways. Annie, 49, was the only girl among six children, and she says she was the family's punch line: "I was scape-goated from the beginning, the one bookish kid, the quiet one among braggarts. As an adult, I became the black sheep—the object of lies and made-up gossip. I am the successful one, married to a successful man, with a higher education and a professional career. My mother hated me, and the boys followed her lead. I suppose it makes them feel better about themselves."

What follows are broad patterns; I have given some of them names, but all of them are drawn from psychological research on siblings, which is comparatively robust. Judging from literature—from the ancient Greeks forward and then on to Cain and Abel and into the present—the sibling bond has always been a source of great fascination for everyone. The ante is upped when a mother is unloving.

The Hansel and Gretel bond: Yes, as in the fairytale, and according to Stephen P. Bank and Michael D. Kahn, this is a bond that emerges from shared trauma—such as the absence of loving and supportive parents or the death of one or both parents. Hansel and Gretel pairs are mutual caretakers, protect each other, and actively work at saving each other; it's a dyadic connection that is different in kind from that of an older sibling parenting a younger one. Only a few daughters I've interviewed report having such a close and symbiotic relationship, and then only when maternal treatment was consistent among and between siblings or there was an underlying cause such as a mother's personality disorder or addiction. Even so, anecdotally at least, most daughters who report something approximating a Hansel and Gretel pair also note that these ties often don't outlast childhood as the siblings come to understand the dynamics of the family differently, react to them differently, and be affected in different ways.

That was the case for Ceci, 43, only separated from her sister by 18 months: "My sister was my protector when we were small. My mother was very combative and verbally abusive, and had what I'd call 'tantrums' from an adult perspective. She'd lose it when things didn't go exactly as she'd planned and take it out on us; our father would duck out, either literally by going out or ignoring Mom totally. But Jill's way of dealing with our mother, as we got older, was to placate her. She felt sorry for her, and still does. I got angry and fought back and I resented Jill's 'poor Mom' thing. She still does it, and that's affected our ability to connect to each other. I'd call it a cordial relationship but nothing more."

Rivals to the max: In some families, the unloved daughter's hardwired need for her mother's love and attention creates an inevitable and toxic rivalry with a sibling who gets both. Daughters report that when the rival is a brother, the blow delivered to the soul and self-esteem is not as great; the pain is intensified when one daughter is rejected and another embraced. That was certainly the case for Gayle, now 44, whose sister—just 22 months older—was the "good" child while she was the "bad" and "difficult" one. Her mother meted out affection and reward on the basis of achievement, and her sister, athletic and an A student, easily beat out Gayle who was dyslexic; their mother proclaimed Gayle an embarrassment, both inside and outside of the family. While Gayle was intensely jealous of her sister, her sister suffered, too, given the enormous pressure on her to succeed so that she could garner her mother's love and attention. In this family, it was a rivalry in which there was no winner. At one point, both daughters were estranged from their mother, though Gayle's sister now maintains a relationship with her. Not surprisingly, the two sisters have no relationship to speak of, exchanging pro forma phone calls on birthdays and holidays.

The favorite and the scapegoat: You can call the favorite the "trophy" or "golden" child, but the bottom line is that he or she can do no wrong while the unloved daughter can do nothing right. A terrible and agonizing clarity (which also often prompts self-blame) envelops the unloved daughter when she realizes her mother can love a child who isn't her. One daughter, who was five when her sister was born, recalled the pain and shock she felt seeing her mother with her sister: "My mother would rock her, constantly singing, loving, kissing, and I had never once seen her act like that. I remember watching her interact so lovingly with my sister, and it was like watching a movie I had never seen. It remains that way to this day."

Sometimes, the favorite is simply seen as an extension of the mother, as one daughter explained. "My younger sister was my mother's clone. They liked the same things, looked alike, had the same priorities. My mother was horribly critical of me—calling me nerdy and dull, compared to my sister's charm—and I always felt like an awkward and unwanted guest who couldn't join in. My mother was never interested in me, and when I married and had children, she was equally distant. It was my sister's kids and husband she adored. I speak to my sister twice a year, over the phone, for no more than five minutes."

Sometimes, a daughter will ally herself against another sibling, hoping that somehow doing so will gain her the attention she craves. That was Leah's older sister's strategy. Leah was the middle child, her sister two years older, and she had a brother four years younger. All the attention was lavished on the baby boy, but her older sister's allegiance to her mother and her vigorous efforts to shut Leah out kept her from being criticized and verbally abused as Leah was. "My sister and my mother were a team in the sense that they both adored my brother. I always felt like an outsider looking in, walking on eggshells to make sure I didn't do anything to invoke my mother's withering dismissal of me. I have spent years in therapy, trying to shake the feeling of being 'less than,' with mixed results despite a happy marriage and two wonderful children. My childhood sense of self still dogs me."

In some families, though, the treatment of the unloved daughter becomes a cruel team sport, rendering her a scapegoat. Mary, now 51, was one of four, with one older sister and two younger brothers. While all the children feared their mother, Mary was the one labeled the "bad" one or the "troublemaker," and picking on her or placing blame on her worked well for her siblings as a tactic to deflect attention from themselves. She remarks that, in hindsight, it's clear that "we never had any control or choice about our relationship. We had a master puppeteer." She is estranged from all of her siblings and comments, "If I were to meet them today as strangers, I would not be interested in being friends."

Many daughters believe what they're told about themselves, especially when they are young and they hear these "facts" repeated again and again, like some twisted familial mantra. How could they not? Scapegoating is much more public than the other kinds of maternal abuse, which are usually kept secret; the marginalization of the scapegoated child is institutionalized in a sense and made into family lore. The treatment is rationalized and the reasons for it are often broadcast to extended family and, sometimes, to anyone who will listen. ("Lizzy has always been difficult, moody, and has a bad temper;

she's nothing like her brothers and sisters, and it's no wonder she's not popular the way they all are.") Needless to say, these daughters usually internalize the criticism until there is a moment of recognition—if there is one—when they finally see the pattern for what it is, most usually in adulthood.

The Odd Girl Out: In this dynamic, the unloved daughter isn't actively set upon as in the scapegoat pattern, but siblings co-conspire with their mother to isolate the unloved daughter in order to gain her love and approval. They reinforce and sustain the mother's vision of things. Corinne, 40, recounts the subtle and not-so-subtle ways in which she was marginalized by both her mother and her siblings: "My older sister followed my mother's lead to stay in her good graces. If I succeeded at something—getting good grades, winning the lead in a play—my mother would first deflect the conversation by praising my brother or sister, and then my sister would start in on how my achievement was no big deal. I felt close to my brother, the baby of the family, when he was little, but as he got older, he just didn't have the courage to stand up to Mom and take my side. I always felt, and still do feel, like an outsider mostly."

Here's another story with resonance for many. Rose, 36, was one of three children, and the only girl: "My mother acted as though she didn't have a daughter most of the time, unless she needed me to do something like laundry or walk the dog. I did well in school, unlike my brothers, and so my mother downplayed my achievements, saying that 'being good at school didn't make me smart.' And, for the most part, I believed her, even after I won awards and ultimately a college scholarship. I still have trouble shutting the voice in my head off—the one that says that everything I do right doesn't really matter. I'm an attorney and both of my brothers are construction workers, but that hasn't changed how my mother treats me . . . I'm still the odd girl out."

Daughters who were the Odd Girl Out in their families of origin often report that they have difficulty forging close friendships with women and have trouble trusting their own judgments in relationships generally. They also report that they're highly sensitive to rejection and criticism.

PARALLEL LIVES

Almost all daughters report that, in one way or another, their mothers orchestrated their sibling relationships with deliberation. In some cases, a mother will actively work at making sure that her children don't bond by setting one against the other, or triangulating. As a result, some daughters grow up in households where, despite the fact that the children are under the same roof, sharing day-to-day experiences, and may even be close in age, they end up living parallel lives without any connection to one another. There's no open warfare or enmity as there can be in the other patterns, but there's also little or no emotional connection. One daughter described it as "living among strangers who were related to me, who had the same parents, but we knew nothing about each other at all."

In a similar vein, Cynthia describes her relationship to her sister and brother, who are three and two years older than she. In this family, it was the older sister who was shunned and actively disliked by their mother, the brother who was adored, and Cynthia who was deemed an embarrassment and failure. Their mother was vocal about her opinions, remarking that she neither knew nor liked her oldest daughter or that she had one child too many. And while both daughters struggled with self-esteem, they did not bond. The older sister rebelled, drinking and acting out; the brother internalized everything as a reluctant Trophy Child; and Cynthia, in her own words, "floundered." Her mother used tactics to divide the siblings such as badmouthing one daughter to another or complaining loudly about both to her son. When the children reached adulthood, their mother would never permit them to visit her at the same time, not even on holidays (that is so telling, isn't it?). Cynthia surmises that this "rule" was partly a function of her mother's need to be the center of attention and partly an effort to make sure her children did not communicate directly with one another. Not surprisingly, Cynthia reports that "all three of us are emotionally detached when it comes to our relationship. We would never hug each other, not even after long absence." They mainly communicate by email nowadays, if at all.

SAFE HAVENS AND ISLANDS OF CONNECTION

Some daughters report that members of their extended family—aunts and uncles, grandmothers and grandfathers, even older cousins—gave them a taste of what it might be like to be in a close relationship, feeling both loved and safe. That was true for Adele, 48: "I loved going to my grandmother's house when I was a girl because she was everything my mother wasn't—kind, open, and uncritical. My mom didn't like her much—called her a slob and always harped on how messy her house was. But, oh, I loved that house and her. She would listen to me—I'd tell her all about what was going on at school and what I was learning—in a way that my mother never did. She was my dad's mother and, sometimes, I could see that he was like her in ways, but he was always working and never had time for me. She died when I was 12, and it was a huge blow."

These relationships—and they may not necessarily be with people a daughter is related to, but might be with a neighbor or a teacher—can provide a daughter with a vision of both herself and how the world works that is very different from what she has learned at home. They can act as a corrective to the things she's been told about herself as well as help her see that what goes on at her house isn't what goes on everywhere. That can be both comforting and dislocating at once, as Annie's story makes clear: "I was sent to my aunt's house in Philadelphia when I was 12. My 10-year-old sister, Mom's favorite, didn't go and it was made clear to me that my mother just wanted a break from dealing with me. I was the 'bad' girl. I'm not sure how this all came about because my mother and her older sister—that was the aunt—were always on the outs, but off I went. And it was an eye-opener. No yelling, no screaming, just a calm house and an aunt who loved joking and laughing, and who let my cousin and me have pillow fights and sit with our feet on the sofa. It was both bewildering—how could they be sisters?—and totally wonderful. I am still close to her. She's the mother I wanted, in truth."

Alas, even with these close connections—especially if they are forged with members of the family—it's rare for a daughter to actually confide and directly seek comfort and solace. Both shame and fear that there will be some sort of retaliation keep her silent.

Still, these memories make a difference, and the daughters who have none of them have a tougher journey than those who do. I hoarded my memories of the times I spent with my Tante Jo, my grandfather's sister, when I was a girl; they provided the same comfort as the stories I read and a place where I could retreat in times of stress and regroup.

WHY DISCERNING THE PATTERNS IN YOUR FAMILY MATTERS

Family dynamics can, as we've seen, either mute or amplify the experience of being unloved and unsupported by your mother. Keeping in mind that the idea of experiences "balancing out" is incorrect, nonetheless the existence of one or more supportive connections in your family—whether that's with your father or a sibling, grandparent, aunt, cousin, or anyone else—can make an enormous difference not just in how you see yourself but also in how much or how little you take responsibility for your mother's treatment of you. A daughter who's even caught a glimpse of her own worthiness in someone else's eyes is in a different place from that of the girl who hasn't; she'll still deal with self-criticism and hurt, but if she squints, she can see a different view of herself. Research suggest that these positive experiences—safe havens or "islands" of connection—can be the basis for what's called "earned secure attachment."

The unloved daughter who's had her mother's treatment amplified—by the chorus effect of a sibling or siblings, by scapegoating, by dismissive paternal behavior—will have a longer road out toward healing. She may not have an island on which to build future connections and so must start from scratch. It can be done; it's just harder.

The next step in discernment is looking at you and your behaviors—not the great behaviors that you love about yourself but the ones that trip you up and get in your way—and tracing them back to their point of origin. Yes, sometimes all roads lead back to Mom.

CHAPTER FOUR
ADAPTATION: HOW HER BEHAVIORS SHAPED YOURS

It's actually amazing when it dawns on me that every single relationship is truly seen through the lens of how my mother loved or didn't love me, those things she did love about me, and most especially those she didn't love about me, and how this alone carries into all relationships. How this seems now so very conditional and how I've used this template throughout my life . . . and to stop and begin to realize how I've continued to carry this view of me and even how I treat others. Remembering this all belonged to my mother and what I've "inherited" belongs to me alone to change now.

-Carrie, 55

During childhood and later, the unloved daughter focuses on her mother; she sees herself peripherally and then only in relation to the questions that animate her emotional landscape. First among them is "Why doesn't Mommy love me?" but there are many others that are variations on the theme: "What can I do to make Mommy love me?" or "Who can I be so she'll be happy with me?" She's not aware, of course, of how her mother's treatment is shaping her—how she sees the world, how she reacts to others, how she deals with feeling bad. She doesn't know why she feels so lonely and adrift some of the time. She doesn't understand why she has to bite her lip to stop herself from crying when the girls at school are running ahead of her and she can't catch up, or why she turns to steel instead, willing herself not to feel. She doesn't know why she has trouble making friends. She soothes herself by thinking that everyone must feel this way or that she's fine on her own.

This second stage of discernment shifts the attention from how your mother treated you to how you adapted to her treatment. It's a key step in the journey of healing.

From time to time, I make a point of seeing whether I can still glimpse my mother's daughter in the woman I am today. It's not hard to do when I look in the mirror: Even older, there are parts of me— my cheekbones, the shape of my chin—that recall the contours of my mother's face. Today, at 68, I am older than my mother was when I saw her last, and that was over 28 years ago. My identity as a daughter has long since been replaced by my identity as a mother because the second was of my choosing and a most welcome experience, as the first wasn't.

Many years ago, outside of my real-world achievements, all I was inside was my mother's daughter; that reactive, desperate-for-love girl in her teens and twenties was nothing but a product of her childhood. I was volatile and quick to anger; I self-protected by being funny— bitingly so—and made it clear to everyone I had to call the shots. And then I began to build a life—spurred on and helped by therapy—that shut some doors that needed closing and opened others so that who I was could be someone other than that frightened child, reading books alone in her bedroom. I slowly learned to listen to other people and to be less prickly. The largest sea change came at the end of my thirties when I became pregnant and also divorced my mother. My impending motherhood forced me to look inward once more, isolating those behaviors learned in childhood that were detrimental to my being the best version of myself I could be. `

This isn't to say that the child who was my mother's daughter has been totally erased; I'd be lying if I told you that. But I recognize the legacy, and I can choose how I wish to behave, most of the time. And when automaticity kicks in, I can see it. That's empowering. Perhaps I'm not the best version of myself that I might have been if I'd had a different mother, but I am close to being the best version of myself given the mother I had.

MERCI BEAUCOUP, EVOLUTION! BUT FORGIVE ME IF I DON'T TOAST YOU . . .

We've already seen that evolution explains why aspects of healing are so elusive—how the infant's responses and her brain adapt to wherever she finds herself to insure survival, the child's hardwired need for maternal love, the lasting effects of bad experiences and the way they are stored in the brain, and more. But what about insecure attachment itself? Wouldn't there be an evolutionary advantage to having everyone be securely attached and in charge of their emotions, able to regulate, and connect to others? How to explain the 40 to 50 percent of us who are insecurely attached?

It sounds facetious, but that's exactly what a group led by psychologists Tsachi Ein-Dor, Mario Mikulincer, and others wanted to find out: Was there perhaps an evolutionary advantage to being either anxiously or avoidantly attached since there's no personal advantage? People with anxious attachment, research shows, are more likely to have a higher rate of failed relationships, experience more stress, are less able to cope with their emotions, have lower self-esteem, and suffer both physically and psychologically. They are more prone to depression and disordered eating. Avoidant individuals have trouble with intimacy, don't work well with others, have difficulty maintaining relationships, manage stress badly, and are generally more pessimistic than securely attached people.

So why hadn't insecure attachment been "selected out" by evolution? The researchers hypothesized and confirmed in a series of laboratory tests that, in times of extreme danger, the insecurely attached might contribute something valuable to the communal, tribal living early humans enjoyed. Say a violent storm threatened or a fire broke out. How would the securely attached person react? She or he would stay calm and self-soothe, take comfort that the members of the tribe were near, look to them for guidance, and might, as a result, be slower to act. The fight or flight response—another bit of hardwiring to keep us alive in times of trouble—might actually be tamped down by all of those stable feelings of belonging. Of course, that's not likely to happen to the anxiously attached individual who's always hyper-alert to danger and who, according to the researchers, may act as the sentinel for the tribe—a kind of Paul Revere—when it comes to threat. So while all the securely attached folks would be hugging and singing some forebear version of "Kumbaya," the anxious person would be screaming, "Storm! Flooding! Fire! The worst is going to happen and we're all going to die so run for it!" and presumably the singing would stop and the secure types would all follow suit. Similarly, the scientists hypothesized that the avoidant individual who steered away from close connection and cared only about him- or herself would be focused on the danger and the best way of escaping it so he or she would promote the common good by thinking fast on his or her feet: What to do? Best way out? Which way? That way?—and thereby save everyone else. Whew! We've "proved" why insecure attachment exists!

Unlike attachment theory, which has been proved reliable in an enormous body of literature, this hypothesis is completely theoretical, but I bring it up because there's a dark kind of humor in a peer-reviewed journal article that could easily be called "Finding the Bright Side of A Not Good Thing." In truth, the actual title of the article comes close because it highlights what insecure attachment actually is: a coping mechanism for inadequate parenting when a child's needs aren't met. It's called "The Attachment Paradox: How Can So Many of Us (the Insecure Ones) Have No Adaptive Advantages?" Note that the researchers are included in "us."

That's where the second stage of personal discovery, or what I call "discernment," has to start: the not-so-simple admission that your needs weren't met in infancy, childhood, and beyond by the person who was supposed to take care of you. Yes, the very person you might still long for or mourn. You cannot begin to understand your behaviors today—how you react to people, think about connections as well as perceived threats, see yourself, set goals for yourself, deal with failure and success, manage emotions—without seeing how you developed the coping mechanisms you did and, more important, what they are. Not only are the circumstances different in every house, but also each daughter comes to the party with her own personality. Once again, we'll start with the most general observations.

ASSESSING GROUND ZERO

While some unloved daughters recognize their mothers' behavior relatively young—by late adolescence or young adulthood—the preponderance of women, anecdotally at least, do not. That said, even when a daughter recognizes the lack of love and attention, as I did, she usually considers it a specific problem, not one capable of affecting her in myriad ways. Daughters who come to the recognition later in their lives—and these moments of epiphany happen anywhere from late twenties and thirties to forties, fifties, and beyond—have been aware of their unhappiness or malaise but haven't understood its point of origin. They may become aware of the problem through a series of failed relationships, for example—in which they are treated as their mothers treated them—or their attention is drawn to the problem by someone pointing it out.

The truth is that none of us is able, at the beginning at least, to see more than the broad strokes of the problem. Without a working knowledge of psychology, there's no way that the true wounding is visible to the naked eye.

IT'S THE LACK OF LOVE WE FEEL, BUT THE REAL DAMAGE LIES ELSEWHERE

Whether we deny it, fight against it, or recognize it, it's the lack of our mother's love in childhood and later that we feel most keenly. It may make us angry, frustrated, desperate, despairing, and/or determined to somehow get it from her, but that's our focus. We feel her lack of support if she's ignoring us; we smart from the blows if she's combative when all we want is love; we go along with the plan of pleasing if she's self-involved or controlling in an effort to get what we need.

But the lasting effects aren't just about love and its lack. We think they are, which is why some of us continue to engage our mothers because we believe that will fix things. We're wrong because we are not looking at the real effects. What are they? They're about what we didn't learn in infancy and childhood. They're about what we did learn instead of the things we needed to learn. That's where the real psychological damage, the hobbling stuff, resides.

UNDERSTANDING THE EMOTIONAL CONSEQUENCES OF LACK OF ATTUNEMENT

In the first chapter, we saw how, in the "Still Face" experiment, infants and toddlers emotionally collapsed in the wake of their mothers' withdrawal—becoming frantic at first and then, depending on how well they were able to self-soothe, turning away from the stress-inducing lack of interaction either quickly or slowly. Keep in mind that these were infants accustomed to attunement. What about those infants for whom attunement is absent most of the time, all of the time, or unreliably present? That brings us back to the findings of the "Strange Situation" and the core of attachment theory.

Perhaps the single best statement—and the most eloquent—is from the authors of *A General Theory of Love*. I continue to quote it because there is simply no way I can write it better than they did. Here it is, and please spend a moment letting it sink in: "The lack of an attuned mother is a nonevent for a reptile and a shattering injury to the complex and fragile limbic brain of a mammal." Yes, it's true for monkeys, and it's true for us. We're born with the hardwiring for emotional connection, but we need interaction—an attuned parent—to activate it so it develops properly.

Lack of maternal attunement affects us on a myriad of levels, the most obvious of which are the mental models formed in our brains about how relationships work and make us feel. These representations—internalized, unconscious, and absorbed by the brain to insure the individual's survival—are among the most lasting of the unloving mother's legacies, though not the only one. They are hard to deal with not just because they're unconscious (which, thank you, is bad enough) but also because they're stored in the brain's default position. So even if you've recognized them and their consequences on a conscious level, either through therapy or on your own—"I am afraid of emotional demands and connections; they make me anxious and I have to deal with triggers; I know that I panic when someone withdraws"—when you're stressed out, the likelihood is you will revert to the default position nonetheless.

That's the first giant step you have to take as you begin to discern: recognizing your default position of stress and how it's affecting your ability to live the way you want to. Understanding that your childhood experiences cause you to panic quickly when someone acts in a way you perceive as less than loving, and fully realizing that you need to check whether your perception is actually founded in the present or simply an echo response to the past and the way your mother used to treat you. Or alternatively, when someone gets too close for your comfort or makes demands on you, you actively pull away and shut down when you really want to live differently. Those intersections of past and present must be identified first.

BEYOND THE MENTAL MODELS OF RELATIONSHIP

Science tells us that we're in control of about 40 percent of the factors that contribute to our happiness, and much of that has to do with our ability to manage stress and negative emotions, and to be able to self-regulate effectively during those times when life gets hard. But without attuned connection, a child doesn't learn to self-soothe effectively, nor does she learn that negative emotions—fear, sadness, anger, among them—are a part of life and can be dealt with.

Instead, as a child, she either turns away from those feelings or she becomes totally immersed in them; neither strategy allows her to manage her feelings, and both put her, one way or another, at the mercy of her emotions. The behaviors associated with insecure attachment—anxiety or avoidance—are, in fact, coping mechanisms learned when we were young, but you will be quick to note that they are ineffective ways of coping. And, of course, what's laid down by the initial lack of maternal attunement only gets hardened and cast in cement as the daughter gets older and more articulate and she tries to claim her feelings only to have her mother marginalize, deny, or put them down. Practically all unloved daughters—regardless of whether their mothers were essentially dismissive, combative, self-involved, emotionally absent, enmeshed, unreliable, or controlling—report that they were told in ways that were both subtle and obvious that their feelings were "wrong" or didn't count or that the real problem was that they were too sensitive or exaggerating. Maternal verbal aggression is often used as a way of maintaining control and often targets a daughter's efforts to voice her feelings and have them recognized.

What didn't happen in infancy and childhood—that healthy dyadic dance of mother and child that leads to the daughter's being able to regulate her emotions—is often further complicated by the daughter's sometimes deliberately distancing herself from her feelings just to avoid being a target, especially if there's scapegoating in the home. Many daughters learn—as I did—that showing vulnerability simply amped up the volume for painful interactions, whether that was with their mothers or with their siblings. A very young child can adopt this as a way of making life easier without, of course, understanding the consequences. Here's what Fern, 37, recounted: "In our house, tears were a sign of weakness. I was picked on by my mother and my brothers, and I was probably six or so when I realized that crying egged them on. So I taught myself not to cry. I'd dig my nails into my palm or bite my tongue, and somehow, feeling that pain made it easier not to cry. I didn't realize until a few years ago, when I went into therapy after my husband left me and I had two kids to take care of, that I had cut myself off from feeling almost everything. People said I was calm and so impartial and fair but, really, I was a zombie."

Cutting yourself off from what you're feeling—even if it's a defensive gesture that helps in the short term—only compounds the damage that the original wounding caused. While the mental models of relationship are recognized first as we move into the stage of discernment, our inability to manage emotion may be harder to see. After all, we're used to either being flooded by the waters or protected by high walls. And we've been reacting this way for so long, years past childhood, that we've come to think of it as normal. Another consequence is that many of us have problems knowing what we're feeling—a key component of what's called "emotional intelligence." Understanding emotional intelligence—and why each of us needs to cultivate it, given the deficits of our childhoods—is part of discernment.

SEEING YOUR EMOTIONAL BLINDERS

Here's the thing: If your upbringing has made you feel that you have to quash, deny, or push off from your emotions, is it any surprise that instead of helping you to navigate life—which is what emotions are supposed to do—they're consigning you to a leaky boat in stormy seas, either some or all of the time?

In the best of all possible worlds, our thoughts and emotions work in tandem to mutually enrich both the processes of thinking and feeling. That's how John D. Mayer and Peter Salovey define emotional intelligence: "the ability to perceive emotions, to access and generate emotions so as to assist thought, to understand emotions and emotional knowledge, and to reflectively regulate emotions so as to promote intellectual thought." The idea here is that "emotion makes thinking more intelligent and that one thinks intelligently about emotions." (By the way, the definitions I'm using are drawn from Mayer and Salovey's original research, not the best-selling book by Daniel Goleman.)

As you read about the branches of emotional intelligence—there are four, and they become increasingly complex—think about your own abilities so that you can start to discern where your own deficiencies lie and begin to work on them. The first branch of emotional intelligence is straightforward and emanates from the positive, secure childhood attachments.

* Able to identify your own emotions
* Able to identify emotions in others
* Able to express emotions and needs accurately
* Can distinguish between faked and real emotions, honest and dishonest expressions of emotion

This first branch is all about perception, and the extent of your skills in this branch affects most of your interactions with others, whether they are strangers, colleagues, friends, or real intimates.

The second branch includes the ability to use emotion to inform thought and action. Again, this involves not only knowing what you're feeling with some accuracy but, additionally, trusting in both your knowledge and the legitimacy of your feelings, not always an easy task for an unloved daughter. This second branch includes:

* Using emotions to prioritize thinking
* Using emotions as aids to judgment, assessment, and memory
* Managing mood swings (optimistic and pessimistic) to expand your point of view
* Using emotional states to encourage fresh ways of looking at problems

It should be clear to some daughters that this is the area in which their abilities begin to falter—especially when it comes to using emotions to sort through and prioritize and to manage mood swings. By and large, it's not just that unloved daughters have trouble identifying what they're feeling (branch one) but that the self-trust necessary to rely on those feelings as outlined in this second branch is often missing or impaired.

The third branch of emotional intelligence is even more nuanced, and affects our ability to know ourselves in depth. It includes:

* Being able to label emotions with precision and understanding the relationship between words and feelings
    * Being able to interpret emotions
    * Being able to understand complex or blended emotions
    * Being able to recognize the transitions between emotions

Some situations arouse emotions in us that are relatively easy to pinpoint and label; we are sad when our dog or cat dies, hurt when a friend forgets our birthday, disappointed when something we were looking forward to falls through. But an argument with a close other—a spouse or partner or intimate friend—may involve not just one emotion but many, some of them coinciding and others washing over us in waves. We may feel angry, sad, and even guilty either in simulcast or at different moments, making it hard to keep track of both what we're feeling and, more important, what actions we want to take based on those feelings. Is it any wonder many unloved daughters lack the skill set this branch of emotional intelligence demands?

The last branch of emotional intelligence involves the ability to regulate emotions and to use emotions to stimulate intellectual growth. That includes:

* Being able to stay open to both pleasant and unpleasant feelings
* Being able to engage or detach from an emotion depending on its usefulness to the task at hand
* Being able to monitor emotions in yourself and others
* Being able to deal with emotions, both positive and negative, without either exaggerating them or repressing them

This is called "metacognition"—being able to think about thoughts and thought processes—and it's the one form of emotional intelligence that's most out of reach for many unloved daughters. It affects their ability to make decisions and wise choices, to know themselves wholly, to feel compassion for themselves, to still self-criticism, and to form close and lasting relationships.

EMOTIONAL INTELLIGENCE AND REAL LIFE

People who are high in emotional intelligence (and securely attached) are able to act in ways the rest of us might not. Say you've just met someone—a very charming person, who's well turned out, a successful professional, a bit quiet but fun to talk to, and attractive in a low-key way. He's not overtly pushy or preening either. You see him a few times yet, afterward, when you think about him, you can't quite put your finger on why you don't have a good feeling about him, but you don't. (It could equally be a woman, by the way.) The emotionally intelligent person tries to identify that feeling: Did he seem insincere because he seemed to smile easily? Or was it the way he kept redirecting the conversation every time you brought up a new topic? Or was it his tendency to talk over you?

You can't come up with an answer quite yet, but the next time you meet for drinks and dinner, you're paying close attention. He picks out the restaurant, where he's a regular. You sit down at the table and order a glass of wine and he smiles and says, "No, try a cocktail. They're famous for them." "Okay," you say. Light banter and conversation ensue, and then you realize that you're feeling controlled. It comes to you that he's scripting and directing the conversation. He insists you order a specialty not even on the menu. That seals it for you, and you're out of there.

What I've described is meeting and getting to know a covert narcissist, and how a woman could use her emotional intelligence. The truth is that someone less adept would probably not just miss the warning signs but actually misread them as positives: how skilled he is at keeping a conversation going, how thoughtful he is to order for you, how responsive he is to everything you say. This is especially true if your childhood experiences have made you detach from your feelings or have made you distrustful of them. Emotional intelligence helps inform many decisions and choices beyond relationships and the occasional spotting of a narcissist, of course.

The good news is that emotional intelligence is a skill set that can be worked on and improved. First, though, you need to examine your own facility at both labeling and managing emotions.

HOW DO *YOU* THINK ABOUT EMOTIONS?

People high in emotional intelligence are good at labeling their emotions—distinguishing discomfort from embarrassment, anger from fear, frustration from resentment, neediness from anxiety, and the like. Studies, such as those conducted by Lisa Feldman Barrett and others, show that people who think about emotions in a less nuanced way, labeling them as unpleasant or pleasant ("That made me feel bad" vs. "That made me feel good") have much more trouble both regulating their emotions and benefitting from knowledge of them. The truth is that the more clarity you have about what you're feeling in a given moment, the better you'll be at not just managing the situation you're in but also deciding on your future actions.

Be honest in your appraisal of how you think about your feelings—nuanced and detailed, somewhat detailed, simplistic, or something in between—because that, too, will add to the growth of your discernment.

MENTAL MODELS AND EMOTIONS

Please remember that what we learn in childhood about relationships—how people connect and act—not only gets internalized but also gets generalized into a worldview. If you grow up believing that people are generally responsive and thoughtful and that you are deserving of respect and likeable, your emotional responses to challenging situations—and how you tend to see other people's motives—are going to be very different than if you've grown up thinking that people aren't trustworthy and that they're likely to take advantage of you. I've deliberately made this as black-and-white as possible for clarity.

While the anxious-preoccupied daughter desperately wants connection, intimacy, and relationship, deep-down her internal models don't permit her to ever let her guard down fully. She learned to self-protect in childhood so, in adulthood, she's like a sailor who goes onto the water on a perfectly clear and cloudless day but can't enjoy herself because she's constantly scanning the horizon for storm clouds. That's what the anxious daughter does in every relationship she has—whether it's with a colleague at work or the next-door neighbor, with a friend, or with a lover. She needs constant reassurance and is highly volatile. It's estimated that roughly 15 to 20 percent of us are anxiously attached.

These are unconscious processes, so that the woman experiencing these feelings and thoughts believes she is acting reasonably and thinking things through when, in fact, she's not. The truth is that her behavior is being triggered automatically, and unless she gets a bead on the dynamic, she'll continue to put stress into every relationship, often to the breaking point. Anxious people are likely to be triggered when things don't go according to the plan they had in mind; their anxiety makes them inflexible so when there's a discrepancy between how they imagined things unfolding and what actually happens, they become emotionally reactive, evoking an outsized response. Anxious people are also prone to catastrophizing—not just imagining the worst possibility but also blowing it up, which evokes a cascade of emotion.

You have a fight with your husband in the morning, and you think to yourself, *Now I've done it. He's going to leave me for sure*, and then this thought morphs into what your life will be like without him and how no one is ever going to love you and you become frantic, sending email after email to him in the office. Or you're at work and you've totally muffed the call with an important client, and you begin thinking that you're going to get fired—your boss made it clear how key the account was—and that no one will ever hire you again.

The avoidantly attached daughter has developed other unconscious coping mechanisms in response to her childhood treatment which are maladaptive in different ways. The two types of avoidant styles—dismissive and fearful—reflect differences in unconscious motivation. Those with a dismissive style tend to see themselves as solo voyagers, not interested in long-term connection; they see relationships as a hassle and the people who need to be in them as weak. They feel superior. The fearful avoidants actually long to be in a relationship but because they see people as untrustworthy, they fear the vulnerability and potential emotional pain that might ensue from intimacy. Like the anxious daughter, the fearful one is easily triggered and prone to misread other people's motives and intentions, unable to access what she's really feeling deep inside other than her fear. It's estimated that roughly 25 percent of us are avoidantly attached.

NOW, ABOUT THE UNCONSCIOUS PROCESSING OF EMOTION . . .

Emotional processing happens on both a conscious and unconscious level, and the most recent research asserts that people who are better able to navigate life are those who use explicit and conscious processing of emotion to self-regulate in times of challenge and stress. What does explicit processing entail? Anett Gyurak, James J. Gross, and colleagues explain: The person who can process explicitly is (1) aware of the cues that elicited the emotional responses, (2) aware of the emotions she's experiencing, (3) aware of how regulating the emotion consciously affects her behavior.

Studies show that this ability to regulate emotion consciously improves mental health, increases the level of coping, and actually reduces stress and reactivity in ways that suppressing emotions does not. (This actually happens on a physiological level, as neuroimaging studies show; activity in the amygdala is actually reduced by explicit processing of emotions but not by suppressing feelings.)

Let me give some real-life examples: You and a friend get into a tiff about an event you're planning together, and you are really about to lose it on her when you suddenly think about the fact that she's under enormous stress financially and you consciously tone down your feelings and words. Do that often enough—consciously regulate your feelings—and it may even start to happen without your thinking about it. Or, alternatively, you realize that you're as angry as you are because she's belittling you in the same way your mother did, and that's tipping the scales and making you nuts. In that moment, you get what's triggering you, and, yes, you consciously take a deep breath and begin to let go of the anger.

That's conscious regulation of emotion in action. For all the reasons I've outlined, this is generally not an unloved daughter's strong suit, but the good news is that emotional regulation—learning to read cues, labeling emotions, and becoming conscious and aware of how feeling impacts behavior—are all skills that can be learned.

SELF-CONTROL, EMOTIONAL PROCESSING, AND MENTAL MODELS

For our emotional intelligence to be functioning optimally—permitting our thoughts to inform our feelings and our emotions to inform our thinking—we have to be able to self-regulate sufficiently so that we're able to control our impulses. Again, impulsivity is hardwired into the species—that fast, unconscious "thinking" that has you react to the car ahead swerving on black ice before you've consciously regis-tered it, the pump of adrenaline when you feel physically threatened—and that resides in the amygdala, part of the limbic system. To avoid certain bad impulses—that drink, those cookies, those cigarettes, that temptation you're trying to avoid—we need the cool processing provided by the prefrontal cortex where the slow process, cognitive thinking, takes place. The prefrontal cortex is the home of executive function, and it's the latter that provides the brakes—what we usually call self-control or willpower—for the impulse. It will not surprise you that there's evidence that our childhood experiences—specifically those connected to our mothers—also affect our self-control.

To eat the marshmallow or not? That was the dilemma posed by Walter Mischel and his colleagues to a large group of four-year-olds over 50 years ago at Stanford University in an experiment so famous that it's now known simply as the "Marshmallow Test." Each child was seated at a desk; there was a single marshmallow on a plate and, beside it, a bell. The researcher then told the child she had to leave and the child was free to eat the marshmallow and ring the bell. But, she promised, if the child waited until she came back, the reward would be a second marshmallow. The wait, by the way, was 15 to 20 minutes, which is a very, very long time if you are four and there is a marshmallow sitting in front of you, absolutely begging to be eaten.

Videos online testify to the agony and the anguish. A few kids give in right away—they succumb to the temptation even as the door swings shut. Others touch and stroke the marshmallow lovingly, lick its edges, and then finally give in. But 30 percent of the children manage—by closing their eyes, covering their faces, fiddling with their hair and clothes, and otherwise distracting themselves—to hang in until the researcher comes back and get the coveted second marshmallow.

What ultimately made this experiment famous is that Mischel and his colleagues tracked these kids through high school and after, and discovered that those who could resist the marshmallow for those 15 minutes had a different skill set than their peers. They were better planners, had higher SAT scores, were more self-confident and could manage their frustrations better, and were more focused. In short, the self-control they exhibited as four-year-olds was a reliable predictor of how much self-control they would have as adults. The marshmallow-resisters had a bright and shiny future, which got educators and psychologists alike all excited about teaching willpower as a skill.

What this boils down to is to be able to outwit the impulse to snarf that candy and take the long view. Once you've mastered that, you're in great shape for mastering many of life's challenges, including setting and achieving your goals, resolving conflicts, planning, and, yes, recovering from setbacks and failures.

But does the experiment only measure self-control? Perhaps not. What if, as Celeste Kidd and her colleagues hypothesized, your decision to gobble or wait had as much to do with your beliefs about how the world works and people act as anything else? How much of your decision about the marshmallow hinged on other factors—your belief that the researcher will actually keep her promise and give you a second marshmallow, for example, or your assessment that no one else in the room will take your marshmallow and eat it if you don't? Is it your self-control or your view of the world that's being tested?

That's exactly what Kidd and her colleagues wanted to find out. In their study, the marshmallow task was preceded by an art project, one involving crayons and the other, stickers. The experimenter produced a worn-out set of crayons and then gave the child the choice of using them or waiting for a brand-new set. For the second project, the researcher produced one small sticker and then gave the child the choice of using it or waiting for a new set of multiple stickers. In each case, the children were confronted with a reliable or unreliable experimenter. The reliable experimenter delivered on her promise (a fancy tray of art supplies or brand-new and abundant stickers), while the unreliable one came back, apologizing, saying there'd been a mistake and the child would have to make do with the crummy crayons or single sticker.

The children were then given the marshmallow task, and the results were revelatory. The kids who'd discovered the experimenter was unreliable waited a mean of three minutes before eating the marshmallow; those in the reliable situation waited twelve. More important, only 1 out of 14 children waited the full 15 minutes in the unreliable situation and got the second marshmallow; 9 out of the

14 in the reliable situation waited the 15 minutes and got the second marshmallow.

While the researchers don't talk about attachment in their article—they talk about unreliability—I think all of this makes terrific sense. Attachment theory explains a great deal about human behavior, and perhaps the ability to exert self-control is yet another area where what we learn at the beginning affects both our abilities and mindsets, in childhood and long after. To a small child, an emotionally unreliable or inconsistent or cruel parent doesn't just demonstrate her nature, but the nature of the world and relationships. If you're used to broken promises, it makes sense that you'd eat that marshmallow pronto. Not surprisingly, that's also what Annie Bernier and her colleagues found in an experiment that looked at both self-control and executive function in infants. (Yes, there's evidence that a year-old baby has executive function in a rudimentary form.) Surprise, surprise: The more responsive the mother was to the child's needs, the better she communicated, and the more she was able to allow the infant some autonomy along with support, the greater the demonstration of self-control and executive function by the child.

So if self-control has been an issue for you (you can't resist shopping or buying things you don't need, that bag of cookies gets eaten pronto, you can't give up those cigarettes, you're faced with that empty wine bottle at the end of the night), yes—Mom's a part of that. But she's lurking in the shadows, too, when you can't focus on the long-term when you're planning to make a shift in your life or when you need to hunker down and concentrate. Self-control is bound up with the ability to set goals and to follow through with them as well.

Once you've figured out if and how the issues of self-control and mastery of your emotions are working in your life, there's very good news. These are skill sets that can be worked on, improved, and acquired. We'll be focusing on just that in Chapter Seven.

LOOKING AT YOUR ATTACHMENT PATTERNS

Consider the following four statements—developed by Kim Bartholomew and Leonard Horowitz—and decide which of the four describes you most accurately. You may, in fact, agree with more than one since attachment styles actually aren't as discrete as the categories make them seem and there may be some overlap.

A. It is easy for me to become emotionally close to others. I am comfortable depending on others and having others depend on me. I don't worry about being alone or having others not accept me.

B. I am comfortable without close emotional relationships. It is very important to me to feel independent and self-sufficient, and I prefer not to depend on others or have others depend on me.

C. I want to be completely emotionally intimate with others, but I often find that others are reluctant to get as close as I would like. I am uncomfortable being without close relationships, but I sometimes worry that others don't value me as much as I value them.

D. I am uncomfortable getting close to others. I want emotionally close relationships, but I find it difficult to trust others completely, or to depend on them. I worry that I will be hurt if I allow myself to become too close to others.

If you have answered A as the way you most usually feel, you are securely attached. If you have chosen B, your answer indicates dismissive-avoidant attachment. If you have chosen C, you are more anxiously-preoccupied than not. D corresponds with fearful-dismissive attachment.

UP CLOSE: ARE YOU ANXIOUS OR AVOIDANT?

Please keep in mind that the three types of insecure attachment— anxious-preoccupied, fearful-avoidant, and dismissive-avoidant—are not as cast in stone as the categories would seem to imply nor does every individual fit neatly into one or another. These tendencies may mix or change over time or within or across relationships, so as you begin to think about your own attachment style, please keep that in mind.

Compared to the secure person who manages upset reasonably well, the anxiously attached woman is rarely on an even enough keel to do so. For those with anxious attachment, even a trickle of pain or disappointment feels like a tsunami, threatening to pull them under. They are not only always on high alert and worried about getting hurt or abandoned but they also have a habit of exaggerating and misreading the cues offered up in all manner of situations.

This is what Patti told me: "I am always quick to jump to conclusions, and I keep losing friends because of it. I take everything to heart so when someone doesn't call me as she promised, my head doesn't think things like 'she got busy' or 'maybe she forgot.' No, I end up writing a whole script about how she's not really my friend or she's using me or something. And then when I do talk to her, it's my script I am answering, not her words. I keep working on this in therapy but it's a lifelong habit."

Anxiously-attached daughters of hypercritical and demanding mothers usually have trouble with any kind of criticism and, moreover, often see criticism where none is intended. Any comment that sounds even vaguely critical can throw the anxious person into an overreactive state of high alert, which often has the unfortunate consequence of escalating into an argument that was highly avoidable in the first place. Take this scenario: Anne is about to go grocery shopping and as she's heading out the door, her husband calls out: "Do you have your list? Don't forget the milk!" She doesn't answer but feels instantly picked on, the way she was as a kid when nothing she did was ever good enough for her mother. Now, she did shop without a list last week and did forget the milk, which created chaos the following morning, but did he have to bring that up? By the time she's done shopping, she's in a full snit, and when she gets home, she starts yelling at her husband, asking why he's always criticizing her. He is, as you might imagine, bewildered.

Anxious attachment is filled with paradoxes and contradictions. On the one hand, you are a scaredy cat on the prowl and alert to rejection, slights, and criticism. You feel intensely vulnerable all the time because you really want the close connection and ties you didn't have growing up, and you desperately want validation. On the other hand, you are also very volatile, quick to pick a fight, apt to be jealous, and subject to emotional highs and lows. All of that has to do with what you didn't learn in childhood: how to manage and regulate your negative emotions. So when you're on the defensive, you slip into high offensive and start the rollercoaster on the track. And you're really apt to play tit for tat because, somehow—wrongly—you feel that's just and it makes you feel more in control; it confirms your view of the world, the one you learned as a child. So when someone doesn't call you back right away, then leaves you a message, do you wait to return the call so he or she "will know what it feels like"? When you've reacted because you felt slighted and the person—it could be your spouse or partner, a friend or colleague—tries to ask what happened, do you roll your eyes or disparage him or her, just as your mother did you?

Unloved daughters who spend their childhood on tenterhooks with mothers who are sometimes attentive and available and sometimes not—asking whether the Good Mommy or the Bad Mommy will show up today—become anxious and always on the prowl for validation and reassurance. That's not true for the daughters of consistently unavailable, hostile, or intrusive mothers. The experts call this type of attachment "avoidant."

These women are coming from a different place. Their experiences have taught them that needing someone puts you at risk, that rejection is painful, and that people are untrustworthy and unreliable. They armor themselves by being wary of intimacy and connection or avoiding closeness altogether. They stay outside a relationship, even while appearing to be in it.

But there are differences. Psychologist Kim Bartholomew expanded the theory by suggesting that there were, in fact, two kinds of avoidant attachment, fearful and dismissive, and they are distinguished not just by their views of themselves but of others. The fearful avoidant has a low opinion of herself, and while she really does want intimacy and close connection, her fear of rejection trumps all because she thinks highly of other people. If she's nothing and he is something, why on earth would he want her? Ditto in the realm of friendship: If Deidre is smart and accomplished and very popular, why would she possibly be hanging out with me? This unloved daughter comes across as needy and insecure and tends to be passive in relationships; she doesn't pick fights the way an anxiously attached woman does. Her inner voice is filled with internalized self-criticism.

In contrast, the dismissive-avoidant has a very high opinion of herself, on the surface at least; she's not hesitant to voice her opinion that relationships aren't very important to her and she's fine on her own, thank you very much. She is proud of her self-reliance. That stance, though, is a protective one, meant to defend the fragile self within from rejection or emotional wounding. That said, unlike the fearful-avoidant, the dismissive doesn't want an intimate relationship or friendship, preferring instead to be emotionally invested in other pursuits such as career, work, and hobbies. These folks, by the way, are the ones the popular culture identifies as narcissists much of the time.

Let me repeat that these three types of insecure attachment—anxious-preoccupied, fearful-avoidant, and dismissive-avoidant—aren't as fixed as the categories would seem to imply, nor does every individual fit neatly into one or another. These tendencies may mix or change over time or within or across relationships. That said, take a look at the following descriptions and see how accurately they reflect your self-portrait. Please remember that this isn't an opportunity to drown yourself in self-criticism; it's about knowing yourself a little better.

You prefer short-term connections, even hookups, to intense relationships: The true avoidant prefers relationships that aren't intimate or close. You're often attracted to people who aren't available—because they're married or live across the country or are otherwise off limits (like your girlfriend's boyfriend). When you're in a new relationship, you tend to idealize an old one which you left because the grass is somehow always greener where you're not. Dismissive-avoidants may sometimes be in relatively long-term relationships but maintain their independence and back off from commitment; they don't want to move in with their lovers because they need their own space; they don't like long-term plans or anything else that sounds as though they're in it for the long haul. If you're a true dismissive-avoidant, the "work" of making a relationship succeed is not your thing because, at the end of the day, you don't think closeness is all that important.

You have different ways of pushing your partner off: If you're dismissive, you get claustrophobic easily and quickly. When you're involved with someone, there's always something missing—he's not smart, polished, or ambitious enough—and that makes you sure that there's someone better for you out there. The avoidant is quick to come up with a list of flaws about her partner, is always on the lookout for greener pastures, and often, she will head out for them. Avoidants are not good candidates for Fidelity of the Year awards, as the next trait makes clear.

You like sex but hate to cuddle: One study showed that the dismissive-avoidant has sex for very different reasons than either the fearful-avoidant or even the anxiously attached. Let's start with the anxiously attached: She understands having sex as a validation of her being loved. Alas, this is actually not so great since, at its best, sex is about the dyad: your needs and desires, and his needs and desires. Not happening: The anxious girl is in bed to be loved. The fearful-avoidant falls into much the same trap; again, all *me* and no dyad and then she panics. And then there is the dismissive. She is just there for the sex. Does it surprise you that these avoidants tend to cheat? That's exactly what one study showed. The truth? Commitment, the need for closeness, and valuing the intimate ties we have are all that keeps us at home in bed and not elsewhere; this avoidant lacks all three.

You're proud of not needing emotional support or closeness: If this is you, I think you know who you are. Yes? The real question is whether you want to stay that way.

While the focus in this chapter is on you and your behaviors, in the next one we'll be looking at the partners and friends you choose. Not surprisingly, attachment styles play an enormous role in this part of your life as well.

DISCERNING YOUR PATTERNS OF BEHAVIOR AND THEIR POINTS OF ORIGIN

Remember that insecure styles of attachment grow out of coping mechanisms adopted during childhood to deal with the stresses of the familial environment; rather than feel the repeated sting of her emotional needs not being met, the insecurely attached daughter usually distances herself emotionally in order to self-soothe and to protect herself. Using cool processing—thinking about *why* you felt as you did, not *what* you felt—and seeing yourself as if from a great distance, think about your childhood self and your mother's treatment of you. Focus on how you protected yourself and coped.

Keep in mind that the more aggressive your mother's behaviors were and the more abusive her treatment—especially if your mother was controlling, combative, or dismissive—the more likely it is that you will have adopted some kind of self-armoring in order to defend yourself. In a similar way, consider the degree to which your view of the world is one as a possibly threatening place, where the default position for people isn't decent behavior but potential antagonism or some kind of duplicity. With that in mind, think about your own attitudes, especially under stress:

• Are you likely to jump to conclusions about people's motives and intentions? Do people sometimes say that you're making a mountain out of molehill? Are you?

• When you get into a disagreement with someone, is it important to you that there be a clear winner? Or are you capable of settling your contentions with give-and-take? Are you likely to give people the benefit of the doubt, or do you think that makes you seem weak?

• Do you worry about people taking advantage of you? If so, why?

• When someone apologizes to you, are you able to put whatever happened between you aside or do you always hold a grudge?

• How sensitive to criticism are you? Are you able to tolerate constructive criticism, or does any criticism feel like a put-down?

• Are you happier being by yourself because dealing with other people is ultimately just a hassle?

The children of mothers with less aggressive styles of interaction or who withdrew from emotional connection or withheld affection—who are emotionally unavailable, for example—will have very different kinds of defense mechanisms and, not surprisingly, different views of the world. If your mother's behaviors—her treatment of you, her responsiveness—were distant and unconnected, ask yourself the following questions as you consider how her behaviors limned yours.

• Do you always expect people to disappoint you, whether it's at work, in friendship, or in an intimate relationship?

• Are you uncomfortable being alone? Do you know how to entertain yourself and feel good about yourself when no one else is around?

• Do you have trouble saying no to people and then feel put upon when you've done what they've asked?

 ◆ Do you require a great deal of reassurance from people you're close to?

 ◆ How often do you fight with intimate partners or close friends? Do you consider yourself quick to anger, or do you think you're pretty even tempered?

 ◆ Are you able to set boundaries in relationships, giving yourself and the other person space? Or does your own neediness drive some people away?

 ◆ Do you feel inadequate much of the time? If so, how does that affect your behavior?

RECOGNIZING THE WOUNDED SELF

One of the paradoxes of this journey is that it's hard for all of us to see the ways in which we've been wounded. To begin with, seeing the initial wound—that we were unloved and our needs were not met—is hard enough, requiring us to dismantle the tunnel vision of what we considered normal, the cultural onus, our desperate need to belong, and, yes, our hopefulness that we'll just wake up one day and it'll all be magically fixed.

Then there's the problem of seeing ourselves clearly. Every person on the planet finds this task challenging, but the lucky ones are those who see the parts of themselves that are hidden from view—both the good and the bad—reflected in the mirrors that intimate relationships provide. This, too, is a challenge for many unloved daughters.

But piece by piece, bit by bit, we can clear away the debris left behind by childhood and polish our own inner mirrors to catch a glimpse of the girls we were, the women we are, and the women we want to become.

Chapter Five
Flashes of Recognition: Patterns and Partners

I've been in one lousy relationship after another, including two marriages. I was miserable and unheard. But it didn't occur to me that this had anything to do with my mother or my childhood until recently. I considered myself unlucky, and no more than that. Can you imagine? I turned 46 and finally sought counseling and discovered that what I thought I'd left behind was still with me.

-Ellie

Often the first insights a daughter has into how she's been affected by her childhood experiences are gleaned from the relationships she chooses to be in. This self-knowledge can begin to emerge in late adolescence, young adulthood, or later adulthood. These perceptions aren't always welcome because they deny what she believes or what she wants to believe. She may think her childhood is behind her because she's growing up at one point, and fully adult and out of the house at another, but she's wrong. Her ties to her family of origin may be weak, frayed, or nonexistent so she figures she's out of there, but in an important sense, she's not.

It's at this moment that we start *distinguishing*: recognizing the patterns of behavior we adopted in childhood and seeing how they play out in our adult relationships. These relationships exist across a spectrum of closeness from strangers to acquaintances to friends to close friends and intimate partners, lovers, and spouses. Our growing understanding of how we're connecting to others may add to our malaise and unhappiness at first because it underscores that we're still not free of our mothers' influence. But while it may feel like a step backward, it's actually a necessary stride forward.

Until we're aware that we are driven and attracted to others by unconscious patterns, we're not likely to connect the dots and see how our choices and actions in the present are connected to our childhood experiences. Sometimes, we stumble upon the truth because we start seeing patterns in failed relationships as we register that we're attracted to the same types of partners again and again, with the same unhappy-making results. They may be people who are controlling or withholding, ones who require being "won over" in some way just as our mothers did, or they may be unreliable. We may find ourselves in a series of relationships, either romantic or not, that reveal our chosen person to be high in narcissistic traits or emotionally withheld. We may find ourselves surrounded by people who criticize and marginalize us as we were criticized and marginalized in childhood. It's only then that we begin to distinguish the echo effect of our childhoods.

This is what Lily, 41, wrote about why it was hard to see the patterns: "My first husband was outwardly nothing like my mother; he was gregarious, accomplished, witty, and well read. He courted me with flowers and surprise gifts, and I fell hard. He seemed to want to protect and care for me. I felt supported and like I'd found my prince. But after we married, I realized he was controlling, not caring. He bossed me around very openly, put me down if things weren't done his way, dismissed my feelings and thoughts. I started having panic attacks as I had when I was a kid. My doctor sent me to a therapist, and guess what? I'd managed to recreate my childhood by focusing on the external ways my husband was different. I was lucky to get help and luckier still to have left."

Strategies we unconsciously adopted in childhood to manage our feelings—yes, attachment styles—can animate our connections to other people in broad ways. They shape how we react to a boss's criticism or to a challenge posed. They're present when we meet someone new or when we're with an old acquaintance. They affect how we deal with crisis and stress. Unperceived, they may isolate us and stop us from getting the love and support we've always craved.

THE PROBLEM WITH FRIENDSHIP

My own neediness trips me up in friendship. I'm always the pleaser with girlfriends. I give 100 percent and they give 10 percent, and I feel angry and used. It happens again and again, and it never stops surprising me.

-Patti, 57

Unloved daughters often have trouble choosing and making

female friends, and for some, this remains a lasting problem. It may come down to trust: If the first female in your life was emotionally untrustworthy, can any woman be? This, too, can become a terrific deficit in a daughter's life since research shows that having close friends correlates with psychological health throughout the lifespan and, perhaps most important to these daughters, can imbue them with the sense of belonging they lack. Additionally, friends can act as role models to emulate, close advisors and confidantes, supporters and cheerleaders—which everyone needs, especially these daughters. Friendships are particularly important in times of stress and transition. Not surprisingly, that's what a study of first-year college students conducted by Vanessa M. Buote and others found: that those who were open to friendships and achieved them did better. In truth, we probably didn't need a study to confirm that.

The tenor of her friendships or the lack of them in a daughter's life may also provide the first inklings of how broadly her childhood has affected her. That was the case for Jamie: "I was pretty much a loner in my small high school. I figured I just didn't fit into any of the cliques that dominated the social scene. I wasn't popular or an athlete, or a Goth or into music so there didn't seem to be a place for me socially, but I didn't care. I was convinced college would be different and, on the surface, it was. I had roommates, suitemates, and, when I joined the newspaper, what seemed to be a ready-made group I could belong to. But it didn't take long for me to realize that I couldn't do the kind of intimate sharing and chitchat my suitemates did, sitting around in their sweats and PJs, telling stories. I froze. I didn't know what to say. Should I share how my mother yelled at me all the time and my dad went out to bars alone? So I sat there. The newspaper group was fine when we were working, but when people tried drawing me out, I froze again. I think they thought I was stuck up. Junior year, I was so depressed that I went to a therapist and a light bulb went off in my head."

Jamie, though, was relatively lucky because she was on to the problem by the time she was 20, and got help for herself. Many daughters don't see themselves clearly enough to understand why friendship is such a challenge; they're still having trouble distinguishing the patterns and not seeing cause and effect. What you didn't learn in childhood—how to set and maintain healthy boundaries, how to keep yourself on an emotional even keel, how not to be overreactive or super-sensitive to the stray remark, how to trust—all plays out in female friendship and gets in the way. "I think it's exhausting to be my friend," Robin, 39, admitted. "I forget that other people need space and it's hard for me to ramp down my neediness. I think I demand too much of everyone and that's why I have trouble keeping close friends. I'm going to have to teach myself how to do 'give-and-take,' you know. It's something I don't really know how to do."

But the ability to distinguish these patterns is also affected by the code of silence. It, too, must be dragged into the open and understood for the groundwork of healing and recovery to be laid.

UNDERSTANDING THE EFFECT OF THE CODE OF SILENCE

Who would have believed me? My mother was a pillar of the community, well regarded. She was careful not to let outsiders see her screaming rages, or the way she picked on me relentlessly. I didn't want anyone to know either. I was deeply ashamed and afraid.

-Erica, 43

As discussed in the second chapter, a key common experience is the sense of being singled out, of being the only unloved child in the world. I have said here and elsewhere that I have come to believe that this feeling of aloneness, of separateness from others, is actually as damaging to the unloved daughter as the absence of maternal love. Beginning in childhood and continuing even into adulthood, most of these daughters bear the awful burden of thinking that they're the only ones affected in this way. Their hurt is amplified by a code of silence that surrounds this taboo subject. And they tend to keep silent themselves. Why is that?

The reasons vary according to the daughter's stage of life. In child-hood, there are three reasons a daughter keeps her silence. The first is that little girls learn about the myths of motherhood—that all mothers are loving and more—and believe them. Of course, if all mothers are loving and she's unloved, there has to be something terribly wrong with her for things to be the way they are. She understandably feels ashamed, and her unloving mother becomes the big secret the child feels she has to keep to herself. If she doesn't, she might end up being even more alone. The second is that a child's world is very small, and it's ruled by her mother, whom the child has made Queen because she needs her love and approval so badly. Her mother is also the last word on how the events in that little world are to be understood: "You were naughty so I had to punish you" or "Good girls don't break things, but you did" or "My life would be so much better if you were like your sister." These statements or variations on them shame the child and underscore her sense of unworthiness and inability to do anything right. She despairs of ever getting her mother to love her and worries that, maybe, her mother is right about her and then no one will ever like or love her. That's a good incentive to keep your silence. The third is her mother's enforcement of the code. Most of these mothers care about appearances, worry about what other people think, and need admiration—and all of that makes them invested in keeping what goes on at home under wraps. Many unloving mothers make sure their daughters look and sound good in public, and they pay attention to behaving lovingly in public, which is all the more confusing to a child. Who will ever believe her if she tells?

In adolescence and adulthood, the daughter may stay silent for many reasons, the most important of which is that her need for her mother's love remains unabated, and she's still trying desperately to win it. Confrontation—articulating what's never been acknowledged—is, for many daughters, out of the question because it's giving up and conceding that she will never get the prize she's after, her mother's attuned affection. The key thing is the core conflict: that a daughter's growing recognition of her wounds (and who wounded her) absolutely coexists with her continued quest to gain her mother's love and support. The next reason, which is also compelling, is that the daughter wants to be "normal" and fit in. Probably the last thing an unloved daughter will do during adolescence and even later is to share information that will set her apart. That can even be true with romantic partners.

Additionally, she's afraid no one will believe her or, worse, say it's her fault her mother didn't love her. The sad truth is that this fear is more legitimate than not. Generally, people really want to believe the mother myths, especially the aspect of unconditional maternal love, and they're inclined either not to believe an unloved daughter or to think she's exaggerating. The most otherwise understanding friends and lovers, especially if they had loving or even good enough mothers, often don't get it. They sometimes believe that it just couldn't have been as bad as you say because "look at how you turned out" and other statements like that. People have trouble believing the truth, which is that, sometimes, there's a little girl still mourning the mother she deserved under that outwardly polished and successful exterior.

I didn't confide in anyone, not even my boyfriends, until I was in therapy in my early twenties and I began to realize that my mother's lack of love for me reflected on her, not me. That perception, while immediate, didn't change the way I interacted in a consistent way because I still wanted and needed her love. Ironically, it was only after my book *Mean Mothers* was published (I was 60!) that a college roommate confessed that she'd had a cruel and withholding mother. We'd shared a room the size of a closet and had been friends that sophomore year, but never said a word about our mothers. We only broke the code of silence 40 years later.

As you begin working on distinguishing how these old patterns work in your present, think about the role the code of silence plays in your life and what you might learn by confiding in a friend if you haven't. A good therapist, of course, can be the ideal confidante. But keeping the silence can both feed your sense of shame and impede your ability to distinguish the patterns.

RECALIBRATING YOUR EMOTIONAL GPS

I keep dating and choosing men who end up treating me exactly as my mother does. It starts out great, but eventually I feel as lousy about myself as I did when I lived under her roof. Can this be fixed? How can I stop? I want to be happy but I don't seem to know how.

-Kim, 35

There's nothing more dispiriting than a failed relationship, especially if you keep recreating your childhood in your intimate relationships. How do we end up choosing people who treat us as our mothers did, when we're trying so hard to get out from under? Why do we find ourselves in the company of friends and lovers who seem to be so attentive and appealing at first and then reveal themselves to be very different? Why aren't we drawn to caring and kind people instead of controlling and manipulative ones?

The truth is that each of us is drawn to what we know, even if what we know and have experienced makes us unhappy. We all gravitate toward the familiar (see the shared root with the word "family"?). For a securely attached individual whose primary connections taught her that people are loving, dependable, and trustworthy, this is just dandy. But for those of us who are insecurely attached, the familiar can be dangerous territory.

A study by Glenn Geher suggests that all of us tend to choose a romantic partner who is similar to our opposite-sex parent. In his research, he not only asked participants to self-report on how their romantic partners were like their opposite-sex parents across various categories but he also interviewed the parents as well. The shared characteristics he discovered between his subjects' partners and their opposite-sex parents were robust, and not merely coincidental. Needless to say, when romantic partners were like parents in good ways, relationship satisfaction was high; when the similarities were related to negative characteristics, however, relationship satisfaction was low. So marrying Dad isn't really a foolproof option.

When we meet someone new, it's not just our unconscious models that are in the room or at the bar; there are conscious assessments, too. So the question remains: How do we end up marrying Mom if she's been critical, unavailable, manipulative, or high in narcissistic traits? That's exactly what Claudia Chloe Brumbaugh and R. Chris Fraley asked: How do insecurely attached people attract mates? After all, we *all* want a securely attached partner—one who's emotionally available, loving, supportive, dependable—not an insecure or clingy one, or someone who's detached and uncommunicative. How do we get roped in?

The researchers suggested that what happens is a combination of misreading by one partner and a fair amount of strategizing and even dissembling by the insecure partner. They point out that anxiously attached people may seem fascinating at first; their preoccupation with themselves may easily be confused with self-disclosure and openness, which facilitates a sense of connection. Similarly, an avoidant person may come across as independent and strong. In a series of experiments, the team discovered that avoidants—despite the fact that they don't want emotional connection—actually made lots of eye contact and used touch more than securely attached people in order to seem more appealing in a dating situation. Avoidants also use humor to create a sense of sharing and detract from their essential aloofness. Although the researchers didn't use Kim Bartholomew's distinction between fearful and dismissive avoidant types, it's clear that the fearful avoidant—who both wants and fears emotional connection—would be the hardest to read and identify. Eventually, though, the leopard will show his spots.

Our working models of relationships not only shape how we act but how we remember acting, actually skewing our recall, as Jeffry A. Simpson and his colleagues discovered, which makes it even harder for couples to get along when the working models of two romantic partners are different. After measuring the attachment orientation of each individual, Simpson's team had each member of the couple identify a significant conflict in the relationship and, choosing one from each list, had the couple engage in a conflict-resolution discussion, which was then videotaped. Right after the discussion, each person rated how supportive or emotionally distant he or she had been. They were then asked the same question one week later. What the researchers found was that the more distress there was in the conflict discussion, the more the individual's working models acted as a filter. Anxious people rated themselves as being more supportive when they remembered the discussion than they did initially; avoidant people reported themselves as being more emotionally distant. "What individuals respond to in relationships is not what they actually said or did during an interaction with their partner," the researchers surmised. "Rather, what they respond to is memories of the interaction filtered through their working models." This research explains why it is that if we have, indeed, partnered with someone whose internalized scripts are very different from our own, the discord is likely to be endless, with little resolution in sight without some kind of intervention.

Some questions to ask yourself:

* Is there an underlying pattern in the relationships I choose to be in?
* Are my reactions and responses basically the same in every relationship no matter how different the person is?
* Do I tend to be attracted to the same kind of person over and over again?
* How long do my relationships—whether they're friendships or romantic liaisons—last? Do they tend to end in the same ways?

DISTINGUISHING OTHER PEOPLE'S ATTACHMENT STYLES

Our working models don't just act as a filter on memory as that study showed; they're fully operational every time we connect with anyone. Our understanding of someone's motivations, our interpretation of their words and behavior, our reading of their emotions and motions are poured through the sieve of our working models. Unless you begin to be aware of your own attachment style—anxious or avoidant—you are working from cue cards in a language you don't speak. If your relationships aren't working for you, the chances are good that you're choosing the wrong partners without understanding why.

Unfortunately, both the limitations of our working models and the cultural depiction of romantic love often interact on an unconscious level to insure some pretty disastrous choices and consequences. From *Romeo and Juliet* to *Fifty Shades of Grey*, romance is portrayed as all-consuming, obliterating the boundaries between yourself and the other. But as science knows, a healthy, sustaining, and truly intimate relationship depends on two people being at once both interdependent yet capable of autonomy. Paradoxically, as the work of Brooke Feeney has shown, by being *both* dependent and autonomous, people actually become more empowered and independent, setting goals for themselves they might not otherwise have.

There's evidence that this interdependence isn't just metaphoric or a matter of living lives that are intertwined on many practical levels. As Daniel Wegner and his coauthors write, "But on hearing even the simplest conversation between intimates, it becomes remarkably apparent that their thoughts, too, are interconnected. Together, they think about things in ways that they would not alone."

These relationships are those of partners who have a secure base. They are skilled communicators, want intimacy and closeness, are good at managing and defusing conflict, can manage their emotions, and aren't given to game-playing. The sad truth is that the insecurely attached daughter, especially if she is looking for Passion and Romance (accompanied by the strains of "Someday My Prince Will Come"), is not likely to be attracted to someone securely attached. That reasonable and stable way of dealing with things can, when filtered through the sieve, look dull, passionless, and even boring; secure people don't create a lot of drama and, all too often, insecurely attached people mistake drama for passion or excitement. Instead, absent conscious awareness, it's much more likely that the unloved daughter will be attracted to someone who's insecurely attached himself. Even if she is attracted to someone secure, without awareness there's unlikely to be a happy ending.

Much of relationship stress—not to mention discord, fracture, and rupture—can be understood as the result of people with very different attachment styles getting together. Put two securely attached people together and you can cue the violins and, all things considered, they are good to go. Of course, this doesn't mean that they won't ever disagree or fight, or that they will necessarily stay together forever. It does mean that they have a home court advantage in terms of being able to communicate, a shared goal of needing and wanting real intimacy, and are less likely to engage in some of the more toxic behaviors—demand/withdraw, belittling their partner, making criticism highly personal, and the like—that bedevil relationships and are, according to John Gottman and other experts, the fuel for divorce.

But combine one securely attached person with an anxiously attached person and get ready for some real challenges and don't forget to fasten your seatbelts. That was the case for Mike and Susie, who had been dating for two years. Mike had been doing his best to quell Susie's constant need for reassurance and her anxiety about whether he really loved her. When his work required him to travel ten days out of every month, Mike suggested they move in together as a sign of his commitment. But living together didn't help. Susie would call or text him during working hours, even though he'd told her he couldn't respond. When he didn't answer, she would get progressively more wound up. Their arguments became constant, covering the same ground over and over—with Susie complaining that she wasn't important to him, that she needed to hear from him immediately, and Mike saying that he was doing all that he could and that she was being crazy and that he felt suffocated—until, finally, Mike moved out and ended the relationship. Of course, the ending might have been different had Susie understood how her own emotional history animated her present. She might have recognized her behavior as prompted by old triggers rather than things Mike was actually doing or saying.

A secure man may initially be attracted to an avoidant partner—she may seem fiercely independent, even mysterious, and a challenge—but will conclude, sooner or later, that the thrill of the chase isn't worth it and that his needs aren't being met in terms of intimacy and sharing.

But the real tinderbox of mismatches is that of the anxiously attached with the avoidantly attached. It's a predictable disaster in the making, with one person reacting with super-charged neediness, clingy behavior, angst, and protest anger and the other—already inclined to keep at a distance in relationship—feeling the need to run for the hills, while being content to play the game at least for a while. The avoidant may like the feeling of control or the rush of power that pushing a needy person around can give some people. Each person in the relationship in this case locates his or her need for intimacy—and understanding of what constitutes closeness—at opposite ends of the spectrum.

Luckily, there's no shortage of excellent research and information on attachment styles, and perhaps the key to either disentangling yourself from a "bad fit" relationship or seeing if it can possibly be salvaged is understanding the motivations that underlie the behaviors of the anxiously and avoidantly attached. Here are some of the characteristics that science has discovered:

Anxious and avoidant people have sex for different reasons:
That's exactly what a study by Dory A. Schachner and Phillip R.
Shaver clarified. Previous research showed that avoidant people were
less likely to fall in love, more likely to play games and manipulate,
and preferred noncommittal casual sex. Additionally, an earlier
study by these authors showed that while avoidants were likely to
try to poach someone else's guy or gal, it was only for the purpose
of short-term sex and self-aggrandizement. In this study, Schachner
and Shaver hypothesized and showed that avoidant people would be
motivated to have sex for status-related reasons or to maintain control.
In contrast, anxious individuals were motivated to have sex because
of their fear of abandonment and need to feel valued by their partner;
in this scenario, having sex is a way of tamping down fear and feeling
cared for.

It's interesting that, albeit for wholly different reasons, both the
anxious and the avoidant see sex as being about the self, not the
partner or the dyad. That observation is borne out and underscored
by a study conducted by Gurit Birnbaum and others.

**They experience sexual activity differently, with different conse-
quences for relationship:** The Birnbaum study looked beyond the
motives for having sex and focused instead on how the anxious and the
avoidant experience sex, and how, for each, sexual activity connects to
relationship. In this case, the participants ranged in age from 17 to
48. What's interesting about this line of inquiry is that, as the authors
note, while it's true that empirical evidence links sexual satisfaction to
the quality and stability of a romantic relationship, clinical evidence
suggests that "harmonious couples can have relatively distressed
sexual interactions whereas other couples have turbulent relationships
but great sex." They go on to write that a theoretical framework for
understanding the role sex plays in romantic relationship, particularly
the interplay between sexual activity and relational problems, appears
to be lacking, and they suggest that attachment styles might provide
one. The results were illuminating. Their first study had participants
self-report scales of attachment orientation and then answer questions
about sexual experience, relational issues, sex-related issues, and

feelings and thoughts about pleasure. They found that highly anxious people reported focusing on their own needs while wanting their partner's emotional involvement but also reported aversive feelings during sexual intercourse and doubts about being loved. Avoidant people reported low levels of pleasure and pleasure-related feelings, and strong aversive feelings during sexual intercourse; they, too, were focused on their own needs. In the second, smaller, study, 50 participants kept a diary for 42 days, reporting on both sexual activity and relationship quality each day, as well as their feelings and thoughts after having sex. Not altogether surprisingly, a good sexual experience, especially among women, decreased relational anxiety while a not-so-good one increased it. Either way, the authors noted that, for the anxiously attached, sex functioned as a barometer for the quality of the relationship. That wasn't true for avoidants, for whom both good sex and bad sex alike did not affect their view of the relationship. This led the researchers to conclude that avoidants have sex for "relationship-irrelevant" reasons. So much for trying to increase a feeling of intimacy with an avoidant.

People who are insecurely attached are diminished by connection, not made stronger: This is perhaps the least discussed aspect of the bigger differences between the securely attached and those who aren't. As the work of Brooke Feeney makes clear, securely attached people who can depend on their partners actually become more independent and more able to take chances and risks because they know they will have support if there's a setback. For different reasons, the anxious and the avoidant don't experience this kind of personal growth through connection.

Another study found similar results, this time focusing on energy. The researchers posited that because securely attached people are more skilled at managing negative emotion and because managing negative emotion uses up energy and self-control, the securely attached would be more energetic. In contrast, the insecurely attached are using their energy to deal with triggers and activations of the attachment systems—whether that's "I'm being abandoned!" or "I'm being encroached!" Using primes on participants—visualizing either a securely attached person or an insecurely attached one—and then having the participants write about the experience and report on how energetic they felt, the researchers confirmed their hypothesis over a series of experiments.

This actually makes perfect sense. Just spend a few minutes visualizing what you feel like with an emotionally demanding or withdrawn person compared with someone who is available and grounded, and check your own energy levels. Yes, it's exhausting to either deal with emotional outbursts on the daily or do cartwheels 24/7 to get someone's attention.

Questions to Ask Yourself About Sex and Intimacy

• Think about your own reasons for having sex and the role sexual connection has played in your present or past relationships. Do you and partner argue about how much (or how little) sex you have, and has this been a pattern in previous relationships?

• Do you get anxious or feel rejected when your partner doesn't seem to want to make love? Or, alternatively, would you rather not have as much sex as your partner demands?

• Think about whether your sense of self is expanded or diminished by having sexual relations. That, too, is part of the work of *distinguishing.*

• If your lovers or friends have complained that you're too clingy or distant, or it's an observation you've heard frequently from others, it's important for you to consider whether the appraisal is correct.

Confronting your own patterns of behavior isn't always easy, but it will help you achieve what you want: a relationship with the right balance of interdependence and autonomy. The key is to disarm the automatic nature of your responses, but that can only happen *after* you've *distinguished*—recognized and understood your behaviors and what drives them.

Examine your reactivity: Because this behavior is largely unconscious, you need to get a bead on whether your reactions are actually being fueled by your experiences or your unconscious reading of those experiences. For example, a study by Lorne Campbell, Jeffry A. Simpson, and others showed, through a series of experiments, that anxiously attached people were much more likely to perceive greater conflict in their relationships on a day-to-day basis; more likely to report feeling hurt or sensitivity; and more likely to be negative about the future of the relationship than those who were not anxiously attached.

Questions to Ask Yourself

• Are your childhood scripts feeding your daily adult dialogue? Is your partner really as unreliable as you think and is the relationship really as rocky as you think it is at moments, or are you making the drama by being overly sensitive and reactive?

• Are your fears of getting hurt or misled making you push off from your partner?

• Are you taking your cues from the past or the present?

HOW IS YOUR ATTACHMENT STYLE AFFECTING YOUR RELATIONSHIPS?

Research shows that our attachment styles don't just play out in the bedroom but, more importantly, affect how we deal with crises, large and small. How does attachment affect our behavior when someone lies to us? We might as well start there since the number-one torpedo to relationships and the leading cause of divorce remains infidelity at almost 22 percent, as a study by Paul R. Amato and Denise Previti showed.

Most of us assume that the immediate and ultimate deathblow to a relationship is one person's deception, especially about something important, but research shows otherwise—only about 23 percent of relationships founder directly after the discovery of deception, and it turns out that attachment style plays a key role. That's what a study conducted among college students by Su Ahn Jang, Sandi W. Smith, and Timothy R. Levine set out to examine, using a narrow definition of deception: "a case in which a person produces a message with the intent to mislead a relational partner about a matter of some consequence to the partner or the relationship." What they looked at is way beyond the white lie, and includes intentional activity as well.

It'll surprise no one that in this crisis, securely attached individuals addressed the issue with their partners directly and, as a result of these communications, were unlikely to end the relationship on the spot. Talking is constructive and while it may not defang the pain of deception, it helps the victim gain perspective. The anxiously attached talked around the issue but they, too, were unlikely to split that second. It was the avoidants—some 45 percent of them—who were saying *au revoir* immediately, leading the investigators to conclude that "avoidants terminate relationships most often, as they tend to avoid the personal after relational troubles. It seems that it is not important what exactly is said; it is important that couples not stop communication all together after the discovery of deception."

Questions to Ask Yourself

* How does your attachment style shape your response to crisis or betrayal?
* How does it affect your ability to communicate with your partner?
* Do you tend to talk around issues or are you capable of addressing them directly?
* Do you simply consign the crisis to "elephant in the living room" status and avoid discussion entirely?

BECOMING MINDFUL OF YOUR AND YOUR PARTNER'S BEHAVIOR IN CONFLICT

In hindsight—and no, I didn't see it until after we split up— my ex revealed himself when we disagreed on anything, big or small. I couldn't voice an opinion without his laughing at me, rolling his eyes, trying to make me back down. When I didn't, he'd belittle me, call me dumb, tell me he was sick of my endless complaints. If that didn't work, he'd leave the room. Over time, I got braver and he got more abusive. It took 12 years, but I finally reached a tipping point.

-Erin, 48

Securely attached people are more able than their insecurely attached counterparts to successfully de-escalate, negotiate, and resolve all manner of conflicts, from small emotional flare-ups to outright warfare. It helps, of course, that they have a positive view of both themselves and others, which facilitates a willingness to explore solutions, a belief that the other person will do his or her best to be honest and direct, and a general optimism about the value of close connection and intimacy. They're better at applying their emotional intelligence—allowing their emotions to inform their feelings and their feelings inform their thoughts—when there's a conflict. They are also better at leaving a sinking ship when they identify one.

Because insecurely attached people have skill deficits when it comes to managing negative emotion, one way of pinpointing your and your partner's attachment styles is to focus on how you disagree or fight. Marital expert John Gottman has long made the point that he can predict with 95 percent accuracy whether a marriage will survive based on *how* a couple fights, not whether they do. Ask yourself the following questions about yourself and then about your partner in an effort to further distinguish your attachment styles:

◆ Does discussing tender issues on which you and your partner disagree make you anxious? Are you overcome by fears that your disagreement will escalate out of control?

◆ Are you generally inclined to "let sleeping dogs lie" and avoid discussion and a possible confrontation as much as possible?

◆ Who is more likely to initiate a discussion, no matter how difficult, about something in the relationship?

◆ Are you able to stay calm in a discussion, or do you get defensive or aggressive almost immediately? Are you likely to be goaded more by your partner's active response or by his dismissing you?

◆ Do you stonewall in fights? If so, how does your partner respond?

DO YOU RECOGNIZE TOXICITY WHEN YOU SEE IT?

Not long ago I got a message from a reader who asked, "Can you be in a toxic relationship without knowing it?" Well, yes: It's possible for insecurely-attached women who have grown up with toxic treatment to normalize certain behaviors because they're used to them.

Have you ever noticed how easy it is to go blind to familiar things in your surroundings? How you stop noticing the pile of boots and shoes by the back door if it's been there long enough? Or how your eyes can glide over the clothes hung on the exercise equipment without noticing them? These are mundane and homely examples of how we all sometimes "normalize" disorder. When you grow up with toxic behaviors—the verbal put-down, the silent treatment, the nasty humor that's meant to make you feel small—it's not unusual to get so used to them that you don't even consciously register them. That can remain true even in adulthood.

The familiar feel of various kinds of abuse is further complicated by the fact that the insecurely attached daughter is also prone to misreading the cues in relationships—interpreting a rollercoaster type of connection with an avoidant person as highly passionate, mistaking controlling behavior as stable and focused, or not recognizing emotional manipulation when she experiences it. Among the behaviors an unloved daughter who's not yet connecting the dots between past and present may miss are the following. Feel free to change the pronouns from masculine to feminine because these patterns are not gender based and pertain to all relationships, not just romantic ones.

He discounts or marginalizes your feelings: One of the most consistent mantras of the unloving and verbally disparaging or abusive parent is "You're too sensitive," and it's one of the easiest to believe and internalize. Emerging into adulthood, many daughters simply take this as a "truth" about themselves, and when their partner or love interest uses the same or similar words, they often acquiesce. These words—or ones like them that suggest you're exaggerating or are a drama queen or thin skinned—should be a wake-up call that you've found yourself back in your childhood room in a very real sense.

He treats you with contempt or belittles you: You might not even notice it because you grew up hearing it, but contemptuous language and gestures aren't part of a healthy relationship. That includes eye-rolling, sneering, or laughter meant to intimidate you or denigrate your responses or even your complaints, or speaking to you with heavy sarcasm ("It's funny that you of all people would have the nerve to tell me to be a better listener" or "Since when are you an expert on relationships?"). These behaviors might be even harder for an insecurely attached woman to spot if they are used only intermittently or at moments of discord, which makes it easier for you to rationalize the behavior.

He withdraws when you make a demand: This most toxic pattern of connection is so widely recognized by psychologists that it actually has its own acronym: DM/W. Demand/withdraw is often a pattern between daughter and mother, especially when the child gets old enough or has the courage to confront her mother. In this pattern—and I am drawing from memory here—the daughter asks the mother why she's treating her badly, and the mother withdraws and denies that it's happening, says nothing at all, or says "I will not talk about this" and leaves the room. This is a relatively rare pattern among the securely attached because they understand that give-and-take is part of the process of connection, but it is common among the insecurely attached. The pattern not only cuts off discussion—assuming that the demand is a legitimate one that addresses a need one person has—but also has escalation built into it since the person making the demand will likely become more frustrated and the louder she gets, the more her partner will withdraw. (By the way, although men sometimes take on the demanding role, studies show it's more likely that a woman will be in this position.) Each party feels aggrieved in this scenario. If every discussion you have with your partner devolves into an argument with the DM/W pattern in place, you need to be looking for an exit.

He manipulates your insecurities; Another legacy of an unloving mother is deep-rooted insecurity about one or more aspects of the self, which can coexist with real-world success and achievement, and is easily triggered. "I'm really self-conscious about my weight," Maggie confided, "and in my last marriage, whenever I complained about anything, my husband would fight back by hassling me about how much I ate or how I looked fat or how other women looked so much better than I did. It took therapy for me to see the pattern. He wanted me to be docile and when I wasn't, he attacked me."

He projects his feelings onto you: Does this scenario sound familiar? You are supposedly "discussing" why he's so against getting a new stove when the oven hasn't worked in months and you can see that he's folded his arms tight against his chest and that he's working his jaw muscles and you ask him why he's angry. Instead of answering, he turns toward you and accuses you of being angry, not just now but all the time, and he keeps on going until it turns into a full-blown tirade about how angry and dissatisfied you seem, and he's sick and tired of "the same old tattoo." Narcissists project their feelings in this way—in his book, *Rethinking Narcissism*, Dr. Craig Malkin calls it "playing emotional hot potato"—but so do other people who simply do not want to, or won't, acknowledge and take responsibility for their feelings. This is, in part, a defensive strategy to deflect blame and fault from one party to another, and it's both toxic and manipulative.

He always needs to be in control: Unloved daughters typically lack the sense of belonging that comes naturally to someone who was raised by a parent or parents who made her feel safe and good about herself. Unfortunately, these daughters are often drawn to men who appear to offer a safe haven—they may seem very sure of themselves, are often successful and driven, are outspoken in their opinions and beliefs—because they mistake control for strength and resolve. Because feeling powerless may be familiar—and echo childhood—a daughter may be slow to recognize that she's being robbed of her own voice and manipulated into making choices she really doesn't want to make. Control can also be exercised with stealth and a light touch as, for example, when one partner consistently "surprises" the other by changing plans the couple had previously agreed on.

REJECTION SENSITIVITY AND REACTING TO THE PRESENT AS IF YOU'RE STUCK IN THE PAST

How good are you at figuring out what makes you act and react? You've already identified your basic attachment style—secure, anxious-preoccupied, dismissive, or fearful avoidant—and it's important to distinguish those behaviors that are driven by your emotional history. If you are anxiously attached, one such pattern is rejection sensitivity.

Of course, all humans are hurt by social rejection—we're creatures who need to belong—and studies show that the pain of social rejection engages precisely the same neural circuitry as physical pain. It turns out that the word "heartache" is more literal than not. That said, anxiously attached people are much more likely to have high degrees of rejection sensitivity, which works to shape their behavior in complicated ways. The term "rejection sensitivity" immediately calls to mind romantic rejection—that exquisite pain when someone you love leaves you—but in fact, that's just one component; this sensitivity affects a person on many different levels, influencing her expectations about interactions large and small and eliciting complex behaviors.

The scale developed by researchers Geraldine Downey and Scott Feldman for use in experiments with college students covered a broad range of situations involving the potential for rebuff, ranging from the relatively benign (asking to borrow a classmate's notes, asking your parents for extra spending money, asking a professor for extra help in a course) to ones that involve more personal rejection (asking someone you don't know for a date, approaching a close friend to talk after you've upset him by saying or doing something, asking a friend for a favor) to situations that, should they end in rejection, could really pack a wallop (asking your lover to move in with you, asking your boyfriend if he really loves you, asking someone close to talk to you after a bitter argument). Again, these examples were developed for college students, but they can be adapted for adult life in most cases. The respondents were asked both how worried they were about how the other person would respond and how they thought the other person would react. Needless to say, all of these scenarios were more fraught for those high in rejection sensitivity than those who worried less about rejection.

Other studies have tracked the effect of rejection sensitivity on intimate relationships. One by Geraldine Downey, Antonio Freitas, and others hypothesized that people high in rejection sensitivity would actually get tangled up in a self-fulfilling prophecy. Their focus on possible rejection would elicit outsized and combative reactions to the slightest hint of it and that, in turn, would make lovers and friends head for the hills. And that's exactly what the researchers found.

So if you're sensitive to the possibility of rejection, here are some questions to ask yourself:

* If there's drama in the relationship, how much of it is instigated by you?
* Do you tend to be drawn to people who make your anxiety more acute? Do you often find yourself in the "pleaser" role?
* Can you trace your sensitivity back to childhood experiences?
* How often do you fight with friends and partners? Do you see a pattern?

• What kind of reassurance do you demand of your partner when you've been triggered? Do you escalate your demands?

• Would you like to change your behavior?

DOING AN INVENTORY OF YOUR RELATIONSHIPS

Part of the work of distinguishing includes looking at how many relationships in your life appear familiar—incorporating combat, verbal abuse, manipulation, or dismissiveness—and make you feel just as you did in childhood. Understanding why you are attracted to these people in the first place—the fake comfort of the familiar, the fact that their treatment confirms so-called truths you were told about yourself when you were growing up, the echo of older patterns as you have to prove yourself worthy of their love—is the first step in getting yourself to a place where you can begin to work on changing.

Think about the following:

• Why are you in the relationships you're in?

• Do you always play the same or a similar role in your relationships? What is that role?

• Can you imagine a relationship that would make you happier than the one you're in now? What would it look like?

• What kind of a partner would you like to be able to choose or find for yourself? What characteristics would this person have?

LOOKING TOWARD DISARMING YOUR DEFAULT SETTINGS

In the next chapter, "Making the Unconscious Conscious," we'll be looking at specific strategies and techniques you can learn to begin the process of healing and become more skilled at connecting in new, more consciously aware ways. To live differently and with greater emotional ease and contentment, you have to head in that direction.

CHAPTER SIX
MAKING THE UNCONSCIOUS CONSCIOUS

My wake-up call came when I realized I didn't even like the people I thought I loved. I was trying to so hard to win my mother's approval, mostly unconsciously, through people I loved or were friends with. Invariably, my mother would say how much better these people were and how much smarter they were than me, which set up competition on so many levels. In the end, I didn't even like these people because it seemed I wasn't even in the equation. I kept choosing people to get my mother's approval, and they were just like her. I can see that now.

~Clarissa, 40

Perhaps one of the most frustrating things about the journey of recovery is that, often, it feels as though you're trying to move a five-ton pachyderm by yourself—yes, the proverbial elephant in the living room—but sometimes he's there and sometimes he's not. Unloved daughters actively complain about how long it takes to recognize the lack of maternal love, how it takes even longer to see the effects, how slow the recovery process is, and how these patterns can be resistant to even years of therapy and efforts at self-help. There are reasons it's hard, and that's what we need to look at first. This chapter is about disarming the unconscious patterns of behaviors, along with the triggers for them, and the reality is that we can't run the obstacle course until we can see the obstacles.

RUNNING THE OBSTACLE COURSE

Some of these obstacles, as we'll see, have to do with the brain and apply to everyone whether they are loved by their mothers or not but take up a special place in the life of a woman who's actively trying to recover. We'll look at how the brain itself and our unconscious thought processes can be an obstacle and what we can do to outwit them—and yes, those unconscious processes can be successfully gamed, which is very good news indeed! In fact, just reading these sentences is changing the neural connections in your brain; we have the continuing pliability of that extraordinary organ to thank for that. First, though, we have to look at ourselves and our behaviors. Often, we are the biggest obstacles to our ability to thrive, the boulders that stand in the way. Why? Because of the core conflict: our continuing need for our mother's love and approval. I call it the "dance of denial," and I was once an expert at it, many years ago. It was the only time in my life, in fact, that I actually achieved the status of a prima ballerina. The dance of denial, in my case, went on for just short of 20 years.

UNDERSTANDING AND ENDING THE DANCE OF DENIAL

She was on her deathbed and someone said, 'Do you want to tell Linda you love her?' My mother answered, 'No.' Of course, I rationalized her behavior because it felt better than thinking I wasn't loved. I rationalized her behavior for years, but it never helped my pain. I would tell people that she behaved the way she did because she was sick, because her own mother had been detached, because she was abused. I barely cried when she died. I cried much more when my beloved dog died, in truth. Why did I rationalize? Who wants anyone to know that they were unloved by their mother? I think that on some level I felt that if my mother couldn't love me, how could anyone?

~Linda, 57

It's a testament to both the centrality and complexity of the mother-daughter relationship that, for many unloved daughters, the recognition of their wounding and its source comes late in life. Some women are in their thirties, forties, fifties, and even sixties—and often, are mothers or even grandmothers themselves—before they finally begin to understand how their mothers' treatment of them in child-hood has affected and continues to shape their lives. Others know at a very young age—as I did—that their mothers didn't love them. They "know" it long before they can even put it into words. I was no older than three or four; others say they knew at six, seven, or eight.

But this early knowledge doesn't necessarily bestow an advantage because these children are clueless about why their mothers don't connect to them; in fact, they are very likely to blame themselves for whatever might be wrong, which adds another layer of emotional confusion. Additionally, their perceptions don't stop them from trying to become the kind of daughter their mother would or might love. But they know deep inside nonetheless, and as they get older, they begin to wrestle with the problem. Note the word "begin" because this is a long process, even with therapy.

What gets in the way of a daughter's seeing her mother's behavior as hurtful, destructive, or even willful? Part of it is certainly the hardwired need for a mother's love and approval that is part and parcel of every infant's being. This need doesn't appear to have an expiration date; it lasts long into adulthood and, perhaps, the entire life span. Along with the need, there is often a feeling of deep shame at being unloved and the deep-seated fear that a mother's judgment is correct. That fear—that her mother is right, that she is ultimately unlovable—and the shame that accompanies it underlie much of a daughter's denial. Denial puts her in the position of somehow having to make sense of the relationship, of trying to find a reason other than her own unworthiness for her mother's lack of love. Looking for a reason can keep you dancing, as Kate wrote: "I rationalized how my mother behaved toward me until last year when I turned 37. I wanted there to be a reason for how she treated me, one I could actually get my head around. I don't think you ever want to admit what's going on when you want so desperately to be loved by your mother."

The core conflict can keep a daughter stuck for years. Sometimes the wake-up call—the moment when the rationalization and denial finally stall out—comes when the pain of rejection becomes too much to bear. Sometimes the level of havoc in the daughter's life—wrought by the behaviors she learned in response to her mother's treatment—gets to be too much and in the moment, she suddenly has the clarity of mind to track the chaos back to its source. That was certainly true for Deidre, whose epiphany happened in her late thirties, after she'd been in two emotionally abusive relationships in a row. It was her marrying someone who treated her just as her mother did that forced her to take a long, hard look at her choices. She ended up going into therapy and, ultimately, divorced both her husband and her mother within a two-year period. As she put it: "My mother wasn't able to take responsibility for her actions and I was no longer in a place where I was willing to tolerate either her denial or the emotional abuse. It still makes me sad, but I had to learn to live differently."

Sometimes it's a third-party intimate—a friend, a lover, a spouse—who opens the door to seeing the pattern, as Jenn's story makes clear: "I was living with the man I ended up marrying, and we invited my mother to dinner to celebrate my getting my master's degree. He'd met her before but never one-on-one in this way, in an intimate setting. It was the same old thing with her, but when she left, he turned to me and said, 'Was this Beat Up Jenn Day? I thought we were celebrating.' He then went on to rattle off every criticism and lousy thing she'd said about me—my flat looked slovenly, I'd gotten fat, did I think I was really going to succeed outside of school?—and I burst into tears because I realized I was so used to her being that way that I just sponged it up. He encouraged me to go into therapy, and I did. Unfortunately, my mother didn't want to take responsibility for anything so we are long estranged. It's a pity, really."

Is it any wonder that unloved daughters deny in order to unconsciously protect themselves from recognizing such a painful truth? Yes, that's a rhetorical question.

The dance of denial is also energized by the myth that all mothers are loving, and the rationalization that drives the dance is fed by other people's responses—the people who tell you, as they tell me, that "It couldn't have been so bad because you turned out just fine" or "Stop complaining. You had a roof over your head." My own, thoroughly unscientific take is that people want so badly to believe that one kind of love is immutable, unconditional, and never wavering—given that we all know love in the world is hard to get and harder to hold on to—that they're resistant to giving up that belief. An unloved daughter's story challenges that pastel-tinted vision of the all-loving mother—and there's the biblical commandment to boot.

And it's not just the outside world's reactions that keep a daughter stuck; speaking up and recognizing the truth of a mother's behavior may be made harder by other family members who either don't see the mother in the same way or don't want to come out and call her behavior what it is. The dilemma that Julia, 41, faces has much to do with her family's rallying in their own dance of denial: "My mother's behavior is still excused by my siblings, and they hate me for telling the truth. They explain and excuse her as a victim because of her own upbringing and are quick to tear me down if I challenge the family in any way. This throws me into self-doubt, once again, and makes me feel guilty about my perceptions. I'm still afraid of being punished in some way for thinking these thoughts about the person who gave me life. But I know what happened and what she did; I end up spinning emotionally."

The moment at which the daughter stops denying and starts looking is the first step of what is a long journey—unraveling the ways in which her own behavior was shaped in childhood. Coming to terms with the self and experience requires self-compassion, insight, and emotional fortitude—which, of course, denial does not—and a decision about how to use and process both the information gleaned and the experience. This is what Laura came to understand. "I rationalized my mother's behavior all of my life. I always had an excuse or rationale for why she said or did things. This was all about minimizing me, because if there were a 'reason' for her behavior, somehow it was okay. Eventually, after getting out of the blame cycle and ignoring all the New Age garbage about 'forgiveness,' I decided on honesty and accountability. As long as I was excusing/rationalizing her behavior, I was discounting what it did to me, condoning it as okay because I didn't deserve any better. A-ha! It took a while to figure this one out—I'm 59. I'm a mother myself so I'm tired of being on a pedestal or in the gutter."

It's not just that the unloved daughter truly gets to see her mother once she stops the dance of denial, but that she is finally afforded the opportunity to see herself in full, unobscured by the second-guessing, self-doubt, and shame that looking away from the real problem induces. For many, it's a hard path, but it is a hopeful one, as Alicia wrote: "We are filled with so much self-doubt that loving ourselves and having belief in our worth is so hard. For so long we believed the trouble lay within ourselves. As a mother myself now, there isn't a thing I wouldn't do for my kids, and I won't put a price tag on it.

Loving my kids unconditionally has let me see that I am actually a much more capable and stronger person than I ever knew."

If you are still on the Ferris wheel—making excuses for your mother, cutting her slack, trying to minimize your own pain—you aren't being compassionate to her. You are simply lacking in self-compassion. In order to begin the process of healing yourself, you have to let go of the denial and trade it for recognition. Yes, it hurts. Why it hurts was put eloquently in an email by Deborah, 55: "When I stopped making excuses for her, I also gave up the hope that things would ever change. That she would come around someday. That was a killer. More like experiencing a death, really."

It is the step, though, that every unloved daughter must take to save herself, whether she decides to remain in contact with her mother or not.

THE FEELING OF BEING "LESS THAN"

The degree to which unconscious processes govern much of human behavior will be made clear in the pages that follow. Keep in mind, though, as you read, that while some of these unconscious patterns are universal default settings, the unloved daughter has some that are specific to her experiences. Feeling less than or inadequate—which can impair the ability to assess herself realistically despite outward success—is one. The habit of self-criticism—ascribing setbacks or failures to fixed character traits instead of circumstances—is another. There are others we'll turn to in detail after examining unconscious process generally.

THE BRAIN: YOURS, MINE, AND EVERYONE'S

All of us pride ourselves—yes, I count myself in that number—on making well-considered decisions most of the time and avoiding snap judgments based on little or no information. We think of ourselves as thoughtful and reasonable, but nothing could be further from the truth. Humans are actually hardwired to make snap judgments or engage in what Daniel Kahneman has called "fast" thinking, most of which takes place outside of consciousness.

Fast thinking that is automatic—you're connecting the dots even as your brain registers that there *are* dots—was obviously an evolutionary advantage at a time in human history when staying alive required being alert and proactive in the face of physical dangers and challenges. Remember the example in the first chapter about reacting to a baby's cry—even if you don't have a baby—before you've consciously registered there's a baby wailing? Our brains still work that way, which factors into the mix when we consider the road to recovery and disarming the responses we learned in childhood. While I won't provide a comprehensive review of all of the automatic processes associated with the brain, I'm going to focus on the ones that most directly affect how we can begin to unlearn what we learned as children.

THE EFFECTS OF PRIMES AND PRIMING

Did you know that if you have people think about a library, they're more likely to lower their voices to a whisper? Or that the smell of cleanser in the air actually encourages people to clean up after themselves? A body of research attests to the fact that cues in the physical environment evoke specific thoughts and reactions without our being aware of their provenance or even that we're being cued to do and think what we're doing and thinking. It's not hard to see the evolutionary advantage to the brain metaphorically sniffing out danger before it's actually seen, but this trait continues to influence our behavior in important ways. For the insecurely attached daughters, those unnoticed primes are a key to disarming reactivity. Let's take a look at how primes and priming work.

In one experiment conducted by John Bargh and Tanya Chartrand, participants who were primed to complete sentences with words associated with rudeness such as "aggressively" and "bold" were more likely to behave rudely than those primed with neutral or polite words like "respect" and "courteous." Similarly, it's been shown that the physical environment—objects—can cue behavior as well. For example, Bargh and his colleagues ran an experiment that used images associated with capitalistic enterprise (a conference table, briefcases, dress shirts, and ties) to see if they could cue competition among the participants. Primed with images of business, 70 percent of those given the word fragment "c_ _ p_ _ _ tive" completed it as "competitive," compared to 42 percent of unprimed subjects. Alternatively, the fragment could have been completed as "cooperative."

Other cues elicit other reactions. A study by Adam Pazda and his colleagues showed that women were more likely to judge a woman as promiscuous or sexually receptive if she was wearing a red dress, and more likely to display jealousy and mate-guarding behavior than if she were wearing white or green! So if you're sitting at a bar or at a party with your honey and you suddenly find yourself bristling at the brunette in red, it's your brain doing the talking.

If you think about primes and priming in a down-to-earth way, it makes a great deal of sense. We're not reacting just to primes in the environment—the crowded subway car elicits one mood, the calming celadon walls of a sunlit living room another—but also to people's facial expressions and body language. Sometimes, we're conscious and aware of how we're being affected, but sometimes we're not. Imagine you are meeting someone for the first time; you've arranged to meet her in the lobby of a building so there aren't any external primes to elicit your responses. Let's say you call out her name as you approach and she doesn't smile at you or extend her hand; do you assume you've done something to offend her or do you think she's having a bad day and her behavior has nothing to do with you? What if she extends her hand in greeting but her face is stiff and unsmiling; are you likely to read into her mixed signals and feel as though you have to do something to win her over? What if she's on the phone and she keeps on talking for the next ten minutes? Would you register that she's being unspeakably rude or would her behavior make you feel small and inadequate?

For all of us, daily life is made up of dozens and dozens of such moments when we're responding to cues from strangers, acquaintances, neighbors, friends, coworkers, and intimates; understanding how we react to these cues is part of the journey of understanding that comprises making the unconscious conscious. Seeing whether and how you internalize external cues is an important first step in disarming unconscious process.

HOW REACTIVE TO CUES ARE YOU?

All this talk of primes may make you feel that we're all human puppets on strings, but the reality is that some of us are more open to their influence while others are relatively impervious. You need to identify your own reactivity both to disarm primes and to learn how to use them consciously and to your advantage. There's a body of research that explores another theory of personality called "personality systems interactions" (PSI). This theory focuses on how individuals cope in times of stress. Based on a continuum of behavior, it distinguishes between those who are action-oriented and those who are state-oriented.

People who are action-oriented are good at emotional regulation, can summon up positive images of self under fire, and don't rely on external cues. (Yes, this sounds like the skill set of a securely-attached person who's motivated by approach goals. The perspective and the vocabulary are different.) In contrast, people who demonstrate state-oriented behavior flood with emotion under stress, don't self-regulate well, are preoccupied by worries about failing, and are sensitive to external cues. (This description is also similar to the traits of an insecurely attached person motivated by avoidance.) This theory also assumes that these dispositions are learned in childhood.

Now, back to primes. In one experiment, after filling out questionnaires that determined either their action or state orientation, half of the participants were asked to visualize a difficult and demanding person in their lives and to recall both specific incidents and how they felt at the time. (In other words, they were asked to hot-process the encounters.) Then, additionally, the experimenters had these participants write down those observations and identify the difficult person by his or her initials. The other half of the participants were asked to do the same things but focusing on, visualizing, naming, and writing about an accepting person in their lives and how they felt. Then everyone was tested on how quickly they could identify a schematized image of a discrepant face in a crowd—a happy face in a field of angry ones, for example. Then they were asked to identify or not identify (noting "me" or "not me") with a series of positive ("reliable," "creative," etc.) and negative ("impulsive," etc.) traits.

Even after visualizing a difficult person and encounters, the action-oriented people could pick out a happy face in a crowd and identify with positive traits; the priming didn't affect them. The researchers hypothesized that the unconscious self-affirming processes of the action-oriented deactivated the primes. Not surprisingly, the state-oriented *were* affected by priming a difficult relationship, couldn't pick out happy faces, and felt more negative about themselves. Not surprisingly, negative priming makes all the deficits of state orientation worse.

Stop and think for a moment whether this is the case for you. Does stress make you feel worse about yourself, or are you able to rise to the occasion and pull down positive self-images?

Now to the other half of the experiment—visualizing an accepting person. Interestingly, action-oriented people weren't affected by visualizing an accepting person either, but—and here's the important part—state-oriented people not only felt better after visualizing a calm relationship but also identified with more positive traits. And this wasn't the only experiment to show that positive primes might help someone who was normally brought low by negative cues.

The takeaway: Visualizing someone who accepts you in times of stress will increase your ability to manage the situation.

EXPLORING THE POWER OF PRIMES

Research suggests that insecurely attached people (or, using the other terminology, the state-oriented) can actually use priming to stabilize mood, self-soothe, and manage negative emotions more productively. For example, researchers Sander L. Koole and David Fockenberg had participants in an experiment either recall a stressful and demanding period in their lives in great detail, or a calming and relaxing one. The researchers then primed the participants with an equal number of positive and negative words. As expected, the action-oriented dealt with the negative primes the way water glides off a duck's back, *but* the state-oriented who focused on a calming time in their lives were able to defuse the effect of the negative primes *better* than the action-oriented! Just thinking about a happy period in their lives—fully visualizing it—helped them to regulate their emotions with more skill and to be less reactive to negative primes.

Other research has explored how insecure attachment styles can be altered. As you know and researchers point out, your attachment style isn't formed by a single encounter with your caretaker but many, many experiences over a long period of time so that a single intervention or moment in time is unlikely to change it. That said, researchers continue to look at what can be done to change the unconscious reactions of the anxiously and avoidantly attached. One is "earned" attachment, which describes what happens when a person is in a relationship—it could be with a love interest, a therapist or mentor, or some other close person—which effectively breaks down those older mental representations and replaces them with ones of secure connection. We'll discuss that later in these pages, but first, let's look at how you can use priming in the day-to-day.

While some experiments using primes—security- and love-related words or scenarios—have changed participants' reactions in laboratory settings, the changes have been short-lived, lasting only hours. That was not the case in an experiment conducted by Katherine B. Carnelley and Angela C. Rowe, which found the effects of secure priming to last for days. They primed the participants by having them visualize someone with whom they felt secure, had them write about these individuals on two separate occasions, and also had them imagine a scenario in which they were helped by sensitive people when they confronted a problem they couldn't deal with on their own.

In their discussion, the researchers note that simply thinking about secure interpersonal experiences may help everyone, regardless of their attachment style, when they are under stress. (In my experience, that's certainly true.) For the anxious or avoidant, recalling people and interactions in their lives that belied their primary experiences may strengthen these secure mental representations and make them more accessible. The hope is that, through repeated exposure, it's the image of secure attachment that comes to mind when a person reacts to or assesses a situation. Finally, though, the researchers acknowledge that "although repetitive priming of attachment security may change people's cognitions or thoughts about relationships and the self, it may be more difficult to change emotional reactions to attachment stimuli." In blunt terms, that describes the unconscious hypervigilance of both the anxious and the avoidant, and their automatic ways of coping. But those, too, can be disarmed over time with effort.

The bottom line: Your ability to imagine and bring up images of the kind and caring people in your life into your thoughts can facilitate change. For some exercises to strengthen your skills, see page 243.

THE TAKEAWAY LESSONS: RECOGNIZING YOUR TRIGGERS

Disarming your unconscious process is a battle to be fought on several fronts. Following are some potentially helpful strategies:

Focus on your reactivity: Years ago, a therapist had these words of wisdom for me: STOP. LOOK. LISTEN. What he meant was that I had to focus and pay conscious attention to situations that made me feel the way I did around my mother. Instead of allowing myself to go on autopilot—becoming defensive or reactive—I had to learn to step back and process not only what I was feeling but also why.

Use STOP, LOOK, LISTEN as a mental timeout when you are becoming reactive, and ask yourself the following questions:

♦ Am I reacting to something in the present, or has the present moment dredged up something out of my past? Keep in mind that words, tone, gestures, and body language can all act as triggers, blurring the line between the past and present.

♦ Am I seeing the situation clearly, or is my reactivity driving the car that's me?

♦ Am I listening to the intention behind the words, not just the words themselves?

Giving yourself a wide enough berth to be able to examine both the source and nature of your feelings is particularly important for those of us who grew up looking through the wrong end of the binoculars.

If you're having a physical response—heightened anxiety, a pounding heart, or fear—to a situation that isn't particularly threatening, it's entirely possible that your emotions are being hijacked by automatic processes. The only way to know is to give yourself a timeout, hit the pause button, and STOP, LOOK, LISTEN.

Pay attention to situational cues: Work on becoming aware of how you're being affected by the space you're in, along with the situation. It's normal to feel anxious, for example, when you go to the doctor, or irritated when you're standing in line at the bank, but it's key to get a bead on how you are triggered and by what. Ask yourself the following questions:

♦ Does my mood shift when I'm in a crowded room? In what ways?

♦ Do I get energized by being around people or exhausted?

♦ Do I tend to overreact to small annoyances and have trouble self-calming?

♦ Am I hypervigilant to small slights, especially those that echo my treatment in childhood—someone calling me out on my version of events, for example, or telling me that I'm too sensitive?

♦ Alternatively, am I quick to withdraw or get defensive when there's tension or a glitch in communication?

Writing down your observations in your journal using cool processing will also give you greater mastery over both your emotions and reactivity over time. All of these behaviors are learned in childhood and need to be consciously unlearned.

Listen to your body: If you're starting to sweat or your throat suddenly feels tight or you have any other visceral response to a situation, see if you can trace those feelings back to a source or sources. Words or postures in what might seem to be an ordinary exchange to someone else but that recall a childhood experience might be triggering you. For example, when someone cuts me dead in mid-conversation—saying something like, "I don't want to talk about this now," or stonewalls by going silent—all of my buttons are automatically pushed because it's my childhood revisited; I have to consciously remind myself that my reaction is being heightened. Beginning to untangle the unconscious responses you learned growing up from what are appropriate and measured responses to what's happening now is key to recovery.

Use self-priming and visualization to increase your security: Follow the lead set by research findings by visualizing, in times of stress, secure connections, people, and places. Remember that securely attached people do this automatically and unconsciously; you can get the same effects by using conscious processing. See pages 243-244 for more.

Don't normalize abusive behavior: Daughters who experienced verbal abuse in childhood and were bullied, taunted, or gaslighted, sometimes have trouble recognizing toxicity in adulthood. Your tendency to excuse or normalize abusive behavior is an important pattern to bring to consciousness so that you can set clear and immutable boundaries and recognize toxic behavior when you see it. If someone is using disparaging words or gestures, excuse yourself and practice STOP, LOOK, LISTEN. You don't have to start World War III; all you need is to say something like, "I'm taking a break now. We can continue this discussion when you don't feel the need to put me down." Setting boundaries is a matter of practice, and you will get used to doing it in time.

Getting off the merry-go-round by recognizing more unconscious patterns: The more you know about the human brain and its special bag of tricks, the better you'll be at disarming unconscious patterns inherited from childhood. These habits of mind aren't limited to unloved daughters, of course, but they definitely stand in everyone's way when it comes to making good decisions, managing emotions successfully, and becoming happier with yourself and your life. For the unloved daughter, still struggling with the fallout from childhood, they are real stumbling blocks. Again, these are unconscious mental processes that can be disarmed by conscious recognition.

REALIZING THE POWER OF INTERMITTENT REINFORCEMENT

If you ever took an introductory psych course, you might remember an experiment involving three very hungry rats conducted by B. F. Skinner, but if you missed it, here's the scoop. Each cage holds a single rat and is equipped with a lever. In the first cage, when the rat pushes the lever, a food pellet is always delivered. Once the rat realizes that food is a sure thing, he loses interest in the lever and goes about his business unless he's hungry. In the second cage, the lever has been disconnected, and when the rat pushes it, nothing happens. He pushes again and again, and the result is the same and, not surprisingly, he loses interest in the lever. It's what happens in the third cage, though, that has a lesson for us. Sometimes the lever works and delivers the pellet, and sometimes it doesn't. It's a totally random pattern, but the intermittent delivery gets the rat totally fixated on the lever and increases his persistence. He'll keep on pushing.

This is true of humans, too. Nothing makes us more persistent than getting what we want *some* of the time. Combine that with two other common habits of mind—recasting a loss as a "near win" and being overly optimistic (which humans are)—and the chances are good that you are going to stay on the emotional carousel forever.

Consider your relationship to your mother or anyone in your life who is disappointing you, big time—and has been for ages— in terms of behavior, empathy, reciprocity, or anything else, and imagine a conversation or a meeting that goes much better than you expected and even makes you feel hopeful that things are about to change. Your inner optimist is smiling, and you're going to try harder because, maybe, this is the time things will *finally* turn around. That's intermittent reinforcement at work. Intermittent reinforcement keeps people at slot machines because winning now and again makes them believe that if they persist, they'll hit it big. It's especially true in relationships: When you get just a tiny taste of what you want, you're suddenly in it to win it even though nothing has really changed. It goes without saying that intermittent reinforcement keeps the dance of denial going and gets your hopes up but also sets you up for second-guessing and rumination when it's clear things haven't changed a bit.

How to tell intermittent reinforcement from real change? By looking at what's happened realistically and paying attention to whether or not you're reading in. One occasional moment that seems promising doesn't foretell a trend. Questions to ask yourself:

◆ Has the person really changed tacks, or is he or she simply less derisive, less withholding, than usual?

◆ What exactly is different about the person's treatment of you? Be sure that it's not your optimism or hopefulness kicking in and making you upbeat for no reason.

◆ Are you ready to talk to the person directly about his or her behavior? And to discuss the kinds of changes you'll need to see if the relationship is to go forward? If you're not ready, then you are effectively deciding to stay on the merry-go-round.

Simply recognizing how intermittent reinforcement can keep you stuck is a step toward disarming it.

GETTING A HANDLE ON RUMINATION

Did you know that the brain actively searches for unfinished business and works to counteract any efforts you make at subverting unwanted thoughts? That's exactly what Daniel Wegner discovered when he wanted to tackle the question of why, when we try *not* to think of something, it ends up being all we can think about. The answer has a fancy name—"ironic processes of mental control"—but it comes down to this: Your brain searches for the very thought you're trying to suppress. In one experiment, Wegner and other researchers told participants not to think about white bears while they were performing a task. Do appreciate the fact that most of us don't spend a lot of our time thinking about white bears most days, so the fact that those who were told not to think about them thought about them once a minute is quite something! In another experiment, participants were first instructed to think about white bears and then not to think about them. Guess what? They thought about them *more* when they were told not to. Avoiding a specific thought seems to have a priming effect. Yikes!

So if you, like many of us, find yourself up in the middle of the night stewing and second-guessing about that last run-in with your mother or someone else, keep in mind that those ironic processes are out to destroy your every effort to stop thinking about her or him. You might want to register the fact that rumination can also feed into self-criticism—that habit of mind that ascribes failures to flaws in your character, rather than events. So how to stop this particular merry-go-round from spinning?

Science shows that while distraction doesn't work, concentrated focus on something that really absorbs your interest does. Planning in detail—whether that's the garden bed you want to dig, the redecorating and repainting of the kitchen you want to do, or even a strategy for how you're going to handle emotional conflict in the future—can stop the white bears in their tracks.

In a paper called "Setting Free the Bears," Dr. Wegner suggests other strategies as well:

◆ Use positive-focused visualization to calm yourself.

◆ Assign yourself a "worry" time. To be honest, I don't think this would work for me, but it does work for other people. Book a time to worry—say 20 minutes—and focus on everything that's bothering you.

◆ Invite the white bears in. This is the technique I've found the most useful; it involves confronting those worries and worst-case scenarios that have been keeping you up and driving you mad. Forcing yourself to confront them, seeing what would actually happen if they came to pass, and what you can do about them if they do, pushes worry out of the shadows and into the light where you can use slow thinking to figure things out. If you have close and trusted intimates with whom you can discuss these scenarios—it really helps to hear yourself clearly—all the better.

Rumination keeps us stuck and prevents us from acting. It's as simple as that, and if you can stop the merry-go-round and begin to plan and set goals for yourself, you will make real progress.

THE DOWNSIDE TO FOCUS

Yes, I know that culturally we praise people who are able to focus and persist, but the truth is that it all depends on what they're focusing on and whether, as the old saw has it, they're "missing the forest for the trees." It's one of the few adages that actually incorporates some psychological truth. This information is especially pertinent for those of you who are anxiously attached and tend to be vigilant and focused on details as a way of directing your behaviors.

In addition to wrongly believing that memory is like a photograph, rather than the patched-together quilt of details that it is, we also like to think of ourselves as having panoramic vision: a capacity for seeing the big picture as well as the small detail. Well, that turns out not to be true, as an experiment conducted by Daniel J. Simons and Christopher Chabris showed, published in a paper wittily called "Gorillas in Our Midst." (They later wrote a book as well, titling it *The Invisible Gorilla*.) They had participants watch a video of people playing basketball, and told them to either count the dribbles or the passes, thus forcing them to focus on a single detail. The video lasted two minutes, and about halfway through, a student in a gorilla costume walked into the middle of the game, thumped her chest, and exited. The researchers asked participants to report the number of bounces or passes, and then asked about the gorilla. Only half of them saw it! That is the downside to focus.

More experiments followed, and they all showed that when we're focused on the detail, more than half of us will miss something important. This process is called "inattentional blindness" and it underscores that our brains are not reliable in the way we think. There are just too many details for our eyes to take in so the brain fills in for us and, sometimes, we end up missing the forest for the trees. Inattentional blindness affects all of us, but since you're on a voyage of self-discovery, ask yourself the following questions:

◆ Am I counting "passes" and "dribbles" in my relationship, rather than looking at patterns of connection?

◆ Am I able to see the bigger picture when I think about my relationships, focusing on the abilities of close others to respond to me and meet my needs, or do I tend to get stuck analyzing and reanalyzing specific quarrels or disagreements?

◆ Do I only think about my relationships in times of stress? If so, how does that affect my focus and ability to see clearly?

◆ Am I able to see myself clearly when I think about my role in relationships, or do I get bogged down by focusing on what was said and done to me?

TROUBLESHOOTING YOUR EMOTIONAL INTELLIGENCE

Two important consequences of negative childhood experiences are the lack of support for the development of emotional intelligence and the presence of dynamics that actively impair it. (For a fuller discussion of emotional intelligence and its four branches, please review pages 96–98.) It's not unusual, by the way, to discover that you have deficiencies in all four branches, especially if your childhood experiences required you to actively deny your feelings. Similarly, if you had to squelch your feelings in order to keep the peace or minimize fractiousness, you're not likely to have easy access to them now, nor will you have the appropriate skill set for managing them. Children who were subjected to continuous gaslighting also have specific deficits—not believing or trusting their feelings—which have to be addressed. Self-doubt—which all unloved daughters suffer from in one degree or another—also undercuts the ability to recognize and manage negative feelings. Samantha, 47, shared her childhood experience, which will be familiar to many: "Being emotional was frowned upon by both parents. Being strong was never showing what you were feeling. My mother and father mocked me and my brother for crying, and I was picked on for feeling 'too sad' too often. Yes, they both told me that they'd give me a reason to be sad if I didn't quit it. As an adult, I don't always know what I am feeling. Sad and angry seem to blend, and both make me feel ashamed. Weird, isn't it?"

The good news is that studies show that emotional intelligence is a skill set—and can be built upon and improved. So take a personal inventory and ask yourself these questions:

♦ *How adept am I at recognizing my feelings?*

Some situations in life prompt emotional responses that are relatively straightforward, and in these cases, labeling what we're feeling isn't very challenging. Your beloved pet dies, and waves of sadness wash over you. But more complicated events—a fight with your spouse or close friend, or a massive and very public failure in your work life—may evoke a range of different emotions, either sequentially or in simulcast, or a blend of feelings. In these situations, identifying your feelings requires the kind of dexterity that a game of pick-up sticks does; you need to label and identify your different feelings in the moment.

♦ *Do I oversimplify when I think about emotion?*

A study conducted by Lisa Feldman Barrett and her colleagues found that people who think about their emotions on a simple continuum with good and pleasant on one end and bad and unpleasant on the other —thus differentiating among them in broad strokes without nuance—had much more trouble managing their feelings.

Is this you?

* *Do I back off from thinking about feelings or emotional situations?*

It's been suggested that motivation may also be tied to poor emotional differentiation. People who are made uncomfortable by their emotions and are motivated to avoid emotional situations tend not to be able to differentiate their feelings very well, as a study by Yasemin Erbas and others showed. On the other hand, people who recognize that they're not good at labeling and identifying their emotions may actually want to approach emotional situations in the hope of improving their skills. This result led Erbas and her team to conclude that volition and motivation have a lot to do with your ability to differentiate your feelings.

THE IMPORTANCE OF NAMING YOUR FEELINGS

It turns out that labeling your emotions—putting your feelings into words—actually causes physiological changes to a part of the brain, the amygdala, literally tamping down reactivity, as an MRI study by Matthew D. Lieberman showed.

So, ask yourself these key questions:

* Do I avoid talking about my feelings? Does talking about my feelings make me anxious or uncomfortable?

* How good am I at making fine distinctions such as realizing that I'm more ashamed than embarrassed, or frustrated instead of angry?

* What's my response to emotionally complex situations? Am I able to untangle all of my various feelings and recognize their source? Or do I just shut my brain off?

* Do I see the big picture?

* When someone asks what I'm feeling, am I able to answer?

* Do I avoid being specific about what I'm feeling on purpose, or is it a question of not knowing what I'm feeling?

* How hard is it for me to say "I'm angry" or "I love you"? Is one easier than the other?

THE QUESTION OF EMOTIONAL CLARITY

It's not just how skilled you are at differentiating your emotions; what matters, too, is how much emotional clarity you possess. What is emotional clarity? It's an enhanced or greater ability to "identify, discriminate between, and understand the type of affect (e.g., anger vs. frustration) and source of affect one typically experiences." While this sounds like emotional differentiation, it's actually a bit different since this is a skill associated with reflection, as opposed to labeling and identifying in the moment. One research study by Matthew Tyler Boden and others found that the two skills were not just different but unrelated. While being able to distinguish your feelings with accuracy will guide your behavior (realizing you were frustrated and not angry will lead you to apologize to the unwitting target of your hissy fit), understanding what kinds of events yield different emotions and outcomes —seeing the big picture—will give you more control over your choices and actions.

For the unloved daughter, the "big picture" is the emerging portrait of your childhood, and how your behaviors were formed in response to the way you were treated. As you become clearer about what happened, you will also be able to see triggers and echoes in your responses. Becoming conscious of outsized reactions that are reflections of the past—words that remind you of things your mother says or said, being put down in a familiar way, being told that the problem lies with you—is key to honing your ability to disarm the old patterns and begin to live differently.

Questions to ask yourself:

+ *Am I a skilled emotional manager?*

If you're pretty sure that you're not, start practicing STOP, LOOK, LISTEN. You need to focus on whether negative emotions insinuate themselves into your life, throw you into a ruminative loop, and end up internalized. If so, the likelihood is that you're "state-oriented" and not as good at managing your emotions as you need to be. On the other hand, if negative emotions are something you can cope with—not by brushing them off but by dealing with them in the day-to-day—the likelihood is that you're "action-oriented." Coping skills are key to both achievement and satisfaction, and understanding how well you cope is critical.

If you're prone to emotional flooding, use self-calming techniques, such as visualizing a supportive person, to stop the cascade. If you tend to wall yourself off, visualize a calming environment to stay emotionally open and permit yourself to feel your emotions.

♦ *Do I have a bead on my moods?*

Moods affect each and every one of us; they impact how well we manage our emotions, as anyone can attest: Get to the office in a bad mood and just see how a minor irritant can escalate into major drama. Unlike emotions, which have an identifiable source or cause —I'm happy because I got a raise, or I'm sad because I messed up my presentation—moods are much more diffuse, harder to think about, and to pinpoint. Becoming conscious of your moods and their effect on your actions and reactions is another way of honing your emotional intelligence skills. Engage in quiet self-reflection and focus on what is causing you to feel the way you do.

Understanding moods is also key to affective forecasting.

RECOGNIZING YOUR (CLOUDY) CRYSTAL BALL

One specific area of reactivity is your anticipation of future events and how you prepare for them emotionally and psychologically. This could be a discussion you're going to have, a party or meet-up you plan on attending, or even a move you're preparing for such as a new job or a new place to live. Not surprisingly, unconscious processes play a role in shaping these responses, too. It turns out that all humans—whether our needs were met in childhood or not—aren't very good at predicting how we'll act and feel in the future. Yes, once again, the securely attached have an edge over the insecurely attached, but understanding this human shortcoming will be helpful as you work on disarming triggers and move toward reclaiming your life.

How good are you at anticipating your future reactions? How skilled are you at predicting how happy something will make you or, for that matter, how unhappy you'll be? This skill is what the experts call "affective forecasting." Psychologists Timothy Wilson and Daniel Gilbert determined that affective forecasting has four distinct parts:

1. Our ability to predict whether our feelings will be positive or negative

2. Our ability to predict the specific emotions we'll experience

3. Our ability to predict how intense those feelings will be

4. Our ability to predict how long those feelings will last

Not surprisingly, most of us are pretty good at the first—figuring out whether we'll feel great or dreadful when a future event takes place. But that's where most people's success rate starts and stops. Again, your emotional intelligence is going to factor in for the second part—some people are better at identifying emotions with precision than others—but generally, people oversimplify when they think about what they'll feel in the future.

Why is that? Few things in this life ever deliver emotions that are pure with no shade of gray; even apparently joyous events such as a wedding, a graduation, or a birth may also evoke unanticipated feelings such as loss or anxiety. Some examples: You're thrilled for your friend who's getting married, but you worry about how your relationship with her will change. You've graduated and are happy, but you're also feeling angsty about what's next. The new baby is delicious and you're delirious with happiness, but you're also worried about how well you'll parent. Our thinking about the future is both more simplified and more black-and-white than what life actually presents.

Humans also fall prey to what experts call "the impact bias." Basically, we overestimate how future events, both good and bad, will affect us emotionally. We honestly believe that something good—getting the dream job, finishing school, moving to a new house—will lock in happiness forever. Thanks to what's called either the "hedonic treadmill" or the "happiness set point," the new thing that seemed to promise eternal happiness becomes, rather quickly, something we're used to and thus stops making us happy. The dream job becomes the job you go to five days a week; graduating gives way to what to do next; and the house is where you live. Predictably, as we get used to positive changes, the intensity of feeling diminishes and our happiness fades. That's the bad news, but there's good news as well.

The impact bias operates when bad things happen, too, and as a result, we recover from setbacks that we were once sure we could never come back from. We misjudge not just the depths of the misery we're going to experience but also how long the misery will last. That's largely a function of what Wilson and Gilbert call our "psychological immune system," which permits us to make sense of (or rationalize) bad things when they happen unexpectedly. This, too, happens unconsciously.

There's not much you can do about the impact bias except to know that it's there and factor it in because the chances are good that whatever you're looking forward to or dreading isn't going to be either as good or as bad as you think. But if you want to get better at predicting your emotional state, some troubleshooting is called for. Wilson and Gilbert have pinpointed the most common sources of forecasting errors, a list from which we can all benefit:

◆ *Your imagined anticipation of what will happen is an epic fail.*

Technically this is called "misconstrual," and the bottom line is that we're not likely to be anywhere close to predicting how we feel if the reality of what happens is completely different from what we imagined. You're sure that the vacation to Corfu will make you 1,000 percent happier, but you didn't factor in the 15-hour delay at the airport, the lousy weather, or your stolen wallet.

◆ *Your focus is wrong.*

This is called "framing," and it happens when we focus on a detail that we believe will influence our feelings but doesn't. You move and you're sure you'll feel happier not dealing with your oh-so-nosy and invasive neighbor. But then you find your neighbors at your condo unwelcoming. You hadn't planned on that.

◆ *Your expectations are either too high or too low.*

The easiest example is the movie or novel everyone is touting and you're really looking forward to loving it. *Not.* Obviously, this can equally apply to anything you're anticipating.

◆ *You're misled by your current mood.*

This is pretty obvious once you know about it: Our mindset at the time affects our thinking about the future. The best antidote to this forecasting error is being aware of the mood you're in and making sure that your ability to perceive your emotions—yes, that's emotional intelligence again—is working optimally.

LOSS AVERSION, SUNK COSTS, AND GETTING STUCK

Culturally, we put a high premium on staying the course, persistence, and grit, and we tend to be dismissive of those who quit or give up; that's why you're more likely to be surrounded by people who believe that "winners never quit and quitters never win" even though you're actually struggling with letting go. The truth? The deck—yes, the unconscious processes that drive the car that is you and everyone else—is totally stacked in favor of hanging in, even when it makes us feel lousy. We can all thank evolution for that (and, yes, I am being ironic.)

Humans are famously conservative, preferring to avert possible loss even when considering potential gain, as the work of psychologists Amos Tversky and Daniel Kahneman showed, earning a Nobel Prize in Economics for the latter. Moreover, when we contemplate change, we're likely to frame the discussion in terms of what we already have invested instead of the possible gains we might reap from moving on. Focusing solely on our investment—which could be time, money, energy—gets in the way whether we're thinking about leaving a marriage, another relationship, a job, or even selling a clunker car we've repaired again and again. The fancy name for this habit of mind is the "sunk-cost fallacy," and we all do it. It's called a fallacy because the investment made is long gone and can't be recouped by either staying or leaving, but that doesn't stop us from thinking this way. It prevents us from looking forward.

The only answer, again, is conscious awareness of your automatic thought processes.

Ask yourself the following questions:

◆ Do I worry a lot about time wasted or spent?
◆ Is what's keeping me in place my investment or my real desire?
◆ Am I able to see beyond where I find myself and into the future?
◆ How afraid of loss am I? Which possible losses worry me most?

CUEING INTO YOUR REJECTION SENSITIVITY

Being overly sensitive to rejection, as reviewed in detail on pages 132-134, can also become a destructive self-fulfilling prophesy, especially if you are very reactive or combative when you perceive either a slight or the hint of possible rejection. It's hard to disarm that hypervigilance—especially if it's what protected you in your family of origin—but it can be done.

Again, the path to disarming is built on conscious awareness. Use the STOP, LOOK, LISTEN technique if you find yourself suddenly tense with anticipation that someone is actively pushing you away or about to exclude you. Use self-calming techniques such as visualization to get yourself on more emotionally stable ground as quickly as you can. Once you've begun to relax a bit, ask yourself the following questions:

- Am I reading into what he or she said?
- Am I taking the words out of context?
- Am I mistaking banter for seriousness or otherwise misunderstanding the speaker's tone?
- What exactly was the speaker's intention? Can I tell?
- Can I stop myself from reacting and simply ask what he or she meant?

More advanced strategies will be detailed in the next chapter.

TACKLING SELF-CRITICISM

Becoming aware of your habit of self-criticism—ascribing the things that go wrong in life to your innate character flaws or characteristics, rather than errors in judgment, simple mistakes, or complicated and hard-to-read circumstances—is central to the process of disarming. Most of the time this internalized voice echoes that of your mother or the other family members who derided or mocked you and made you feel inadequate and never good enough, no matter what you did. If constant criticism or derision was part of the daily fare, the reality is that you may employ this kind of thinking without even being conscious that you are. Yes, it's part of how children normalize their experiences so as to be able to get through them.

Self-criticism sounds like this: "I didn't get the promotion because I'm just not smart enough." "The relationship failed because there's nothing lovable about me." "I will never make anything out of my life because I'm nothing but a failure as a human being." "No wonder everything went wrong because I'm not capable of doing anything right." Is this you?

Ask whether your own impulse is to blame yourself or to attribute failure to your flaws when things go south because this, too, is learned behavior and may be an extension of self-criticism. Alternatively, you may also duck personal responsibility and be unwittingly quick to pin blame on others. Attribution involves finding a cause or reason for the untoward and, sometimes, being content that there's no reason at all and accepting that stuff just happens. Blaming is about finding someone to pin the bad stuff on. If you were raised in an environment where the blame game was always played, your reaction may be unconscious and automatic.

Let's say the family car was vandalized one night while it was parked in the driveway and the windshield smashed. Parent #1 is angry about the windshield but writes the incident off as an unlucky encounter with random neighborhood thugs. Incident over. In another household, Parent #2 has to blame someone. It turns out that Nancy was the last kid to come home and she didn't leave the porch light on so the vandals had the cover of darkness. In the telling, it now becomes Nancy's fault that the car was vandalized. Does this sound familiar?

Ask yourself the following questions:

◆ When things go wrong, how important is it that someone be blamed or punished?

◆ How sensitive to criticism am I? How often do I overreact?

◆ Am I able to tell the difference between criticism that is meant to be constructive and criticism that is meant to diminish me?

DISARMING THE SELF-CRITICAL VOICE

Recognizing the voice is the very first step, and you move on and out from there. Next, you need to begin to talk back to the voice—and yes, some people actually do this literally, speaking aloud with other explanations for why something has gone awry or failed. (You may not want to do this in a public place. Generally, talking to yourself in this way draws a fair amount of unwelcome attention!) Using your journal to analyze a situation or event—discovering why things went wrong or ended badly if they did, or why your expectations weren't met—is another way of establishing a different pattern of response.

We'll examine specific strategies in the next chapter, especially on pages 173 and following.

YOUR PERSONAL DEFAULT SETTINGS

While it's possible to draw generalizations—valuable ones, as it happens—about our experiences and the effects of an unloving mother's behaviors, each of our experiences has elements that are unique and individual. Spend time thinking about which of the unconscious processes reviewed in this chapter constitute your own personal default settings. With that information in hand, you'll be able to develop effective strategies for learning new behaviors. You may well discover that things about yourself that you considered personality traits—the way you hesitate, your fearfulness, even your tendency to procrastinate—are actually responses to your childhood experiences.

In the next chapter, we'll be looking at precisely how you can reclaim the power to live the best life you possibly can.

Chapter Seven
Reclaiming Your Power

For me, the continuing challenges are shutting off the critical voice in my head that stops me from doing anything that seems vaguely challenging because I'm sure I'll fail and the problem of not trusting anyone. I always think people are out to trip me up.

-Ana, 41

While it's true that all of us felt powerless in our childhoods and many continue to into adulthood, we're ready to start reclaiming our authentic selves once we have gone through the processes of discovery, discernment, distinguishing, and disarming. We can thank the magical power of the brain—yes, that very same brain that can sometimes lead us down the garden path—because of its changeability, which is more literal than not.

This chapter focuses on the changes you can make, starting now, to how you manage your emotions, use your emotions to inform your thoughts, set goals for yourself, choose the company you keep, and live your life. Every strategy offered on these pages is founded in science, much of it behavioral. Some of what you'll be reading will run counter to what you've read elsewhere—why you should give up on affirmations, for example, or how positive thinking can set you back—but I'd like you to give me the benefit of the doubt and, more important, have what science knows be part of your arsenal going forward. Let's start with the things you have to stop doing.

THE BIG QUESTION YOU HAVE TO STOP ASKING

If there is a single question that hangs over an unloved daughter's life, it's certainly this one: "Why doesn't my mother love me?" And understandably, for almost all of us, finding the answer becomes a search no different from the knights seeking the Holy Grail. Why is that? Because a definitive answer would help make sense of what happened at your house and to you and, maybe, offer up the magic formula that could allow you to fix everything, as one woman wrote me: "I thought that if I knew why she didn't love me, I could somehow change the unlovable parts of me and then she would love me. Mind you, I was still thinking this way in my forties, long after I became a mother myself."

But the impulse to make sense of what's happened also can easily become another cycle of justification, rationalization, and normalization on the daughter's part, one that keeps the music ever playing for the dance of denial. Yes, there's an aha! moment when you read a self-help book or an article and you decide your mother's a narcissist or has borderline personality disorder, and you breathe a sigh of relief because now you think you know why she shunned or shamed you. Here's the problem: With that supposed answer in hand, you think you're getting closer to resolving and understanding your childhood experiences, but the reality is that the answer doesn't move you forward at all. Why? Because your focus remains on *her* when it should be on *you*.

It's for that reason that I ask that you stop asking the question and stop looking for the answer. You have to stay focused on how you adapted to her treatment and how you can give up the behaviors you unconsciously took on and exchange them for new ones. Why she did what she did isn't your concern; *you* are your main concern. Asking the question reinforces your false belief that there's a definitive answer, which there isn't; mothers don't love for many reasons or none at all. But each possible answer only reflects *her*; it was *never* about you. So please stop asking.

I know it's hard not to ask but it's something you *must* do.

SAY NO TO POSITIVE THINKING

I'm not asking you to throw out those inspirational magnets and mugs—the ones that say things like "Every cloud has a silver lining" or "What doesn't kill you makes you stronger"—but I do want you to put them away for the moment. Yes, I know the cultural wisdom advocates coping with disappointment and pain by looking at the bright side, but the truth is that positive thinking isn't actually always good for you. Let me explain why positive thinking should be off the table *especially* when dealing with the special circumstances an unloved daughter confronts.

◆ Humans are hardwired for over-optimism anyway

It's called the "optimism bias," and it basically means that we are inclined to think that bad things will happen to us (and those close to us) less often than they will happen to other people and that, conversely, good things will be more likely to happen to us than to the average person. (This is true even if you are a glass-is-half-empty person and inclined toward pessimism.) First noted by psychologist Neil Weinstein in 1980, it's been looked at different ways over the years. Needless to say, it feeds right into the dance of denial and other tactics unloved daughters adopt when dealing with the core conflict.

A fascinating experiment, detailed in 2012 by Tali Sharot and others, demonstrated that there is actually a location in the brain for the optimism bias, the left inferior frontal gyrus (IFG). Negative information, they posited, is processed by the right IFG. When they delivered intercranial magnetic stimulation to the left IFG—thus disabling study participants' founts of optimism—they were able to demonstrate that people were more apt both to let in negative information and to pay attention to it.

Unloved daughters, especially those who are still hopeful that somehow the crisis can be resolved, are very vulnerable to using positive thinking to override the realistic appreciation of the circumstances they find themselves in.

The takeaway: Positive thinking can stop you from being realistic about your circumstances and get in the way of the emotional work you have to do.

◆ Optimism feeds the illusion of control

This one is really interesting and unexpected. Humans are loaded with cognitive biases, including the tendency to credit our successes to our own actions and to attribute our failures to outside sources or situations beyond our control. But did you know that being a bit down in the mouth about our prospects may actually stand us in good stead as an antidote to all that optimism? That's what a series of experiments conducted by Lauren B. Alloy and Lyn Y. Abramson found. Depressed subjects had a more accurate view of their own agency than nondepressed participants.

When you curb your enthusiasm, along with your optimism, you can recognize that you're hardwired to connect dots that aren't actually connected. Inculcate some realism into how you view your actions and the progress you're making. It's also important that you become clear about which aspects of your life you can control and which you can't; yes, the Serenity Prayer is right in calling that wisdom.

♦ *Positive thinking can be a distraction from the work at hand*

Thinking positively—reaching for that silver-lining script or putting on those rose-colored glasses—not only skews our ability to assess situations critically but also encourages us to avoid or distract ourselves from dealing with negative fallout. Whether your coping skills are largely anxious or avoidant, the last thing you should be doing is looking away from the difficulties at hand.

GIVE UP ON AFFIRMATIONS AND ASK YOURSELF QUESTIONS INSTEAD

I personally have nothing against affirmations, but research shows that asking yourself "Will I...?" is far more effective and motivates you more than repeating "I will do X or Y" again and again. I know it's contrarian, but please trust me on this. Throughout this chapter, we'll be using this technique and apply it to goal-setting.

STOP COUNTING YOUR BLESSINGS

You're probably yelling at me by now, but hear me out. Research shows that subtracting your blessings, rather than counting them, is far more effective when you're trying to self-regulate and stop yourself from sliding into an ocean of despair, maintain a level of happiness, or feel grateful. Researchers Minkyung Koo, Sara Algoe, Timothy Wilson, and Daniel Gilbert (the latter two are gurus on the subject of happiness) asked a simple question: Was it how people thought about a positive event that affected how happy they were and how happiness could be sustained? They posed a question: What if, instead of counting your blessings, you subtracted them? Guess what? In their fourth study, which examined romantic relationships (all of the participants were in relationships they considered satisfying), the researchers had individuals either write about how they met, how they started dating, and the like or write about how they might not have met or ended up together. It was the second task—the exercise of subtraction—that yielded an increase in positive affect.

The takeaway: If you're using thinking about the good things in your life to self-regulate, you'll feel happier and experience more gratitude by thinking about what your life would be like without those things or those people.

LET GO OF PLEASING AND APPEASING

No one wants more drama in her life, but if your coping mechanisms include appeasing difficult or toxic people or continuing to try to please them, you have to put those behaviors on hiatus immediately. Historically, appeasement doesn't work for countries, and it doesn't work for people either. This is not a call to start a new world war and to engage in open hostilities with all the difficult people in your life, but it's a reminder that you must work on setting boundaries if you're not ready to throw in the towel and simply ban those people from your life.

Boundaries are healthy and shouldn't look like mini versions of the Great Wall of China. Begin by thinking about your goals and then put them down on paper. For example, one of your goals might be to maintain less contact with more civility or to set forth some rules that would govern your interactions with these folks. Setting boundaries doesn't have to include aggression or anger—in fact, it shouldn't—although you should prepare yourself for pushback, especially if you are dealing with people who are used to controlling or manipulating you. (Please note: If you are living with an abusive person who could do you physical harm, please consult a therapist or counselor before attempting to put boundaries in place). You need to stop pleasing and appeasing at this moment because acting in this way disappears you, your needs and wants, your feelings and thoughts. These are unhealthy patterns that can get in the way of your growth and development.

STOP NORMALIZING ABUSIVE OR TOXIC BEHAVIOR

You might not even be aware that you're reacting to abusive behavior in unhealthy ways, especially if you grew up around abusive people.

Take a look at these behaviors that unintentionally fuel the continuation of abuse and see which ones are part of your personal repertoire. The time has come to cull them from your unconscious scripts.

♦ *Accepting that you're "too sensitive"*

You've heard these words all of your life and whenever someone says something hurtful, you end up taking responsibility for being hurt and your pain becomes your problem, not the person's who wounded you. Similarly, an intimate tells you that you're "too serious" or that you "can't take a joke" after he or she has said something that absolutely withers you, and you accept that statement as accurate. Stop right now.

On the other hand, if you tend to be overreactive, practice the STOP, LOOK, LISTEN technique so that you can get a handle on what you're bringing to the party. This doesn't mean that you should believe it's "your fault," but you should work on finding balance. Context matters, and as you become more confident about identifying those moments when you actually are being "too sensitive," it will be much easier to identify the people who are using those words to manipulate and control you.

♦ *You still don't defend yourself when you're falsely blamed or put down*

If you were scapegoated or the daughter of a hypercritical mother, duck and cover may have been your first line of defense during childhood and you may be very sensitive to any kind of criticism at all. But that needs to stop if you're going to move forward because you need to be able to tell the difference between criticism that's used as a weapon and critical commentary that is meant to be helpful. Paying attention to a person's language and tone can help you distinguish one kind of criticism from the other. Criticism that intends to marginalize you is highly personal, often expressed in sentences that begin with "You always" or "You never," which are then followed by a laundry list of your flaws. The criticism is never limited to something specific but spins out into generalized statements about your character such as "You always forget to do what you've been asked to do because you're selfish and unmotivated by nature." Criticism that is meant to be constructive is specific, offered as a suggestion, and is usually part of a dialogue: "I think there were ways you might have handled that blowup with him differently such as explaining why it's so frustrating" or "It would be better if you didn't get defensive because that leads to escalating the tension."

• *You still rationalize when you're stonewalled*

Children who are ignored or made to feel invisible in childhood often have trouble recognizing what psychologists know to be the most toxic pattern in relationships and a sure sign of trouble: demand/withdraw. The unloved daughter tends to tolerate stonewalling precisely because it's so familiar to her and to rationalize her partner's behavior by thinking that he's simply too stressed to talk things through, to blame herself for choosing the wrong time or tone to initiate a discussion, or to castigate herself for making a demand in the first place. This kind of tolerance just adds to an already unhealthy dynamic; stonewalling is never an appropriate response.

• *You still question your perceptions*

Children who are mocked, marginalized, or gaslighted in their families of origin don't just suffer from low self-esteem; they're also quick to retreat when challenged because they're deeply insecure about whether their perceptions are valid and to be trusted. Second-guessing themselves is the default behavior. Gaslighting can make a child deeply fearful, as I was, especially of being "crazy" or damaged in some profound way. This again cedes all power to the narcissist or manipulator who needs to control you.

That ends the list of the behaviors you need to give up. Now we'll shift our attention to the behaviors and skills you'll want to master and acquire.

STRATEGIES FOR SKILLFUL EMOTIONAL MANAGEMENT

Whether you cope with negative feelings by pushing off from them or get utterly swept up in them, it's clear that you will need a new set of skills to finally move out of that childhood bedroom that's been replicated in your head. Becoming emotionally resilient is the goal here so that you can weather the crises life throws at you—whether a minor setback or something major like a job loss, the illness of a loved one, a breakup or divorce, or anything else disruptive—and become adept at setting new goals for yourself and achieving them. It's the antidote to being stuck.

These strategies can be used alone or in combination. You will have to see which ones work best for you.

IN THE THICK OF IT: NAMING YOUR FEELINGS

Putting your feelings into words is the basis of talk therapy, of course, and as we've already explored, being able to label and identify your emotions precisely is a key component of emotional intelligence. A study conducted by Matthew Lieberman and others showed, via MRI imaging, that naming emotions actually decreased activity in the amygdala—the more primitive part of the brain where emotions are stored and where reactivity begins—and increased activity in the prefrontal cortex, the part of the brain where thinking and executive control take place.

This means there's a strategy that permits you to exert control and manage your feelings. Knowing what you're feeling—distinguishing anxiety from fear, shame from anger, etc.—allows you to tamp down the emotionality your amygdala is fueling and have access to the thinking part of your brain instead. That access lets you assess and understand the situation using reasoning: "I am anxious because he's acting out of character." "I am scared because this reminds me of my childhood." "I feel shame because she's right about my overreaction." "I am angry because her tone is nasty and bullying." "I feel threatened by his tone." This type of thinking permits you to exert some initial control over your emotional responses and opens the door to being able to manage your feelings in the moment.

USING COGNITIVE REAPPRAISAL

We've already seen that suppressing negative emotions and thoughts is a flawed strategy that only increases rumination and anxiety because when you try not to think of a white bear, you can think of nothing else. But science suggests that one helpful tactic is what's called "cognitive reappraisal." Let's say you're in a really stressful situation—about to be interviewed for a big job opportunity or in the middle of a fight with someone you really care about—and you are just flooded with emotion. What can you do? You pull back and you mentally reappraise the situation as being less threatening than it appears. You remind yourself that this job isn't a make or break situation (there will be other opportunities after this one, and the world's not going to end if you don't get it) or that the person you're arguing with looks tired and stressed, too, and this can be defused with some effort without your totally losing it.

Cognitive reappraisal allows you to cool down your emotions—think of it as taking a deep breath, but with your mind—and calm down enough to start sorting them out. Getting a handle on why you are feeling what you're feeling requires cognition and applies the brakes to the way your emotions are hijacking your brain. It allows you to get back into the driver's seat.

So is cognitive reappraisal as effective as naming emotions? It turns out it isn't. That was shown by an experiment by Katharina Kircanski, Matthew D. Lieberman, and others that looked at the comparative usefulness of labeling your emotions, cognitive reappraisal, and distraction with a group of participants who suffered from arachnophobia, an acute fear of spiders. They did so by having the participants approach a Chilean rose-haired tarantula, which had a six-inch leg span, in the pretest. (No, the number of inches is not a typo, and you could not have paid me to be a participant!) They began five feet away from the spider at first, were instructed to approach it continuously, and then—as the last step—were instructed to touch the spider with the tip of their index finger. Then, in a subsequent test, they were exposed to a different spider but one just as large and were randomly assigned to use affect labeling ("I feel anxious the disgusting spider will jump on me"), reappraisal ("Looking at the little spider isn't dangerous"), distraction (looking at furniture instead of the spider), or given no verbal instruction at all while they looked at the spider. The strength of their emotions was measured by skin conductance response. (Skin becomes a better conductor of electricity when something happens that is physiologically arousing, and arousal is part of emotional response.) The researchers found that naming and labeling emotions reduced the skin conductance response more than other techniques.

That said, affect labeling did not offer an advantage when it came to self-reported fear, which was described after each test.

So while cognitive reappraisal should be part of your emotional tool kit, naming emotions remains the go-to strategy.

MINDFULNESS

Yes, this has become a buzzword of sorts and is very much in vogue but it has science to back up its usefulness. You may have read magazine articles or books about mindfulness and meditation as an approach to life—a concept drawn from Buddhism—but let's take a look at what it means in terms of emotional regulation. Being mindful means that you are intentionally and exclusively focused on ongoing sensory, cognitive, and emotional experience without judging it or elaborating on it. It's total awareness with acceptance. Studies show that mindfulness reduces stress, stimulates positive emotions (producing joy and tranquility, among other feelings), and increases cognitive flexibility. These are all very good reasons to reach for a yoga mat.

I'm going to offer a demurral here, however. At the end of your journey, mindfulness may be a good technique to manage emotions and maintain emotional equilibrium, but it's not likely to be an effective one if you are still working through identifying your reactions and your basic attachment style. It will surprise no one that, despite the benefits mindfulness bestows on people, it comes relatively easily to the securely attached (they're better equipped to accept and have compassion for themselves) and is problematic for the insecurely attached. Why is that? Because the strategies that the insecurely attached use—pushing off from emotion and suppressing distressing thoughts for the avoidant and desperately trying to maintain connection with a cascade of anxiety for the anxious-preoccupied individual—diminish the capacity for mindfulness. The ways insecurely attached people have of coping make it very hard for them to be open, aware, and nonjudgmental, which lie at the heart of mindfulness.

That was shown in an experiment by Jon G. Caldwell and Phillip R. Shaver, who hypothesized that the deactivating strategy of avoidants and the hyperactivating strategy of the anxiously attached predicted lower levels of mindfulness and found exactly that. *But* having made that discovery, the same researchers set out to examine whether mindfulness could, in fact, improve the regulation of emotion in insecurely attached women. It turned out that the experiments' participants, who were part of a three-day intensive program (eight hours a day, with focus on exercises, understanding of both mindfulness and attachment, guided meditation with images of secure attachment, writing and discussion of unhealthy attachment scripts, and more), showed significant improvements in rumination, emotional clarity, emotion regulation, and mindfulness.

This seems to suggest that initial intensive training is actually necessary for the unloved daughter to make use of mindfulness as a self-help regulatory technique. Keep it in mind as you get further along in the journey; taking classes might be a good idea, too.

SHUTTING DOWN THE CRITICAL TAPE

As studies show, self-criticism is often the result of a child's internalizing the harsh and abusive verbal assessments of a mother, but it might be a father or siblings as well. It also grows from the messages conveyed by both actions and inactions (hostile encounters or withheld comfort or support). Unloved daughters with verbally aggressive mothers often report—and I can attest to this from my own experience—that shutting off the tape loop of self-criticism in your head is surprisingly difficult, even with a therapist's help. Among the legacies unloving mothers bequeath is the unhealthy default setting of self-blame when life goes south, made worse by the fact that insecurely attached daughters have difficulty regulating their emotions.

What to do about uprooting and silencing the critical voice? This is, anecdotally at least, one of the hardest things to learn. Following are some strategies for you to consider.

+ *Recognize the voice*

Bring your thoughts into consciousness and make them explicit, Say them out loud. Write them down. Realize that the voice is that of a person who didn't love you. She is an interloper.

+ *Challenge the voice and the thoughts*

Giving voice to the internalized words and even writing them down so you can see them in black-and-white make it clear that they only have power because you believed them to be true as a child. Argue with what was said, pointing out that you're neither stupid nor lazy, not a burden or a bother or whatever untruths were pounded into your head. Say the words out loud if you are alone.

• *Countermand the voice with facts*

These old habits of self-criticism pop up when you're feeling down and stressed because you've experienced a setback, rejection, or have failed at something. Disarm your reactivity by identifying your emotions or using cognitive reappraisal first. Then sit down and analyze why the stressful event happened. Writing down alternatives to the automatic response of self-criticism may give you more of a handle on silencing it, especially if you're able to take responsibility for your mistakes without devolving into self-criticism. Let's say that someone has broken up with you, ending a friendship or intimate relationship, and the default settings in your head are telling you that you're unlovable, lacking in charm, and unattractive. Take on the voice by seeing what happened as a neutral observer might. For example: "The relationship ended because I chose someone who did not listen and probably didn't want to be in a close relationship with me under any circumstances. It had nothing to do with my failings or my appeal. It had everything to do with the fact that I chose the wrong person."

Learning to accept both your strengths and your weaknesses and seeing setbacks as part of life are essential to your healing.

• *Practice self-talk*

Remind yourself of your own strengths and talents, which your mother and perhaps the rest of your family ignored, scoffed at, or marginalized. (My own mother, who was self-conscious and worried about how smart she was, always denigrated my academic achievements, except when she could brag about them to her social circle.) Write them down and put the list somewhere you see it every day and read it aloud. If you're having trouble coming up with a list, ask a friend or intimate to tell you what she or he admires about you. Remember that what you internalized was meant to make you feel small and lousy about yourself.

EXAMINE YOUR BELIEFS ABOUT THE SELF

Do you believe that personality—yours and anyone else's—is inborn and fixed, or do you believe that people are actually capable of growing and changing in meaningful ways? This sounds like a philosophical question, but it isn't because your beliefs can enhance or diminish your sense of self and influence your behaviors, as the work of Carol Dweck has shown.

Think about your beliefs carefully. If you actually believe that personality is set in stone, silencing that critical voice will be next to impossible because your belief gives what was said to you in childhood a boost of credibility.

According to Dweck, our theories about the self influence not just how we respond to specific situations but also how we process and think about them. So spend some real time asking yourself whether you believe that personality is fixed or is malleable and capable of change before you continue reading. Think about your attitudes toward yourself—your personality and traits—as well as those of others. Dweck notes that people who believe that personality can change confront challenges confidently, stick to difficult tasks, and bounce back from failure more easily.

YOUR BELIEFS AND DEALING WITH REJECTION

In an interesting bit of research, Lauren Howe and Carol Dweck discovered that people who embrace the idea that personality is fixed have more trouble recovering from rejection than those who see personality as fluid and changeable. The reason, as they write, is that these people see rejection as "revealing a core truth about themselves," and that prolongs their suffering.

The people who believe that personality and character are fixed are unlikely to believe that they can grow and learn from rejection, and the researchers found that some people actually still had lingering pain as long as five years after the rejection took place. Many actually want to edit the failed relationships out of their history, believing that anyone who knew the story would somehow be encouraged to reject them, too.

Do you recognize this pattern in yourself? It's an important question to ponder. This is how Carole, 51, answered: "I'd like to believe that I can change, but then I look at all the failed relationships in my life and I wonder. I'm starting to see that I'm actually driving people away with my need for reassurance and always looking over my shoulder in fear. If I can't fix that part, I think real change is going to be impossible."

I answer that by saying that what was learned can be unlearned, and despairing of change is not just unproductive, but incorrect. Unlearning is hard, to be sure, but definitely possible.

TURN DOWN THE HEAT: DEALING WITH REJECTION SENSITIVITY

One of the best discussions of rejection sensitivity I've read describes it as "hot" reactivity, which is completely emotionally fueled. (Yes, this is the same terminology used in the discussion on how to reframe memories using cool processing.) Ozlem Ayduk and a team that included Walter Mischel (who ran the famous delayed gratification "Marshmallow Test" described on page 103) wanted to know if children who had successfully been able to delay gratification would actually be more skilled at managing rejection sensitivity.

You may remember that the children who managed to resist the marshmallow did so by distracting themselves—looking away, singing, staring into the distance, whatever worked. The researchers suggest that people high in rejection sensitivity can also use strategic rerouting of attention, away from those cues that are clanging, "Rejection imminent! Arm yourself!" and instead pay attention to situational cues that contradict the rejection sensitivity (such as appreciating body language—"He's smiling at me so why I am panicking?"—and tone of voice) and be able to take cognitive control.

Note that this is a deliberate cooling strategy, which is different from thought suppression. As we know, thought suppression only serves to jump-start the brain to search for the thoughts you're trying to tamp down and ends in a ruminative loop, as Daniel Wegner's "White Bear" experiments showed. Learning to cool down consciously and with effort works.

BECOME FLUENT IN THE LANGUAGE OF SELF-COMPASSION

It's been suggested by many that self-compassion is a successful strategy for those trying to recover from childhood and who need help stilling that critical voice. Additionally, self-compassion has been shown in studies to bolster resilience from failure and to support self-improvement. What is self-compassion exactly? Just as compassion involves feeling for the plight of others, and extending caring and understanding to them, self-compassion directs caring toward the self in the same way. According to researcher Kristin Neff, self-compassion requires that you see your pain in the larger context of humanity's experiences—and as a part of them. It necessitates that you treat yourself with the same loving-kindness your compassionate self would offer to others. (This understanding is drawn from Buddhism, as you probably know.)

What's important is that self-compassion isn't anything like self-pity because self-pity focuses on the self as separate from others, and promotes a "poor me" point of view that paints the self as worse off than anyone else. Self-pity is more self-involved and selfish than not.

Self-compassion also doesn't involve self-aggrandizement or puffing yourself up to make yourself feel more important because that stance, too, sees the self as separate. Self-compassion is displaying empathy toward yourself and your experiences.

Neff describes self-compassion as having three parts, which I'll paraphrase:

• Extending kindness and understanding to yourself, rather than judgmental criticism

• Seeing your experience as part of the larger human experience

• Keeping yourself aware of your painful feelings without over-identifying with them

The problem, though, is that all three of these steps are hard for most of you. (If they're not, skip this part. I'm troubleshooting for those who struggle with self-compassion.) The reasons why self-compassion is difficult aren't hard to see. The first step relies on self-love and self-esteem, which are usually in short supply, and if you're used to being self-critical, it's not likely that you'll be nonjudgmental when it comes to assessing yourself. The second is complicated, too, because most unloved daughters feel isolated and singular and aren't likely to believe that their problems are like those of most other people. The third step, as we've already acknowledged, also presents a hurdle since you have to be able to manage negative emotions first in order to achieve that equanimity and balance. That said, self-compassion can be learned and accomplished.

Since research shows that self-compassion really does help people deal with challenging times and stops rumination—another thing most unloved daughters suffer from—how do we build our capacity so we can use it to still the critical voice? Here are a few anecdotal layperson tips, slightly aided by science but informed by experience, which may be of help on the road to self-compassion. As you do these, be sure to use cool processing, which has you recalling why you felt as you did, not what you felt.

• *Get a photograph of yourself when you were little and spend time with it.*

Look at that child (you) and see her as a stranger might. What's cute and appealing about her? Talk to that little girl and give her some comfort and recognize how lonely and sad she was. And while you're there, ask yourself why anyone would ever think that child was anything less than adorable. I've had hundreds of people on my Facebook page do this exercise and not one has found her childhood self less than utterly endearing.

It's fruitful, too, to look at photographs of yourself in late childhood or adolescence. Try as I might, when I looked through photographs, I was unable to see the "fat" girl my mother saw or the supremely diffi-cult one she described 24/7. Again, look at you as a stranger might and remember what she was really like back then—what she liked doing, the books she read, what made her laugh, what she dreamed of, what she yearned for. Getting to know our younger selves in this way supports feeling compassion for ourselves.

• *Focus on at least three things you love about you.*

They can be characteristics or talents or abilities, but they need to be things that make you happy that you are you. Cast a wide net as you think about yourself in this way because you may discover that some of the best things about you aren't big things but small details. For example, it might be the way you can put people at ease or your ability to raid the fridge and create a meal; it doesn't have to be something grandiose like playing Wimbledon, writing a bestseller, or running a major corporation. You can love your hair, the way you transplant seedlings, how you make your child laugh, or the fact that you're kick-ass at your job. If you're stumped, ask a friend or another intimate to help you.

The critical voice reduces you to a series of negatives that helped your parent marginalize or control you; having self-compassion permits you to add in all the other things her characterizations missed.

♦ *Make a drawing, create a collage, or build an altar symbolizing your strengths.*

This may sound very New Age-y to some of you, but expressing yourself in another medium can clarify and strengthen your intentions and requires a different kind of thinking and permits you to see yourself in a different way. If you can't draw, write down words that describe your best you (steadfast, capable, loyal, good cook, expert knitter) and download images or cut out photographs from magazines to create a positive "portrait" of yourself.

Alternatively, you can create an altar—yes, this is very New Age, but I once wrote a book about it—by assembling objects and images that summon up your gifts or what you love or your favorite pursuits. Gather them on a shelf, table, or windowsill, and use the grouping as a visual reminder of what's good about you. You can also build an altar to signify your intention by using symbols of growth and possibility (anything green, a butterfly because of its metamorphosis, seeds or pinecones, a photo of a lotus, for example) along with words that inspire you to action.

♦ *Make self-compassion a goal.*

We will be talking more about goal-setting, but you can work up to being self-compassionate as you would any other goal, such as saving money, cleaning out your closets, or finding a new job. Write your goal down, and come up with steps to accomplish it. Here are some possible statements you could make: "I won't be as hard on myself when things go wrong. Everyone screws up some of the time." "I have to put my mistakes in context and have a better perspective on them. They're not proof I'm worthless." "When someone criticizes me, I have to ground myself and listen and then ground myself again. Is there something to be learned from what he or she is saying, or should I just discard it?"

When you find yourself falling into the old default position of self-criticism, call it out and argue with it and then move your mind into a self-compassionate place. Keep notes on the progress you're making by not reverting to that self-critical point of view, and treat yourself to something you like when you succeed. Yes, it's called positive reinforcement.

 • *Ask yourself: Will I show myself compassion?*

Write the question down and pin it up where you can see it. Remind yourself that this is a step-by-step process and that baby steps are fine but that next time you experience a setback or are down in the dumps about all that you're not, you will show yourself some compassion instead of joining the old critical chorus.

GOAL-SETTING AND SELF-INVENTORY

Rather than simply being hopeful about changing your life, how you connect to others, and how you feel about yourself, you need to stop being vague and set some concrete goals. Science actually knows a lot about goal-setting—there's been lots of research—and which factors play a role in whether a goal can be met. You can set goals in any area of your life: personal strivings, relationship, or work and career. Here are some useful strategies, many of them adapted from my book *Quitting—Why We Fear It and Why We Shouldn't—in Life, Love, and Work*:

 • *Write your goals down.*

Studies show that writing them down makes your thinking more concrete and helps motivation, too. (And while you can type your goals, you engage different parts of your brain when you handwrite so grab a pen.) It's also very helpful to think about your goals in both the short term and the long term because it helps you stay balanced in terms of your realism and your optimism about your progress. For example, your short-term goal might be to reduce your anxiety by exercising, using visualization, and working on managing your emotions more proficiently by paying attention to triggers. Your long-term goal might be to increase the level of intimacy in your relationships by being less anxious about trusting others.

   ◆ *Make sure your goals and abilities are in sync.*

Common wisdom has it that "the higher the bar, the better the jump," but that happens not to be true for everyone. First, make sure the goal you're setting is feasible. Ask yourself whether it's something you can actually accomplish in the time frame you're considering. Do you need to set an interim goal? Or should you lower your expectations, at least to begin with?

Use writing to clarify both your intentions and your plans. This is very important if you've avoided making mistakes or the possibility of failure most of your life; secure people expect glitches to happen and plan for them, which makes them more resilient and able to recover from setbacks faster. So examine your goals carefully.

The work of Gabriele Oettingen and her colleagues underscored that how you think about achieving goals directly affects your motivation. At one end of the spectrum is what they called "indulging": painting a totally rosy picture of what your future will be like when you've achieved the goal, and returning to it again and again in your imagination, embroidering it with details. An indulging train of thought would sound like this: "I will change myself so much that I'll be able to find a partner and live happily ever after" or "I will so wow my bosses that they'll give me a promotion and double my salary" or "I'll just write a novel and it will become a huge bestseller and I'll be rich." At its worst, indulging is no different from pipe-dreaming. At the other end is what they call "dwelling": being so fixed on your current negative circumstances that you can only come up with visions of defeat if you try to change. Neither of these thought processes motivates you to actually achieve the goal. The solution to effective goal-setting is what Oettingen calls "mental contrasting."

USING MENTAL CONTRASTING

Mental contrasting requires you to keep in mind, at the same time, *both* your goal and the future you will enjoy if you attain it *and* the real-life issues that could get in the way of your achieving it. Having both the positive vision and the proactive problem-solving stance in your head simultaneously gets you to a Goldilocks place of "just right"—the correct mix of optimism with healthy realism. Let's say that your goal is to get closer to someone you like but someone you're always locking horns with. You realize you've been overly reactive so you're going to focus on modulating your responses, and you can envision how much better the relationship will be. But you balance that positive vision with the recognition that she is pretty reactive herself so you're going to come up with strategies to keep the conversation going if things go off track. That's where if/then thinking comes in.

One caveat about mental contrasting: Researchers using brain imaging have located the parts of the brain in which mental contrasting takes place, specifically those associated with working memory and intention; they are different from those activated by indulging. This led them to surmise that mental contrasting taxes working memory, which is a limited resource, so they suggest you try not to use mental contrasting when you're thinking about other things or are stressed or tired. Keep that in mind.

BEING PREPARED: THE POWER OF IF/THEN THINKING

The Boy Scout motto, "Be Prepared," is a good one, and while if/then thinking won't help you determine which way is north and won't start a camp fire, it is a game-changer nonetheless and needs to be used to bolster mental contrasting. Preparing for the stumble, the glitch, the setback, or even an unanticipated change in the script is an important and empowering skill. Basically, it's really thinking about Plan B when you're still focused on Plan A: "If X happens, then I will do Y." If/then thinking both permits you to plan and enables emotional and intellectual flexibility.

You can prepare if/then strategies by journaling and planning out on paper if that works better for you than simply thinking about them. Using this approach won't just increase your flexibility but will also decrease worry and anxiety because it gets you past thinking about just a single Plan A but forward to Plans B and C, thus allowing you to roll with the punches if need be. This is especially useful for those women who worry excessively about failing or who still struggle with rejection sensitivity.

SUBSTITUTING APPROACH FOR AVOIDANCE

Once you've recognized that you're motivated by avoidance—you tend to dodge tough conversations, worry too much about failing so stay in place, default to pleasing or appeasing instead of speaking up— you have to become your own best cheerleader. Once again, concentrate on disarming your default positions by reminding yourself of their origins and how they undermine your true strengths and abilities. Studies show that parents transmit a fear of failure to their children, which is hardly surprising if you think about it. If your parent defines and loves you for what you do and not for who you are, you are going to be filled with terror at letting her or him down and being shut out.

Remind yourself that while avoidance is safe, it also keeps you stuck in place. Take a leaf out of the securely attached person's book and remind yourself that a setback or even a failure isn't proof of your worthlessness; it's a call to regroup. Use all the tools at your disposal—reappraisal, self-talk, self-compassion, and mental contrasting—if there's a bump in the road.

LEARNING TO LET GO

You've heard the saying "Quitters never win and winners never quit," haven't you? Well, guess what? It's not true. It's ironic that the culture focuses solely on the virtues of grit and persistence because the reality is that humans are far more likely to keep trying and stay long past the expiration date in all manner of situations that are unhealthy and unhappy-making than they are to leave the party too early. That's generally true of everyone, but it's especially true for the unloved daughter. Securely attached people acknowledge the possibility of setbacks and even failure when they set goals; because they believe the self is malleable and capable of growth, they don't see failure as proof positive of some core and immutable flaw in themselves. This isn't to say that failing doesn't smart—it does—but they don't go down for the count.

The insecurely attached daughter has to work at letting go because until she reclaims her authentic self completely and adopts new goals and ways of managing feelings, she's likely to revert to the default settings bequeathed by childhood, willing to do anything to avoid looking as though she's failed in a public way. Even when she's decided that bailing out is what she needs to do, she may hesitate because she's plagued by self-doubt and ends up staying the course once again.

Bring your beliefs and thoughts about failure and the self into full conscious awareness for clarity. Recognize that letting go of what's not working in your life isn't a sign of inadequacy but an indication of your willingness to head off in a new direction. You're just decluttering for a season of rebirth, which isn't unlike what you do to your closets when the seasons change, only on a larger scale. In this context, the ability to quit without regret and with confidence is a major sign of progress.

REVISITING VISUALIZATION

We've discussed using visualization and other cognitive techniques to help you tear down the walls that keep you in an avoidant lockstep or, alternatively, to help you stop the emotional flooding that keeps you on an ever-turning carousel without balance. Continue to work on developing and strengthening this skill set as you move toward the next stage of redirecting your life. The more you work at calming yourself down in times of stress, the more these strategies will pay out. Keep in mind that securely attached people do this unconsciously—bringing up images of love and support when they're anxious, remembering positive experiences when they're stressed—and over time, this can become a habit for you, too.

Up next are the steps you'll need to take to redirect your life, should you choose to. You may find it useful to return to this chapter and review it if some of these old habits are still getting in your way.

Chapter Eight
Redirecting Your Life: Making Choices

It was only when I realized that I could be free of her influence that I became free and started my life over. Can you imagine? I was 42 and the mother of two boys. I actually considered giving myself a new first name. That's how reborn I felt.

-Christie

With newly recovered personal power and belief in the self comes the hard part: redirecting your intent and energy and deciding what changes you need to make to your life to be happier and more fulfilled. This part of the journey isn't as painful as the stages of discovery and distinguishing, with their truths to be faced, or as emotionally strenuous as disarming and reclaiming, but it does test your newfound trust in yourself. Redirecting your life requires having faith in your own recognitions, trusting your own perceptions, and believing that growth and change are possible. If you're wondering whether you're ready, remind yourself that feeling unsure in the moment is part of the process. Progress remains one baby step at a time and, sometimes, two steps back.

REDIRECTION AND AGENCY

One of the psychological shifts you need to make at this stage, if you haven't before, is seeing yourself as having the agency to effect change and take charge. This will be an important transition for those daughters who have lived their lives listening to others or reacting to situations curated by other people, or who have unwittingly recreated their childhoods in their closest personal relationships and have felt powerless.

One of the key choices—and inevitably tied to other decisions you feel you need to make—is how to manage your relationship to your mother. On the pages following, we'll look at the possibilities open to you without giving advice. While there are commonalities, each daughter's situation is unique and individual to her. Only you can decide what you need to do because only you understand what the situation is from the inside out. You alone will live with the consequences of your decisions, even though their effect will be felt by others.

This isn't the only choice you'll make, of course. But it's the one that needs to be dealt with first, one way or another.

ASKING WHETHER THE MATERNAL RELATIONSHIP CAN BE SALVAGED

As we know, the core conflict isn't resolved by reaching adulthood. It continues to be a war between the hardwired need for maternal love and support, as well as a sense of belonging, on the one hand and the daughter's growing rational understanding of how toxic the connection is and her need for some stress-free normalcy on the other. The battle between those two opposed needs can go on for years. In fact, the conflict can continue even if the daughter chooses to divorce her mother. How counterintuitive is that?

Because the culture sides with the mother—buying into the mythology that all mothers are loving because nurturing the young is instinctual—and puts the daughter on trial, the struggle has a public face in addition to a private one. For the first 18 years of her life, the daughter has no choice but to deal with her mother, no matter what. While getting out of her childhood home is freeing in one sense, it's not a magic bullet. Her wounding isn't salved by independence and her longing for the stability and comfort she needs continues.

In the redirection stage, the daughter has to decide whether to try to save some kind of relationship from the wreckage or to cut bait. Neither choice, by the way, is made in the spur of the moment but is usually preceded by years of thinking about, and going back and forth between, the two alternatives. I call that "going back to the well" because even though the daughter knows intellectually that the well is dry, her impulse is to try just one more time, just in case.

Having waged this particular battle myself for over two decades when I was a young woman—from my twenties through my thirties, to be exact—I understand how much is at stake. On the one hand, there's the tantalizing and ever-hopeful possibility of a reconciliation, accompanied by some long-wished-for recognition by the mother that her daughter really is lovable. Yes, cue the violins for the Hollywood ending. Alas, this is almost always a pipe dream. But many daughters, daunted by the cultural onus of going no-contact and the emotional losses involved, are motivated to try to keep the relationship intact in some way, however imperfect it is. Social pressure is also a factor, as is the daughter's fear of making a mistake and of denying her children an extended family. Keep in mind that the decision to divorce your mother inevitably leads to estrangement with other members of your family as well. We'll look at the fallout separately because it's a huge issue.

Trying to salvage the relationship for most is like navigating an obstacle course. If you try it and fail, do not blame yourself.

UNDERSTANDING THE OBSTACLE COURSE

You have no idea how long I've tried to fix this or how many different ways I've tried. I've tried and tried but I can't. I just can't.

-Melanie, 45

Some daughters choose to keep the relationship going even though it involves maintaining the painful status quo; one daughter explained it by saying, "For me, I chose to salvage my relationship with her because I know beyond the shadow of a doubt that my mother tried the best she knew how but she was crippled by the cycle of violence from her mom and her grandmother. I know some daughters don't have that assurance, though." But when questioned, she admitted that the going wasn't smooth: "It depends on the day. There are still unhealthy boundaries, but what helps is having better coping mechanisms. I developed a support system completely outside of my family." When I asked her whether the exchanges were still hurtful, she replied, "It hurts, but I also worry about regretting not having anything to do with her before she dies. Fear is a terrible motivator. But I choose to keep her at arm's length. I pity her."

But the obstacles, despite a daughter's best efforts, often remain and you need to recognize that your ability to remove or sidestep them is usually very limited. Among the most common roadblocks are:

♦ ***Lack of acknowledgment or plain denial on the mother's part***
Salvaging the relationship has to be a dyadic process, with the full

involvement of both the mother and daughter. Unfortunately, that's not always the case, as one daughter commented: "I'm in awe of people who can continue to have a relationship with their narcissistic mothers. I, for one, couldn't do it. I've been no-contact for almost ten years even though she lives across the street (yes, she followed me here—what kind of madness is that?). But I'm just not strong enough to handle that abuse every day. And my fear is that she'd poison my daughter against me."

Her mother's unwillingness to own her behavior became the linchpin for another daughter in her own middle age: "At the age of 50, I asked myself . . . how long was I going to beg for my mother's love or for an apology or even for an acknowledgment of what went on . . . ? I gave that up and mourned the loss of my childhood and of the mother I never really had. I felt that at 50, it had become pathetic. Pathetic that I allowed myself to chase after that for half of my life."

If your mother is willing to see a therapist with you, it's worth trying. But be prepared for the possibility that she'll take over the session or sessions and try to win the counselor to "her" side. The truth? Your mother has to want reconciliation as much as you do; if she doesn't, the effort will inevitably fail.

◆ *Refusal to respect boundaries*

Maintaining boundaries while trying to save the relationship is often a huge struggle since combative, dismissive, self-involved, controlling, and enmeshed mothers have never observed boundaries and believe that motherhood confers the right to intrude whenever and however. This led one daughter to remark wryly: "All relationships can be salvaged—but at what cost? Some of us aren't willing to pay and pay and pay and pay. . . . "

Setting boundaries inspires some women to go "low"-contact—with few in-person get-togethers and limited communication—but alas, that's often difficult to maintain. One woman wrote, "My mother is as convinced of her right to intrude on my privacy and to meddle in my affairs as she was when I was 12. Never mind that I'm 45 and the mother of three. She just doesn't get it. She orchestrates drama all the time and, frankly, it's intolerable. This isn't working." Mothers who have never respected boundaries are very unlikely to start now.

♦ *Continued verbal aggression, abuse, manipulation, and game-playing*

Alas, without acknowledgment and therapeutic intervention, mothers tend to keep acting as they always have, despite the daughters' efforts to develop new scripts. Ellie reported, with not a little bit of sadness and resignation: "I have tried a 'low-contact' relationship with my mother for over a year. She continued to be manipulative, toxic and would do things to try and drive a wedge between my husband and me. I felt retraumatized every time I had to deal with her either in person or through texting. I made the decision in May to go officially 'no-contact' with her. I immediately felt a weight lifted off of my shoulders. I know without a shadow of a doubt that this is the best decision for my life. I am now working with a wonderful counselor and working on healing myself."

WHEN ALL EFFORTS FAIL AT SALVAGING THE CONNECTION, OR STAYING LOW-CONTACT

Again, this is a highly personal choice: whether to live with the painful status quo or to push forward to break free. It's at this point that many daughters begin to consider divorcing their mothers. It's a moment filled with ambivalence and fear, as well as the hope of living differently.

THINKING ABOUT DIVORCING MOM

It's been five years and I still struggle with feeling ashamed. A part of me still believes that someone better and stronger than me would have found a solution. I feel as though it's my fault somehow at moments. Of course, that's what my mother says.

-Sally, 51

In the court of public opinion, the daughter is always on trial. The societal response to a mother or father who disinherits a child— whether it's someone famous like Joan Crawford, who cut two of her children out of her will, referring only obliquely to "reasons that are well known to them," or your next-door neighbor—is muted and more or less accepting. "Ah, yes," culture murmurs, feeling sorry for the parent, summoning thoughts of an incorrigible or impossible child, a black sheep, the one with whom you tried everything you could think of but nothing worked. There's a collective nod, an acknowledgment that parenting is hard and that children can be difficult to deal with.

In contrast, the adult child who cuts her mother out of her life is judged on the spot, labeled as ungrateful, irrational, immature, impetuous, or acting out. The myths of motherhood are largely responsible for this cultural stance and, combined with the Fifth Commandment, pack a mighty wallop.

As a daughter who wrestled with the question of choosing no contact for two decades of my adult life—cutting off and then going back again and again until I finally bailed at the age of 38—I've seen people change their opinion of me in seconds. It might be a doctor or nurse asking me about my mother's health when she was my age and hearing me answer, "I don't know. She wasn't in my life." Or it could be a new acquaintance hearing that, no, my daughter never met her grandmother, even when she was still alive and living not very far away. Yes, I have a dog in this race and I know the cost. I have been called selfish, narcissistic, and much worse by total strangers. No one likes hearing about unloving mothers. No one.

SOME OBSERVATIONS ABOUT GOING NO-CONTACT

I have spoken to many women over the years, both before writing *Mean Mothers* and since, about maternal divorce. It is, in every sense of the word, a *crucial* decision, and I use the word deliberately because it comes from the Latin *"crux,"* or *"cross."* You are at a crossroads in life by considering this decision. In ancient times, the crossroads was a place of mystery and life-altering, signifying a major decision. This is no different.

Here are three anecdotal observations you need to keep in mind as you think about your choices:

◆ *No one sees the cutoff as a real solution*

While you're unlikely to hear this from most people, the truth is that maternal divorce is a last-ditch effort to establish some normalcy.

It is usually preceded by years of effort on the daughter's part to try to fix things, either on her own or with a therapist's help. Because a daughter never divorces just her mother—she inevitably will lose other family members, including siblings, aunts, uncles, and even her father, as people take sides—it is emotionally highly fraught and very painful. Ironically, maternal divorce is hard and scary precisely because the decision has to draw on self-love and self-esteem, which are usually in short supply. Sometimes, after going no-contact, a daughter will try again. Alas, unless the mother is willing to go into therapy to thrash it out, it rarely works. While going no-contact solves some problems, it inevitably creates new ones.

♦ *The need and longing for a loving mother coexists with the cutoff*

It's not unusual for adult daughters to experience a great sense of loss even though they initiated the break; one daughter described the grief she felt as the final death of her hope that someday her mother would love her. Sometimes, the pain will outweigh the relief the daughter feels and she'll reinitiate contact and get back on the merry-go-round for a time until she finally concludes she must divorce again.

If you have found yourself in this pattern, it's important that you see it as par for the course and not indicative of any failing on your part. Be patient with yourself. The core conflict is resolved by your healing alone. I know it sounds weird but it's true. Going no-contact will not end the core conflict.

♦ *The therapeutic stance toward parental divorce may be insufficient*

Daughters who are in therapy may feel pushed into divorce when they're not ready or, alternatively, feel that their decision to go no-contact isn't being supported or is being actively discouraged by their counselors. My own therapist wasn't in favor of my cutting my mother out of my life, arguing that you can't ever hope to fix a relationship that you're not in. That's both logical and true. In my case, having tried for 20 years to "fix things"—with a mother who categorically denied that anything was wrong except with me—I didn't heed her advice.

There's no one-size-fits-all answer to whether maternal divorce is the right choice for an individual. It's a personal decision.

DECIDING ON DIVORCE OR NO CONTACT

There's terrific anguish in choosing between saving yourself and the losses that accompany divorce. One daughter recounted the terrible turmoil she felt when her therapist suggested she cut her mother out of her life and she realized that, likely as not, she would lose her connection to her father. She talked to her father and he suggested she take a hiatus from her mother, instead of acting definitively, and reassured her that somehow they'd work something out. Nonetheless, she felt shame and conflict: "I also feel like the worst person in the world for even considering cutting my mom out, especially as she is just getting older and may someday really need my help, but I know you have to take care of yourself and sometimes that means letting go of people you wish you didn't have to let go of. . . . So, no, I don't think my relationship with my mom can be salvaged, even though I wish it could be. Since I've never really been able to hear myself speak or even think when around her, and even when not around her because she never really granted me the opportunity to have a voice of my own, I especially don't feel that continuing a relationship with her is a good idea. She just, and I hate to admit it but it's true, has too much power over me as all mothers seem to have over their children. But despite not feeling like I should have a relationship with her anymore, I don't know how to cut ties with her, especially with my dad in the picture."

Other daughters have transitioned from low contact to no contact over time. One woman explained why it was that she thought she was heading toward the final cutoff: "I have chosen recently to go 'low contact' with my mother. This has been very good for my family and continued healing. However, given that I am no longer a source of narcissistic supply for her, my mother has ratcheted up the drama and is constantly testing boundaries. I am actually thinking at this point that it may be best to go 'no contact.' This is a difficult decision, but I have come to the acceptance that she is not going to change and my family and I are better off without her. I think that any relationship can be saved and that anyone who does the difficult work can change, but I think that would be unlikely now, given her age and how entrenched her behaviors are." Again, only you can decide.

Divorcing your mother isn't a solution in the traditional sense because it involves an admission of powerlessness, as Ceci noted: "I can't fix what she's broken. I would like a distant relationship with her, and for my kids, but it's not safe, and our age of connectivity means the distance I'd be okay with isn't possible anyway. And she still smears me to others, and claims our rift is a result of my broken-ness, not her continued abusive behavior. As I said, I can't fix what she's broken." Maternal divorce also doesn't answer the larger problem of being unloved. In truth, going no-contact is the first step in a long process, which, in the best of all possible worlds, includes mourning the mother love you didn't get and so richly deserved, the growth of your own self-compassion, and the stilling of the voice within—inter-nalized from years of criticism and verbal aggression—and replacing it with a tape that says, "You're fine."

At our most optimistic, humans like to believe that all close bonds can somehow be repaired or salvaged so that we're not left with nothing. This is especially true when it comes to a relationship—that of mother and child—that our culture places on a pedestal, separate from all other connections. The pity is that when the damage is severe, it can't be.

SELF-DOUBT AND THE WORRY THAT YOU'RE THE CRAZY ONE

Most of the time, I feel confident that I've made the right choice. But then there are moments when I imagine picking up the phone and calling her and, miracle of miracles, she's so happy I called and everything will be different. Well, I gave into that impulse a few weeks ago after three years of no contact and, after enduring 15 minutes of a blistering attack in which she listed every one of my flaws and explained why I was worthless compared to my sister, who is so wonderful and fabulous, I deleted her number from my phone. I'm going to have to learn to weather those moments, but I'm not leaving anything to chance.

-Diane, 46

If you're wrestling with the decision to go no-contact or you've taken the step and are filled with angst, don't beat yourself up; it's a big decision and, yes, it *should* make you nervous. But there's the good kind of nervous—the kind of self-questioning that goes into a major decision—and the bad kind of nervous that melts you down into a puddle of self-criticism and puts the voice telling you it's all your fault on a loudspeaker. Pay attention to the difference. Keep in mind that unloved daughters—and yes, I'm including myself—really want to be like everyone else. And everyone else, from the daughter's point of view, is comprised of those mother-daughter pairs she sees on the street, laughing and talking, going shopping and having lunch. You know, those people who don't feel depressed on Mother's Day or Christmas and who actually feel loved by their mothers. I bring this up because it's part of the complexity of even considering—much less implementing—a divorce from your mother.

The truth is that the relationships that end in estrangement are not amped-up versions of normal stress or tension in healthy mother-daughter relationships. Stress (and even friction or real fraction) happens in basically loving mother-daughter dyads, particularly in times of transition. There's no question that the mother-daughter connection undergoes a period of transition from late adolescence to adulthood—a body of research substantiates that—as do the relationships between mother and son, father and daughter, father and son.

Mothers used to an authoritarian or controlling style of parenting will certainly feel the friction the most as their daughters begin to make choices that are not necessarily the mothers' own; research shows that mothers may experience lowered subjective wellbeing when daughters outstrip or eclipse their mothers' choices and achievements. In loving and relatively healthy relationships, boundaries are redrawn by both mother and daughter, and acceptance of a child's choices— even grudgingly offered—gets worked out.

These relationships, while not perfect (what connection ever is?), have a pattern of give-and-take, even in times of stress and difference; the unloved daughter is in a very different place.

Unless her mother is willing and ready to take responsibility for her actions and words, past and present, things will stay the same.

WHAT ABOUT GRANDMA? DAUGHTERS AND THEIR CHILDREN

While I actually divorced my mother because I didn't want her to come into contact with my child, many women are ambivalent about going no-contact because they don't want to deprive their child or children of an extended family; not surprisingly, they hold out the hope that, regardless of their mothers' failures at parenting, they will somehow succeed as grandmothers or at least be good enough. That's actually not as crazy as it sounds because the two roles are so different; grandmothers can send grandchildren home at the end of the day, don't have to pay their bills, and can control the degree to which they choose to interact. Sometimes, it works; often, alas, it doesn't. Anecdotally, it seems to work best when there's physical distance, the visits are short, and the daughter stays largely out of the picture.

When a daughter decides to go no-contact with her mother, the problem becomes more complicated. On the one hand, there's the guilt of depriving your child or children of an extended family; on the other, there's the risk that your own offspring can be manipulated to get at you in some way, even getting co-opted to your mother's side. That sounds paranoid as all get out, but it actually does happen, as Darcy's story makes clear: "My husband is an only child with only one surviving parent whom he adores and he really doesn't understand the conflict in my family. There are four children in my family of origin, three sons whom my mother treats well, and me, the scapegoat and disappointment. Make a long story short, I gave in and allowed my kids to see their grandmother, and she filled them with poison about me. But the breaking point came when my husband realized that she was scapegoating my kids in front of my brothers' children. He talked to my mother who called our kids liars and denied it all. My husband's eyes were finally open."

Anna, now 60, lived in the same town as her mother and she felt she couldn't deprive her two daughters of their grandmother. In her case, things were peaceful until her daughters were preteens and they became increasingly uncomfortable with how their grandmother constantly criticized their mother and started telling them that they would have to "take sides." She'd get angry when the girls refused to play along. Ultimately, the girls themselves decided they wanted to see less of their grandparents.

On the other hand, Jane reports that she had success allowing her sons to see her mother and explains why: "I set very distinct rules and boundaries and made it clear to my mother that if she bad-mouthed me or my husband, the boys couldn't visit her anymore. I trusted my father, too, to make sure that happened. My mother treated my brothers well—she considers girls pretty useless and I am a good example—and I figured she would be okay around my sons. It wasn't always easy or a cakewalk, and I can't say that the boys felt close to their grandmother, although they adored their grandfather, but it mainly worked."

Again, each daughter's experience, her relationship to her mother, each family constellation, makes each situation unique. Each of us has to make our own choice.

DEALING WITH FALLOUT (AND NO END IN SIGHT)

I am a pariah in my family—the crazy one, the mean one. My sister and brother have seen an opportunity for themselves when I went low-contact with our mother and worked it to their advantage, painting me as ungrateful, impossible, and yes, a narcissist. Which is pretty ironic, given the givens. Family gatherings became even more impossible, and they waged a campaign for our mother to "fire" me. Ironic, because I had been back and forth in therapy on whether or not to go to the final step. Long story short: She divorced me. It made it harder on me in some ways and easier in others.

～Margaret, 50

For some daughters, divorcing Mom is the very last stop. It was for me; my relationship to my much younger brother, long uneasy, finally succumbed within a few years. With the rest of my extended family an ocean away, I was on my own with my daughter and husband. The core conflict, for me, stopped on a dime because becoming a good mother became my focus.

For many, though, the pain of exclusion continues—hearing about family gatherings but not being invited to them; being gossiped about and then informed of the gossip, especially if they live where they grew up or are still in touch with outsiders who are connected to family members; feeling as though they can never go home again, even back to their old neighborhood. Some still feel real shame about the choices they've made even though they know, deep inside, it was the only choice and they have support in their circle of intimates. But it's over, except for emotional loss and, perhaps, the continuation of the core conflict.

But that may seem like paradise compared to what happens to some whose mothers continue fighting a battle of attrition even when the daughter has opted out. These mothers continue to try to insinuate themselves into their daughters' lives by contacting other family members, their husbands, and anyone who will listen, spreading lies and creating drama. Sometimes, they co-opt friends and neighbors, too. One daughter wrote to say that her mother sent her husband a birthday greeting with a gift card for his favorite restaurants, sends presents on every occasion to her daughter, and calls them both even though the daughter has repeatedly asked her not to. It sounds crazy but it's true. Another daughter recounted how her mother actually tried to convince her husband that she was cheating on him, and offered to help bankroll the divorce! (No, I'm not making this up, but you'd have a hard time getting past an editor's red pencil if you put it in a novel.) Yet another recalled how, when she decided to divorce her husband, her long-estranged mother ended up colluding with him to try to take her children away. (!!! She kept her kids, by the way.) Daughters have even found themselves the victims of smear campaigns at work, which turn out to have been orchestrated by their mothers.

And yes, there are nightmarish incidents when a daughter's children have been co-opted into their grandmother's orbit. When it does happen, it seems to take place at moments of stress in the mother-child relationships—usually the transitional periods of adolescence or young adulthood when there's often tension in even fundamentally close connections—and the grandmother is able to insinuate herself into the mix. That's what happened to Janine: "My mother started to manipulate my daughter when she was 14 by buying her things I couldn't afford, but especially the provocative, sexy clothing I didn't want her wearing. Grandma told her I was too strict, unreasonable, and became her cheerleader, all of which contributed to growing tension between me and my child. She moved out of my house at 18 and into my mother's home. Luckily for me, once my daughter moved in, my mother started treating her as she did me. She was back home in three months and then went off to college. Our relationship is still a work in progress, and she has limited contact with her grandmother. I have none."

There's no data on the mother vendetta, but if it befalls you, please recognize that it's a form of gaslighting and a reflection of your mother's need to continue to control and manipulate you. Even though you've vacated the sandbox, it's no fun for the bully to find herself there alone. Remember that her actions are a reflection of her, not you, and represent more evidence of the toxic environment she needs to create to feel good about herself. Get professional support if you need it, and stay out of the fray as much as you can. Try not to feed into her needs.

EXERCISING SELF-COMPASSION (AGAIN)

Why is it so damn hard not to blame yourself?

~Leslie, 43

Please try to be kind to yourself as you attempt to "resolve"—and the word is in quotation marks for irony because there's really no resolution—your relationship to your mother. Use your goal-setting skills to figure out and make concrete what you want to do. Write it out. Don't be hard on yourself if you second-guess or worry from time to time; important decisions require thinking through. Get help if you need it; therapy is best, but if you can't afford it, a nonjudgmental friend or intimate will do in a pinch. Give yourself time to sort out your emotions and work on labeling them so that your emotions inform your thoughts. If you are anxious about your choices, the best way to quell your anxiety is to remind yourself of the validity of your feelings and why you felt as you did.

Most important, have self-compassion for the hurt little girl inside of you; it's her endless hopefulness that she can somehow make this right that makes this process so agonizing. Here are some ideas for growing your self-compassion at this stage:

♦ *Recognize you're not alone*

Going no-contact can be a lonely place, and if you're still not convinced that your mother's treatment isn't about you, it can be a place of shame as well. I realize it's hard to confide in others, but if there are people in your life you trust, please do. Get professional support if you need it, making sure that your counselor isn't categorically against going no-contact. (Some are.) Remember that your struggles are shared by many others—yes, the percentage of those whose emotional needs weren't met in childhood is somewhere between 40 and 50 percent—so it's likely that someone you know has faced similar challenges even though the taboo nature of the subject keeps everyone mum. Break the silence using newfound discrimination.

♦ *Focus on mothering yourself*

Be good to yourself by being understanding, rather than self-critical. Focus on the progress you've made and use if/then thinking to tackle the moments at which you fall short of your own expectations. Spend time with people you care about and who care about you when you're feeling discouraged. Applaud yourself when you've handled something better than you used to or when you feel you've taken a stride in an important direction. At their best, mothers are their children's life coaches; be your own.

♦ *Begin the process of mourning*

We'll be discussing the need to mourn the mother you deserved in the next chapter in greater detail, but this is the moment to start mourning the mother you deserved. Yes, not your actual mother but the one, absent the lottery of life, you should have had. Mourning in this way can help you gain in self-compassion—it's a way of seeing that your needs were legitimate and that it wasn't because you were too sensitive, needy, or difficult—as well as bolstering your faith in your judgment as you compare the mother you had with the one you needed. Mourning the mother you wanted and deserved can also help you self-mother and provide an image for visualization when you're stressed or nervous.

◆ *Look forward, not back*

Letting go of the past doesn't mean denying that it happened or insisting that it really made you stronger, but it does mean setting it behind you as you move forward. Once you've decided the right way for you to manage your relationship to your mother, recognize that you've reached an important milestone by exercising your agency. If you decided to try to maintain a relationship and it's not working, don't beat yourself up. Keep in mind that the success of your efforts isn't fully in your control; your mother will either cooperate or she won't.

STAYING FIRM AND BALANCED: BOUNDARIES AND TOLERANCE

I'm still struggling with feeling as though people won't like me if I assert myself. I realize that this is self-destructive because I'm the one making myself into a doormat and then get angry at others as if they made me stunt my life. I'm working on it, but it's hard.

~*Celeste, 37*

If you're going to redirect your life in meaningful ways, you will continue to have to pay attention to boundaries—both yours and those of others. Set goals for yourself to manage reactivity if you're still having trouble finding balance in your relationships, and continue to use if/then thinking to prepare yourself for moments that might be stressful or that you know will test your ability to manage your emotions. These could be situations as various as having to address a group at work, going to a gathering where you know very few people, or doing something new and unfamiliar. If you've come to realize that you're still highly sensitive to abandonment, gear up before your partner or spouse goes off on a business trip or if a friend or intimate has decided to take some time off alone to recharge.

Part of setting boundaries entails being very clear about how, in this new stage of your life, you will allow others to treat you and about behaviors you simply will no longer tolerate. Again, work on being consciously aware of your responses to other people's words and actions, checking to see if you're reacting in the present or to triggers in the past. That said, deciding that you won't permit people in your life who try to marginalize or manipulate you or are verbally abusive is a perfectly healthy response and part of redirection.

If you've lived your life armored and wary of others, work hard at becoming more discerning about people's intentions and motives, especially if self-isolating in this way is no longer working for you. If you want and need to have closer connections, you will also have to become more aware of how unconscious processes are driving your choices and substitute conscious awareness in the area of relationship.

PARTNERS, FRIENDS, ACQUAINTANCES: FINDING THE RIGHT ONES

There's no question in my mind that I keep wandering back to where I started. Is it that I'm attracted to people who treat me as my mother did, or do manipulators see me as an easy mark? I've been more discerning of late, getting out of situations that feel familiar the minute I realize that they do. That's progress.

-Miranda, 36

It's at this moment that what you've learned about your own style of attachment needs to be put to work, no longer theoretically, but as information you'll need to draw on as you redirect and reconfigure your relationships to others.

You can set relationship goals for yourself as you would any other goal pertaining to work or life. Begin by assessing your relationships across the board—from the truly intimate ones to those that are much looser or to ties that are shallower—and see whether they are working the way you want and need them to. This isn't a decluttering exercise because the point isn't to get rid of every existing relationship and start over from scratch. (That may be true for some who have managed to recreate their childhood environments, but it's not going to be the norm, although many will find a few relationships aren't salvageable and are impediments to growth.) This also isn't a call to heap all the blame on others; you need to take responsibility for what you bring to the party. This is about taking a realistic inventory.

Following are some strategies, derived from research, that may help you set relationship goals.

◆ *Use abstract thinking, not specifics, when you consider what's missing in your life*

Studies show that people who think abstractly about losses and lacks in their life are more likely to meet their goals than those who think in concrete terms. Let's say, for example, that an important intimate relationship has ended; rather than thinking, "I need a new lover, spouse, boyfriend," think instead about what you miss having in your life. That could be a sense of connection, mutual caring, sharing your life, or anything else, but the point is that if you think about what it is that you want in this way, you'll discover many different avenues for achieving your goal that thinking "I need a new lover" doesn't. For example, a sense of connection can be fostered by group activities, working on a project such as community gardening, mentoring a young person, and many other pursuits. Charles S. Carver and Michael F. Scheier, experts on self-regulation, note that understanding the core desire abstractly makes you far more flexible in terms of achieving your most important goals because it allows you to see different pathways to achieving them.

◆ *Strive for a more complex definition of self*

Studies by Patricia Linville show that people who have defined themselves narrowly—believing that a single role defines them in a primary way—not only have more trouble dealing with the daily stressors in life but are also less resilient and have more difficulty coping with goal-related setbacks. This makes perfect sense. If your marriage has imploded and your primary definition of self has been "wife," there's a good chance you might go down for the count; if, though, your definition of self includes "wife" along with "friend, tennis player, volunteer, singer in the choir, mother, worker, cousin, sister," many of these other definitions of self will help to buffer you from the blow. This strikes me as doubly relevant as you move from defining yourself as an unloved daughter to a more proactive, more engaged self.

Thinking about self-definition in this way will also help you forge new connections, pursue new activities, and—in the process—enrich existing relationships. This is especially true for those women who have kept their troubled relationships to their mothers a closely guarded secret, unwittingly self-isolating themselves in the process, or who have avoided close connections. Remember that attachment styles aren't set in stone.

♦ **Build on the relationships you have**

What you have learned about your own reactivity, triggers, and attachment style can be used to further understanding in your adult relationships as you become more adept at recognizing the attachment styles and behaviors of close others. Part of redirecting your life may include strengthening the relationships you already have and working to make those connections closer and more intimate. If/then thinking is useful if there are relationships that need repairing since you will be forcing yourself to think about the various ways you can reach out and have Plan B and Plan C in mind if your initial response isn't well received.

CHILDREN: FEAR AND JOY (BOTH OR EITHER, TAKE YOUR PICK)

The idea of having a child and becoming my mother and doing what she did to me terrified me. I married someone who didn't want children for that very reason. Now, looking back, I wonder whether I was right about myself. I am kind in ways my mother never was. I am caring. I don't know now what might have happened.

-Linda, 55

In the best of all worlds, the decision to have a child would be a considered one, even though we all know it isn't always. People have children for all manner of reasons, and some are better and more predictive of good parenting than others. Unloved daughters have a different kind of stake in this decision, largely driven by the fear that they will simply repeat their mothers' behavior and continue the cycle for another generation. Is the fear reasonable or unreasonable?

As someone who was afraid and decided not to have a child for almost two decades of adult life and then reversed myself, the answer isn't as clear cut as some would like it to be. Basically, it depends on the daughter herself and the degree to which her behaviors have become conscious and aware. Since parenting is learned behavior, we're more likely to repeat learned patterns if we're *not* emotionally and intellectually present. For starters, it's worth looking at some pretty terrible reasons to have a child. You may recognize some people you know in the description, perhaps even your mother.

- *To have someone who loves you*

I've had a number of women, all of whom had babies very young, make this confession. In most cases they explain that having a baby seemed to offer a respite from the pain of unloving parents or rejecting relationships with lovers or spouses. The real problem, of course, is that the burden of supplying love is shifted onto the child, who is supposed to be emotional first aid for the parent. That is a recipe for disaster.

- *Because someone expects you to*

It doesn't matter who that someone is—a parent, a spouse, or societal pressure. Having a child is a decision you need to own on every level because it is an enormous commitment. The work that good parenting requires is far too intense and demanding to be inspired by anyone's expectations other than your own.

- *To fit in*

Yes, some women actually admit that they were afraid that others would somehow shun or stigmatize them if they decided not to have a child. Perhaps they would seem "less" than women with children. If we are honest with ourselves about so-called cultural "norms," we would recognize that this is actually a legitimate worry for many. Still, it isn't a healthy motivation to commit to parenting.

- *To give your life purpose*

While it's true that raising a child can give your life focus and purpose, it's a lousy reason to have a child. You are the only person who can define what gives your life meaning. It's not an obligation that can be fulfilled by another human being, not even one you give birth to. This reason (and the next) can easily become enmeshment—which involves denying the child the room she needs to become herself and totally ignoring her emotional boundaries—or micromanagement. A child's job isn't to make *your* life look better or richer than it actually is.

• *To establish your legacy*

Historically, dynasty, the protection of material goods and assets, and a need to leave something behind in the wake of mortality have all been reasons to have a child. But that doesn't give them any more emotional or psychological validity. Like those who have children to give their lives purpose, mothers concerned with legacy see children as extensions of themselves and, as reported by many daughters, put enormous pressure on their children to reflect well on them. In this scenario, what the children want—and for that matter, what they feel and think—are largely ignored. As one daughter told me, "It was hugely important to my mother that I be admired so that she could be admired by others for having raised me. She picked my clothes, my friends, even the college I went to, based on how 'enviable' it would seem to her social circle. I became a lawyer because she wanted me to. When I finally realized I hated practicing law, my mother freaked out, especially when I went from this high-paying, prestigious profession to, in her opinion, the lowly work of teaching in public school. She mentions it constantly and belittles me for my choices."

• *To keep your marriage together (or to get someone to marry you in the first place)*

Despite all the articles in the popular press, all the studies, and all the cautionary tales presented in novels and movies, people still appear to believe that a baby can heal a relationship already under stress. Of course, nothing could be farther from the truth. And while disagreements over childrearing aren't among the top three reasons people divorce—those remain infidelity, drug or alcohol abuse, and money—they are extremely common. Here's the thing: Just as lovers wrongly believe they'll simply smooth over disagreements about money, couples tend not to discuss their views about raising children ahead of time.

The good news, of course, is that your original motivation for having a child need not dictate how you parent if you are willing to be honest with yourself and work hard at seeing how your unconscious, unarticulated, and unacknowledged needs—not your child's—are influencing your behavior. With awareness, we become better mothers.

MAKING THE DECISION: YES OR NO?

Having a child was very important to me, and I went on to have three. Yes, I was nervous, but I was also determined to have my kids be loved in all the ways I wasn't. Was I a perfect mother? No, far from it. But my children thrived and I showered them with love, affection, understanding, and support—everything I was denied myself.

~Lorraine, 48

I didn't trust myself enough to bring a child into the world. I was panicked about visiting the same misery my mother had rained on me. I was particularly scared of having a girl and, maybe, if there'd been a way of guaranteeing I would only have a son, I might have gotten up the courage. My mother was fine with my brothers, her sons. Do I have regrets now? Yes, because I am different than I was 20 years ago. And now it's too late.

~Deidre, 46

While the question of whether they'll mother well is what haunts many daughters, if they're aware of how they were wounded, they already have the requisite consciousness not to repeat their mothers' behaviors. If they decide to become parents, these women actually become good ones with practice and effort; alas, the daughters who still normalize their childhood experiences and really don't see the connection between childhood and their own deep-rooted unhappiness are most at risk for repeating their mothers' behaviors at least until they grow more aware. Eleanor, now 59, recounts how she thought "a baby would fix everything" and how she really didn't think about the decision much at all; she was 19 when she had her first child. Her children are now 38 and 36, both have failed to thrive in various ways, and she is loaded with regrets: "Now that I understand how emotionally neglected I was, I understand that I didn't have the tools to be a good mother. I've talked to my children about it, but my the party. This is about taking a realistic inventory.

Following are some strategies, derived from research, that may help you set relationship goals.

♦ *Use abstract thinking, not specifics, when you consider what's missing in your life*

Studies show that people who think abstractly about losses and lacks in their life are more likely to meet their goals than those who think in concrete terms. Let's say, for example, that an important intimate relationship has ended; rather than thinking, "I need a new lover, spouse, boyfriend," think instead about what you miss having in your life. That could be a sense of connection, mutual caring, sharing your life, or anything else, but the point is that if you think about what it is that you want in this way, you'll discover many different avenues for achieving your goal that thinking "I need a new lover" doesn't. For example, a sense of connection can be fostered by group activities, working on a project such as community gardening, mentoring a young person, and many other pursuits. Charles S. Carver and Michael F. Scheier, experts on self-regulation, note that understanding the core desire abstractly makes you far more flexible in terms of achieving your most important goals because it allows you to see different pathways to achieving them.

♦ *Strive for a more complex definition of self*

Studies by Patricia Linville show that people who have defined themselves narrowly—believing that a single role defines them in a primary way—not only have more trouble dealing with the daily stressors in life but are also less resilient and have more difficulty coping with goal-related setbacks. This makes perfect sense. If your marriage has imploded and your primary definition of self has been "wife," there's a good chance you might go down for the count; if, though, your definition of self includes "wife" along with "friend, tennis player, volunteer, singer in the choir, mother, worker, cousin, sister," many of these other definitions of self will help to buffer you from the blow. This strikes me as doubly relevant as you move from defining yourself as an unloved daughter to a more proactive, more engaged self.

Thinking about self-definition in this way will also help you forge new connections, pursue new activities, and—in the process—enrich actions, checking to see if you're reacting in the present or to triggers in the past. That said, deciding that you won't permit people in your life who try to marginalize or manipulate you or are verbally abusive is a perfectly healthy response and part of redirection.

If you've lived your life armored and wary of others, work hard at becoming more discerning about people's intentions and motives, especially if self-isolating in this way is no longer working for you. If you want and need to have closer connections, you will also have to become more aware of how unconscious processes are driving your choices and substitute conscious awareness in the area of relationship.

PARTNERS, FRIENDS, ACQUAINTANCES: FINDING THE RIGHT ONES

There's no question in my mind that I keep wandering back to where I started. Is it that I'm attracted to people who treat me as my mother did, or do manipulators see me as an easy mark? I've been more discerning of late, getting out of situations that feel familiar the minute I realize that they do. That's progress.

-Miranda, 36

It's at this moment that what you've learned about your own style of attachment needs to be put to work, no longer theoretically, but as information you'll need to draw on as you redirect and reconfigure your relationships to others.

You can set relationship goals for yourself as you would any other goal pertaining to work or life. Begin by assessing your relationships across the board—from the truly intimate ones to those that are much looser or to ties that are shallower—and see whether they are working the way you want and need them to. This isn't a decluttering exercise because the point isn't to get rid of every existing relationship and start over from scratch. (That may be true for some who have managed to recreate their childhood environments, but it's not going to be the norm, although many will find a few relationships aren't salvageable and are impediments to growth.) This also isn't a call to heap all the blame on others; you need to take responsibility for what you bring to guilt is HUGE. I feel I did them a disservice by bringing them into my shambles of a world." When I asked her what advice she'd give to other women, she wrote: "Deal with your own demons first. Remember it's not just a baby; it's a human being you're responsible for. Realize that you will need a 'village,' whether it be your partner, close friends, or family. Don't expect children to fill up the hole in your soul. If I'd been self-aware enough to realize I'd been emotionally neglected and the life consequences, I don't think I would have had children."

Lizbeth, a 43-year-old professional, is childless by choice. But the question was one she struggled with her whole life. She's felt the burden of societal expectations keenly but long wondered about her own maternal capabilities. "I remember babysitting girls and watching my friends' younger siblings play with their dolls, and all the nurturing behavior they play-acted. I never knew what to do with my dolls, except to display them, sitting on my bed." By the time she was ten, she figured she was different somehow and started telling her friends she'd never have kids.

But of course, it wasn't as cut and dried as all that. Her own recognition of how she was neglected and emotionally abused in childhood was slow in coming. "Perhaps, if it hadn't taken me almost 40 years to recognize how I'd been affected, I might have started the healing process sooner and that might have led to a different choice and outcome." Instead, she married a narcissist, who treated her as her parents did, and it was only escaping that marriage and going into therapy that permitted her to see the patterns in her childhood. Still, when she reached the age of 40—what her doctor called the outside limit—she and her second husband once again talked about whether to have a child. And once again, she chose not to, with her husband's full support despite his contention that she would make an excellent mother. As to regrets, this is how Lizbeth answers: "I do think it's the right choice for me, despite it being an unpopular one in society. I don't feel like I have a hole in my heart by not having them. I know, too, that if I ever feel I am missing out by not having them, we have the option to adopt. I strongly believe that there are many kids that need good homes if I ever want to take on that challenge."

Another woman and her husband—both with distinctly negative

childhood experiences—immersed themselves in parenting classes and reading up on child development for six years before they finally felt that each of them was ready. All these years later, they are the parents of two young adult women and satisfied that their children were well loved, supported, and tended to.

Other women report changes of heart over the years. One confided that, by the age of 14, she knew she didn't want a child and during her twenties actually consulted several doctors about having a tubal litigation; they all refused her. But by the end of her twenties, she'd changed her mind and describes her daughter's birth "as the moment I was born" and she became "the mother I wanted and needed." For some women, having a child feels like an opportunity to right the wrongs of the past and to become proactive about shaping the future.

Everyone's story is different, and the decision whether or not to become a mother is highly personal, even now when it's no longer considered a stigma not to have children. Indeed, many women and men live very happily without them. What unloved daughters need to remember is that much of one's success as a parent has to do with being emotionally present, no longer burdened by the automatic responses and emotional baggage of the past. That's what permits us to hew to what Daniel Siegel and Mary Hartzell call "the high road" in their book, *Parenting from the Inside Out*, arguably the best book on the subject ever written.

When you're on the high road, you're very aware of the emotional baggage you have in tow and what triggers your own worst responses. You work at being present and rational, committing yourself to thinking things through rather than being reactive. High-road processing tends to present different possible responses to a situation, and keeps you in the driver's seat. Imagine that your child suddenly starts crying when you're in the middle of something you need to get done, and it's irritating you. You register your feelings of annoyance, push them away, and then think, "I need to find out why she's crying. I have to stop what I'm doing and spend a few minutes helping her calm down." High-road processing effectively invites your best self in as your child's parent.

Then there's low-road processing, which has you forget about your emotional baggage and become a quivering mass of emotional reactivity the second your kid starts crying because, dammit, *you have stuff to get done*. Low-road processing hijacks your conscious thought process and ability to be empathic. You just let whatever you're feeling rip, either yelling at her to stop or screaming, "Go to your room now. If you don't stop crying, I'll give you something to cry about!"

By confronting your past experiences—and reading this book—you've already committed to being on the high road. That's a fine start, whether you decide to have a child or children, are already a mother, or not.

REBUILDING: BREAKING OLD PATTERNS AND LEARNING NEW ONES

As you begin to move in new directions, you will need to continue to hone your emotional intelligence skill set. If you are still having trouble identifying what you're feeling—most particularly in times of stress—you need to refocus, using your journal to explore what's going on. If you've become more adept at naming your feelings, the next step is to begin using them to inform your thoughts when you're making a decision or choice. This may feel uncomfortable at first, making you wonder whether you can really trust your perceptions, but just keep pushing through. It takes time to become comfortable with being in command of yourself. It's new, after all.

Start using your emotional intelligence to fact-check whether the direction you're heading in is the right one and whether the goals you are setting will make you happier and feel more fulfilled. Among the questions you may want to ask yourself are:

• Is the hesitation or anxiety I'm feeling a function of unfamiliarity—I'm trying something new—or am I reacting because I've fallen back into old patterns of behavior?

• Am I able to manage my emotions and reactivity as I set new goals, or do I need to refocus on self-regulating?

• When I get frustrated or experience a setback, do I revert to the self-critical tape, or am I able to use self-talk and compassion to get myself going again?

• Am I creating a support system for myself during this period of redirection? Am I letting close others in, or am I acting in old familiar ways?

FINDING YOUR BEST SELF

Perhaps the hardest part of this journey is figuring out who you want to be when your best self shows up. Or when you finally are a grown-up, out from under your mother's influence. While I genuinely hate all that "what doesn't kill you makes you stronger" stuff and I'm always quick to say that I would trade everything I learned in childhood for a loving and supportive mother, there are some aspects of self that *are* forged in positive ways. You might not have seen them before since they were buried under the muck of unhappiness and unhealthy patterns, but they are there, along with the bad stuff you have to get rid of. As you work toward redirecting your life, hold on to the pieces of yourself you actually like.

And have the guts to imagine yourself as you always wanted to be. Why not? You have the tools.

In the next chapter, we'll be looking at what it means to heal and why recovery is an ongoing process that takes time.

Chapter Nine
Recovery and Works in Progress

When will it stop hurting? Will it ever stop hurting?

~Annie, 53

Many daughters—and I include myself in that number—stumble over the word "healing," which means "to make whole or sound, free of injury or ailment." The word raises expectations that are difficult to realize. "Why is the healing so slow, so unreliable?" one woman emails me. "I think I'm over it, and then something triggers my feelings and I am so not over it." "I've had no contact with my mother for three years," another writes. "And while it's certainly better being free of her, I'm still hurting." Another remarks that "I'm still so sad, after five years. Will the sadness ever end?"

REDEFINING HEALING

The idea of wholeness restored spurs on the kind of magical thinking that many unloved daughters indulge in, beginning in childhood when they fantasize that their "real" mothers will show up to reclaim them, as I did. This may include hoping for that moment when everything suddenly changes and they are embraced by their mothers fully and completely with love and nothing needs fixing. Daughters sometimes think that it's only then that they will be made whole, and alas, that is unlikely to happen, and even if it did, they'd still have to heal from their experiences. But perhaps it's not just about expectations and magical thinking; perhaps the larger problem is how we think of healing and wholeness.

That brings me to the Japanese art of *kintsugi*, which takes a very different view of things that are broken or cracked than we do in the West. When something precious is damaged—whether it's Rembrandt's "The Nightwatch," Michelangelo's "David," or a family heirloom—we do what we can to restore it to its former pristine beauty. We want the repairs to be seamless, the cracks or slashes unseen, the object to be fully made whole so that, to all appearances, nothing untoward ever happened to it. *Kintsugi* takes a very different approach, one which we can apply to healing.

The term means "gold joinery," and the technique is used to repair ceramic objects, using lacquer and a precious metal such as gold to join the broken pieces together. It's said to date from the 15th century when, supposedly, a shogun sent a prized object back to China for repair, and it was returned with staples holding it together. Dissatisfied, the shogun set a challenge for artisans to come up with a more aesthetically pleasing way of repair, and *kintsugi* was the answer. In time, these repaired objects became venerated because the visibility of their cracks and breaks testified to their history, making them emblems of resilience, the passage of time, the inevitability of change, and the possibility of transformation. It's the transformative nature of *kintsugi* that's so arresting because by flaunting the object's history, the object becomes more than it was before it was damaged; it becomes a new object that is part of the present but also testifies to its past identity.

I think that the way we think and talk about healing isn't productive; we expect our recovery to render us as "whole" as someone who was well loved and tended to, which, frankly, isn't possible. This kind of expectation fuels our impatience with ourselves when our wounds are reopened by an event or experience, or when we disappoint ourselves and act out in those old, familiar patterns. It encourages us to stay self-critical. It makes us feel that we are less than those who had loving beginnings, forever scarred and needy. It makes us wonder who we might have been if we'd had a loving mother and makes us think that who we are is necessarily inferior and flawed compared to those who were loved.

Instead, I suggest that when we talk of healing the wounds of childhood, we bring to mind the image of a beautiful cup or bowl repaired by *kintsugi*, its cracks and breaks made into shining patterns of great beauty and oneness. That image may help us focus on how our past experiences inform those in the present, to better see how the behaviors we adopted in childhood to cope may animate our behaviors and choices now, even as we move away from the past. As a layperson and fellow traveler, not a day goes by that I don't appreciate how my childhood even now shapes the woman I am, in ways both seen and unseen, good and bad. Rather than seeing them as scars, envisioning those wounds as brooks, streams, and rivers of gold, silver, or copper brings a smile to my face.

As to filling the hole in your heart, the truth is that by changing your behaviors and focus, by bringing more light to bear on your experiences, you change both your perspective and the size of the hole. I don't believe that hole can ever be fully filled in—I expect that I'll be able to see the hole for as long as I live—but I can testify that I no longer see it the way I used to. Other things have filled the hole—the love I feel for others and the love they feel for me, places dear to my heart, books and words that have gentled me, the sound of the ocean, the smell of freshly turned soil, the beauty of flowers, my daughter's laugh—in ways unexpected. I see the hole differently because I have thought deeply about its effect on me and have come to appreciate the woman I became as well as the child and young adult I once was.

One question I often field from readers is this one: "Don't you ever wonder who you might have been if your mother had been loving?" Actually, I don't because the question doesn't lead me or you anywhere productive. It's no different from wondering what my life would have been like if I'd been blond and petite, instead of dark and tall; if I'd been possessed of great musical talent, instead of being utterly tone-deaf; if I'd been a brilliant mathematician, or a brilliant anything, instead of a reasonably smart person. We can't change the facts of our lives. But what *is* productive is looking back at your behaviors in the past and recognizing the degree to which your childhood experiences drove the choices you made and the people you chose to be with. If you can do that objectively—without falling into the habit of self-criticism or beating yourself up—it can permit you to own the narrative of your life in a way that you haven't before.

JOURNALING: CONNECTING THE DOTS

If you haven't been journaling, now is definitely the time to start, and if you have been, it's a good time for a brand-new notebook to write in. Part of recovery entails continuing to refine our understanding of the pivotal events in our lives and seeing them as part of a coherent narrative. The act of connecting the dots functions the way the shiny lacquer used in *kintsugi* fills the cracks in a damaged ceramic object.

Do journal about the present, focusing on how your current behavior is becoming increasingly separated from your past. That will permit you to segregate those recurring behaviors so you can focus on changing them.

MOURNING THE MOTHER YOU DESERVED

Will I ever stop feeling I was cheated of something essential?? Even at age 59, it makes me angry, and my mother died over ten years ago.

~Priscilla

The road that is recovery from a childhood without a mother's love, support, and attunement is long and complicated. One aspect of healing that is rarely touched upon is mourning the mother you needed, sought, and—yes—deserved. The word "deserved" is a key to understanding why this remains elusive for many women; they simply don't see themselves as deserving because they've internalized what their mothers said and did as self-criticism and have wrongly concluded that they're lacking, worthless, or simply unlovable.

When I cut my mother out of my life some 13 years before her actual passing, I began the process of mourning the mother I deserved, which had nothing to do with the woman who gave birth to me. It was what I needed to do to let go and move on, especially because I was about to become a mother myself; by mourning the mother I needed, I validated my unmet needs as well as my feelings.

Losses in life must be mourned and research shows that ritualized mourning promotes healing.

WHY IT'S IMPORTANT TO MOURN THE MOTHER YOU NEEDED—AND WHY IT CAN BE SO HARD

Grieving the mother you needed is impeded both by feeling unworthy of love and by the core conflict. Those who concede the battle—going no-contact or limiting communication with their mothers and usually other family members—experience great loss along with relief. For the daughter to heal, this loss—the death of the hope that this essential relationship can be salvaged—needs to be mourned along with the mother she deserved and didn't get.

The depth of the core conflict can be glimpsed in the anguish of those daughters who stay in the relationship precisely because they fear they will feel worse when their mothers die. Meg's words echo those of others: "If I cut her off and she dies, I'm scared I'll feel even more pain than I do now. What if she changed and came to her senses, and I missed it? Then it would be my fault, the way she always said it was."

Mourning the mother you needed and deserved shifts the focus to you and away from the mother you had. Let's look at what mourning entails because, again, it's a process, not a single step. We can't just light a candle and be done with it.

THE STAGES OF GRIEF ECHO THE PROCESS OF A DAUGHTER'S RECOVERY FROM CHILDHOOD

In their book *On Grief and Grieving*, Elizabeth Kübler-Ross and coauthor David Kessler point out that the five stages of loss for which Kübler-Ross is famous—denial, anger, bargaining, depression, and acceptance—aren't meant "to help tuck messy emotions into neat packages." They emphasize that everyone experiences grief in a unique and individual way. Not everyone will go through each stage, for example, and the stages may not necessarily follow in the expected sequence.

That said, these stages are nonetheless illuminating, especially when seen in the context of an unloved daughter's journey out of childhood, and make it clear why mourning is an essential part of healing.

Denial: As the authors write, "It is nature's way of letting in as much as we can handle." With the experience of great loss, denial helps cushion the immediate blow, allowing the person to pace the absorption of the reality. That's true for death, but it also applies to the daughter's recognition of her woundedness. That's why it can take years or decades for the daughter to actually see her mother's behavior with clarity. Counterintuitively, some women actually only see it in hindsight, after their mothers' deaths.

Anger: In the wake of death, anger is the most accessible of emotions, directed at targets as various as the deceased for abandoning the loved one, God or the forces of the universe, the unfairness of life, doctors and the healthcare system, and more. Kübler-Ross and Kessler stress that beneath the anger lie other, more complex, emotions, especially the raw pain of loss, and that the power of the grieving person's anger may actually feel overwhelming at times.

Unloved daughters, too, go through a stage or even stages of anger as they work through their emotions toward recovery. Their anger may be directed squarely at their mothers for their treatment, at other family members who stood by and failed to protect them, and also at themselves for not recognizing the toxic treatment sooner.

Anger at the self, alas, can get in the way of the daughter's ability to feel self-compassion; once again, it is the act of mourning the mother you deserved that permits self-compassion to take root and flower. That said, continuing to feel anger at your mother's treatment of you will keep you stuck emotionally; see more on this in the section titled "Acceptance."

Bargaining: This stage usually has to do with impending death—bargaining with God or making promises to change, thinking that "if only" we'd done X or Y, we'd be spared the pain of loss. With death, this is a stage to be passed through toward acceptance of the reality. The unloved daughter's journey is marked by years of bargaining, spoken or unspoken entreaties in the belief that if some condition is met, her mother will love and support her. She may embark on a course of pleasing and appeasing her mother or make changes to her behavior, looking in vain for the solution that will bring the desired end: her mother's love. Just as in the process of grief, it's only when the daughter ceases to bargain that she can begin to accept the reality that she's powerless to wrest what she needs from her mother.

Depression: In the context of a major loss, Kübler-Ross and Kessler are quick to point out that we are often impatient with the deep sadness or depression that accompanies it. As a society, we want people to snap out of it or are quick to insist that if sadness persists, it deserves treatment. They write instead that in grief, "depression is a way for nature to keep us protected by shutting down the nervous system so that we can adapt to something we feel we cannot handle." They see it as a necessary step in the process of healing. Since I'm neither a psychologist nor a therapist, I'm staying out of the fray.

The terrain for the unloved daughter is equally tricky; it's normal to feel sad, even depressed, by your mother's treatment of you. This sadness is often given more depth by feelings of isolation—believing you're the only unloved girl in the world—and shame. The shame emerges from the mother myths (that all mothers are loving) and the unloved daughter's worry that she's to blame for how her mother treats her. Just as well-meaning people try to push and prod mourners out of this stage of grief, so, too, may friends and acquaintances in whom the daughter confides unwittingly marginalize her sadness, saying things like "It couldn't have been so bad because you turned out so well!" and other comments of that ilk. (Side note: I have heard this too many times to count. It's the subject of emails I receive from readers who insist my mother must have been a doll . . .)

Acceptance: Most important, Kübler-Ross and Kessler are quick to say that acceptance of the reality isn't a synonym for being all right or even okay with that reality. That's a key point. It's about acknowledging the loss, identifying the permanent and even endlessly painful aspects of it, the permanent changes it's made to your life and you, and learning to live with all of that from this day forward. In their view, acceptance permits us "to withdraw our energy from the loss and begin to invest in life." Acceptance permits the mourner to forge new relationships and connections as part of their recovery.

All of this applies to unloved daughters as well, though acceptance remains, for many, somehow out of reach. This is why, once again, the need to mourn the mother you deserved is crucial to acceptance. Acceptance does not mean to forgive, excuse, deny, or paper over; it means saying to yourself, "It is what it is, and it's about her, not me. I don't have the power to change it or her, only myself."

WHAT DOES IT MEAN TO MOURN THE MOTHER YOU DESERVED?

Just what it sounds like—to grieve the absence of a mother who listened to you, took pride in you, who needed you to understand her as well as she understood you, a woman willing to own up to her mistakes and not excoriate you for yours, and—yes—someone to laugh and cry with. I look at my relationship with my own daughter, and sometimes, I can see how my younger self would have envied her. Even now, it's difficult to look past how my mother squandered countless opportunities; chief among them was actually knowing me.

Studies show that rituals help us deal with loss because performing rituals—literally deciding to take action in the wake of calamity—helps make us feel more in control; a loss of any kind in life robs us of the sense of control, whether it's a literal death or a symbolic one such as the death or end of a relationship, the death of the hope that a relationship can be salvaged or repaired, or the final dashing of a long-held dream or goal. Ritual is as old as humanity itself and, indeed, all religions incorporate ritual for this very reason: to aid and support transition and grieving at a time of loss. That said, we're not talking about religious rituals here—that part is up to you if you choose—but personal rituals. If this sounds a bit too New Age-y for you, let me begin with the science.

In a series of experiments, Michael I. Norton and Francesca Gino looked at whether personal rituals actually alleviated feelings of grief. Personal rituals, as described by the participants who'd experienced loss, were wide ranging and very individual indeed; for example, one person wrote a letter to her ex-lover and never mailed it but later destroyed it to symbolize letting go, while those whose partners had died remembered them in specific ways, such as playing a favorite song and thinking and crying about the loved one or doing something the person used to do. The researchers found that, indeed, enacting rituals alleviated grief, and didn't depend on the person's actually believing in the efficacy of rituals, either; additionally, they found that the specific behaviors that comprised the ritual were less important than performing some kind of ritual behavior.

You can make up your own rituals, of course, or you might want to perform a variation on any of these suggestions.

♦ *Letting go*

In order to mourn the mother you deserved, you need to let go of the mother you had and all the complicated feelings the relationship engendered. You can write a letter to your mother and then burn it in a fireproof container, as one reader did, or toss it into a fireplace if you have one. You can also burn a photograph or image that is emblematic of the relationship. Writing down all your emotions—such as fear, anger, shame, anxiety, and the like—on slips of paper and burning them can also be a ritual.

Similarly, cutting an item of clothing or fabric into small pieces and then disposing of them ritualistically (burying them, for example, or choosing a specific place to throw them away) is another way of letting go, especially if the item has some sort of emotional history or meaning.

Water is highly symbolic—necessary for life in all of its forms, cleansing, an emblem of change and movement—and used in rituals the world over. You can literally "wash your hands" of your childhood experiences or anything else you need to shed; this is something I do with the help of lavender or some other scented soap. If you are lucky enough to live near a body of water, tossing stones into the water and saying words as you do—"Now I am letting go of the bad times with you," "Now my focus is off the past and on the present and future," "This pebble represents the shame and fear I learned as a child and now let go of"—could be very powerful. Do what feels right for you.

Lighting candles plays a significant role in rituals all over the world and many people incorporate them into a personal ritual. Do remember to use them safely; never leave a burning candle unattended, and always place it well away from anything flammable. Candles symbolically and literally illuminate the space, casting out darkness, so you can light them ceremonially to celebrate letting go of your old behaviors or losing the internalized critical voice. Colored candles can also be used symbolically: Red is a symbol of love, passion, and anger; white is associated with knowledge and deliberation; blue stands for the sky, the heavens, spirit, and intellect; and purple, which is a blend of blue and red, symbolizes the connection between earth and heaven and the balance of passion and intellect.

◆ *Mourning the mother you deserved*

The act of mourning the mother you didn't get puts your needs center stage where they should be and will help you manage the complex emotions that are aroused by the recognition. Begin by visualizing this mother and what it would have been like to be in her presence. You can draw on qualities you admire in women (and men) you know that you associate with good mothering, caring, kindness, and attunement. You can also use memories of those who were safe havens in your childhood or who were simply kind to you.

When I visualize the mother I needed, I see someone who is a good listener and kind. If she has one essential quality, it is that she's genuinely interested in me: who I am, what I'm thinking, why I'm drawn to some things and not to others. She's someone who feels good about herself without needing to put others down, open to new experiences, and thoughtful.

If I had been her daughter, I'd have been me but a better version of myself, and much earlier in life.

Here are some possibilities for you to explore as you mourn the mother you needed:

♦ *Write about her, especially what it was like to be with her*

Use your journal to imagine what your life and interactions might have been like if you had the mother you needed. This exercise shines a different light on your experiences and permits you to experience a sense of loss that is more healing than not.

♦ *Create an altar or collage*

Gathering objects that you find beautiful, inspiring, or calming, or ones that symbolize maternal love, and arranging them in a meaningful way to express your thoughts can be another way of expressing what you missed. Similarly, you can collect images to create a collage that does much the same thing.

♦ *Compile a collection of quotations*

Finding the right words to describe the emotional connection you needed doesn't come easily to everyone so using other people's words may help you give voice to your thoughts and feelings and help you process. You can collect these sayings in your journal or handwrite them on pieces of paper and paste or tape them to a piece of foam board or cardboard; you can frame it, too.

One of the nice things about this exercise is that it enables self-mothering and compassion because it has you reading and thinking about the positive and transformative power of love.

SHIFTING PERSPECTIVE: WHAT YOUR MOTHER MISSED BY NOT LOVING YOU

I find this hard to contemplate. I don't care what my mother missed out on. That's for her to lament (which I don't think she really does—or if she does, she blames me as the cause). I care far more about all the time and energy I wasted (there's your wastefulness theme) trying to win her love, be worthy of her time and attention.

~Suzanne, 49

Once you have begun the process of mourning and worked hard at letting go of the emotions that get in your way, I would encourage you to try this shift in perspective: focusing on what your mother missed out on by not loving you or seeing you as you truly are.

Now, this is an imaginative exercise since it's likely your mother never, ever thinks about you in this way and, given the horrified response I got from readers when I first posed the question on Facebook, I am guessing you are saying *"no"* either under your breath or out loud and maybe shaking your head. But here's the thing: If you are thoughtful and reflective, revisiting pivotal moments and experiences in your life will occasionally yield a new perspective. Given my work, I actually believed that the dust had pretty much settled and that I had gleaned every possible insight from the wreckage that was my childhood. Well, never say never.

This exercise is based on my own epiphany of several years ago: the utter wastefulness of the unloving mother and her willful squandering of a unique relationship. I lay the blame for the waste at the mother's feet because she alone has the power to shape the relationship during a daughter's childhood and after. (That's where we started in Chapter One, remember?)

I understood this with utter clarity on a trip to Amsterdam—my mother's hometown—with my own daughter, then almost 28. We were on our way to *Artis*, the zoo, one of my mother's favorite destinations; while she didn't love me, she adored animals. The rain had actually stopped and the sun was shining. We were walking along streets as familiar to me as those in New York, my hometown, talking and

laughing. It struck me how lucky I was to have such a smart, percep-
tive, and funny companion to spend my time with. That I'd had a
hand in her creation seemed nothing short of miraculous.

And then it hit me: This was precisely what my mother missed
because she threw it away. By the time I was my daughter's age, I had
broken off all connection to my mother, for perhaps the second or
third time. That cutoff lasted two years or so, and the final one was
still a decade away. Appreciating my daughter, I really felt the wastefulness of my mother's actions and behaviors, without pitying her. In
a world where true connection is so maddeningly elusive, love is hard
to find and even harder for most of us to hold on to, my mother's
stubborn insistence that I was lacking, unlovable, and had nothing to
offer her (or anyone else) seemed all the more unfathomable in light
of my relationship to the granddaughter she never knew.

There's no doubt that this epiphany has much to do with how old
I am. It's not something I would have understood when I was younger
or, for that matter, when my daughter was younger; I just didn't have
the perspective. I am no longer the wounded child who longed for
my mother's love, though I will go to my grave mourning the love I
deserved and didn't get. My own role as the mother of a daughter has
long since eclipsed the emotional importance of being my mother's
child. This makes it possible for me to consider what my mother missed
in not loving me, without giving her a pass or an ounce of forgiveness.
But thinking about her wastefulness put the focus on me in a different
way. It's now easy to see that I was just as cute, funny, and smart then
as my kid is today except my mother was too jealous and hateful to see
it. She took my accomplishments as an affront unless she could use
them to aggrandize herself.

If you believe that you are ready, I think this can be a useful
exercise. Only you can judge your own readiness to think about your
mother in this theoretical way. Remember that most unloving mothers
never acknowledge their behavior, so the idea of their addressing what
they missed is more or less a fantasy; their denial is too great. But
I think that in the recovery stage, there's value to seeing what your
mother lost. Being able to shift perspective—going from grasping what
you needed and were denied to recovering and healing to pivoting

and seeing what she missed—is like seeing the valley from within it to seeing it from the high hills or mountains that surround it. Are you game to pivot?

In answer to the question "What did your mother miss out on?," one of my readers posted: "I read this and immediately began to cry. What a new idea for me: My mom missed out. I've been so focused on how I've missed out on having a loving mother. But it also touches me deeply because it touches that core belief that I am unworthy. And makes me think: Maybe I'm not unworthy." Many took it as an opportunity to catalogue their gifts and strengths, which I would encourage you to do as well: "She missed knowing me. Knowing how generous and loyal I am." "She missed my empathy. My sense of humor. My drive." "She missed the opportunity to be loved unconditionally, or as unconditionally as possible." "My mother has missed out knowing what a loving daughter she had in me, but it was never acknowledged, for whatever reason. I could have made her life much easier or should I say much more fulfilled, as a mother of seven. I am generous, to a fault, but that much she did know about me, and she used it against me. Does this make sense?"

In a thoroughly unscientific way, I've rounded up the main themes daughters raised in thinking about what their mothers lost by being unloving. There are many more, of course. If you are ready to think about this, it's a reflection that can yield a great deal of clarity. Remember that this isn't an exercise meant to make you feel sorry for your mother but to strengthen your own self-compassion, encourage you to mother yourself, and to see yourself as you truly are.

◆ *Sharing in her daughter's life*

Yes, here is the great payoff for a loving mother—to see the child you've brought into the world make her own choices, succeed and sometimes stumble, and be a part of it all.

◆ *Really knowing her child*

Being intimate with anyone is a terrific opportunity to move past the confines of our own skins and ways of perceiving the world. But there is something very special about knowing someone from the very beginning. This is undoubtedly biased, but the world gets brighter when I see the daughter I know and love. Her insights and reactions remind me of the limitations of my own points of view and help me—even at this age—to keep on growing.

◆ *Watching her daughter flower (and seeing the role she played)*

There's an enormous difference between seeing your child as an extension of yourself or someone you have to "mold" into shape as some unloving mothers do and playing the role of gardener as your child grows. A good gardener provides her with the love, support, resources, and protection she needs to become herself. And yes, it's fine to feel pride in what you've been able to give your daughter.

One daughter offered this insight: "My mother had me because it was the thing to do. She missed the look of love in a child's eye, a warm hug, endless artwork made at school or at home. Mother's Day cards which were made from love, not forced because of another adult telling me I had to do it. Little love notes under a pillow because little daughters are silly that way. Tea parties and long talks of where fairies come from. She missed *me*, but the world has me now. I just need to be a shining star for myself and my daughters."

◆ *Having fun and joy with (and because of) her daughter*

Yes, the dismissive, hypercritical, absent, or "it's all about me" mothers miss out on the fabulous company an adult daughter can be. I'm not being a Pollyanna here and saying my daughter never makes me crazy or that we never fight; we do. The arguments are epic when they happen, but we easily resolve them. The rest, folks, is what my mother missed—the stuff of life that fills your heart with joy and puts a smile on your very soul.

As one 30-year-old daughter put it: "Well, I think that she missed out on a wonderful friendship. I have a couple of girlfriends who have really great and fun relationships with their moms. I was jealous of how easy, nurturing, and natural these relationships were. The relationship I had with my mother was mostly insufferable. So all my life I was jealous of my friends because my mom wasn't my friend. I couldn't talk to her about anything. I couldn't share with her my insecurities. I couldn't count on her support. She was cold, she was judgmental, she was hypercritical, and a lot of the time she was downright mean. Had she been an actual friend or boyfriend, I would have dumped her a long time ago! So my mom missed out on what could have been a

Recovery and Works in Progress

warm and wonderful friendship. A friendship that could have added more meaning and fullness to her life."

In the end, here's the truth: You weren't the only one who missed out. Really. Keep it in mind on your journey toward healing.

THE THORNY QUESTION OF FORGIVENESS

I think forgiveness is a personal choice, and there is no yes or no answer. For me, personally, I think that no matter how I or anyone else defines the word "forgiveness," to me, it feels like it excuses what was done, and I just can't use that word.

-Leslie, 41

There's probably no subject more fraught than the question of forgiveness in any situation where you feel deeply wronged or betrayed. It's especially true when the question is asked apropos of a mother whose cardinal responsibility was to love and take care of you, and who failed you in ways that matter, the effects of which stay with you from childhood into adulthood. "To err is human, to forgive divine," wrote Alexander Pope, echoing what is essentially a cultural trope. The ability to forgive, particularly in the wake of egregious hurt or violation, is usually understood as a marker of moral and spiritual evolution, and is endowed with specific authority by its inclusion in the Judeo-Christian tradition and specifically in the Lord's Prayer.

Recognizing the cultural bias is important since the unloved daughter will feel the pressure to forgive her mother. It can come from close friends, acquaintances, relatives, strangers, and sometimes even a therapist; her efforts to forgive may be fueled by her own need to show herself as morally superior somehow to her mother as well.

But even though there seems to be a consensus that forgiveness constitutes the high road, there's also a fair amount of confusion about what forgiveness is and isn't. Does it absolve a person of wrongdoing or excuse her? Or is it about something else? Is forgiveness about the other person, or is it about the person professing it? Is it about letting go of anger? Does forgiving give you an advantage that vengefulness doesn't? Does forgiving someone turn you into a patsy or an enabler? What's the difference between forgiving and forgetting? Do you have to forgive in order to heal? What happens if you can't forgive?

These are questions philosophers, psychologists, and ordinary folk like you and me have tried to answer.

THE PSYCHOLOGY OF FORGIVENESS

I'm getting to the point of genuine forgiveness because I can't hang on to my abusive past if I want a better future. It doesn't excuse the doings she did to me, but I deserve the freedom to have peace and love in my heart that I never learned from her.

-Deidre, 50

At the beginning of their history, humans were more likely to survive in groups than as isolated singletons or couples so it's been proposed that forgiveness emerged as a prosocial behavior; revenge or retribution doesn't just separate you from the transgressor and his allies but might, in fact, run counter to the communal interests of the tribe. In an article by Jeni L. Burnette and others, the researchers hypothesized that forgiveness as a strategy might have evolved as a function of calculating the risks of revenge against the possible benefits of the relationship. The thinking would go something like this: The younger guy has poached your mate in your tribe of hunter/gatherers, but it occurs to you that he is also one of the strongest men in the tribe and very useful in flood season. What to do? Use revenge as a deterrent against future encroachments or bet on the value of his future cooperation and go with forgiveness? In a series of experiments, the team did find that, among the college students who participated, there was a calculation of exploitation risk and relationship value that fostered considering forgiveness.

Other studies show that certain personality traits actually make some people more likely to forgive than others or, more precisely, more prone to believe in forgiveness as a helpful and useful strategy after someone has wronged you. One article, by the psychologist Michael McCullough, suggests that people who thrive in the realm of relationships are more forgiving. Ditto people who are emotionally stable and, not surprisingly, those who are more religious and spiritual. The researchers also assert that there are specific psychological processes at play when people forgive: empathy for the transgressor, the ability to give the transgressor the benefit of the doubt (being generous in both the appraisal of the wrongdoer's behavior and the severity of the wrong itself), and the tendency not to ruminate about the betrayal or wrong. Although the article doesn't mention attachment, it's worth noting that the insecurely attached daughter isn't likely to be able to process events in these ways.

A meta-analytic review also suggests that there's a connection between self-control and forgiveness. The thinking here is that since the impulse to be vengeful is more "primitive," being constructive instead is a sign of self-control. Frankly, this sounds like the cultural bias at work, but more on that anon.

THE KISS OF THE PORCUPINE AND OTHER INSIGHTS

How can you forgive a mother who not only refuses to acknowledge the hurt you suffered by her actions, but is shocked that you think your childhood was painful and she was cruel to you? I refuse to validate her treatment of me. I choose to self-parent and love the child within. I love her and care for her the way she deserves with kindness and time and care. This takes so much energy and thought and is, at times, difficult. If only I was parented well to begin with. How can I possibly let go of myself and prove her right with my forgiveness? I do not hang on to a bucket of burden and hate, I have worked through and processed my emotions around my childhood and will continue to do so by keeping the little me close, but I cannot offer forgiveness to her while she is in denial of her mean, cruel treatment of me.

- Amanda

Frank Fincham, an expert on forgiveness, offers up the image of two kissing porcupines as emblematic of the human conundrum. Imagine the two on a frigid night, snuggling to stay warm, enjoying the closeness, until one's quill pierces the other's skin. Ouch! Since humans are social creatures, we make ourselves vulnerable to the "ouch!" moment in the quest for intimacy. Fincham carefully parses what forgiveness is and isn't, and his definitions may be pertinent to those of you struggling with the question.

Forgiveness isn't denial or pretending the hurt didn't happen but, in fact, confirms the hurt because forgiveness wouldn't otherwise be warranted. Additionally, forgiveness confirms the act or transgression as intentional since unintentional acts don't require forgiveness. Forgiveness doesn't, Fincham argues, imply reconciliation or reunion; while it's true that reconciliation requires forgiveness, you can forgive someone and have nothing to do with them in the future. Finally—and this one seems important—forgiveness isn't a single act but a process. Why? Because it requires managing all the negative emotions that are a consequence of the act and substituting goodwill for the impulse to strike back. It's a process that involves a considerable amount of emotional and cognitive work and so, as Fincham notes, the statement "I am trying to forgive you" is especially true and meaningful.

THE DOWNSIDE TO FORGIVENESS

I have forgiven my mother time and time again. I went back hoping for a different outcome, but alas, it never happened that way. I understand she wasn't born this person, that things happened, choices were made, something is broken inside her. I feel she's too far gone in this persona of me, me, me. It was a revolving door for me. I tried to get away, but then some crisis would arise, and of course, I was right there to save the day because that's who I am and she was my mom. Then the crisis would pass and things went back to "normal." I lived this way for way too long. I have finally cut ties and phone numbers.

-Susan, 50

Does forgiveness always work? I think you already know the answer to this, either from personal experience or from anecdote; the short answer is "no." But let's turn to research to get a bead on the downside to forgiveness, in an article appropriately titled "The Doormat Effect," which can be considered a cautionary tale for daughters who are considering both forgiving their mothers and remaining in the relationship.

In a bit of contrarian research—the vast majority of studies look at the benefits of forgiveness—Laura Luchies, Eli Finkel, and others looked at whether forgiveness was as universal a panacea as it appeared. Not altogether surprisingly, they found that forgiveness is only beneficial when certain conditions are met—that is, the transgressor makes amends and works to change his or her behavior. If that happens, then the self-concept and self-respect of the forgiving person remain intact. But when the offender doesn't—or, even worse, sees forgiveness as an open invitation to keep breaching the trust in the relationship— the person's self-concept is understandably eroded and he or she will feel used and stupid. Despite the body of research seeming to recommend forgiveness as a panacea, they wrote, "[T]he responses of both victims and perpetrators are influential following a betrayal. Victims' self-respect and self-concept clarity are determined not only by their own decision whether to forgive or not but also by their perpetrators' decision whether to act in a manner that signals that the victim will be safe or valued or not."

Unless and until your mother has come to the table, openly acknowledged her treatment of you, and has vowed to work with you to change her ways, it may well be that forgiving is just a way of reestablishing your status as a doormat if you are still in contact.

THE DANCE OF DENIAL AND FORGIVENESS

While clinicians and researchers agree that forgiveness of transgressions large and small is a cornerstone of maintaining intimate relationships, especially marriage, certain caveats do apply: The relationship must be one of equals, without an imbalance of power, with equal investment and recognition of the benefits of the connection. By definition, the relationship between the mother and the unloved child isn't one of equals, not even if the daughter is an adult. She still wants and needs the maternal love and support she didn't get.

Forgiveness may actually get in the way of the daughter's appreciation of how she's been wounded and her healing. It can become part of the dance of denial, enabling or re-animating the explanations that rationalize and normalize her mother's words and actions ("She doesn't know she's hurting me," "Her own childhood was lousy so she doesn't know any better," "I'm probably too sensitive like she says"). Because the ability to forgive is considered a sign of moral worthiness—setting you apart from the grudge-holders of this world—a daughter may unconsciously believe that showing herself worthy in this way will finally get her what she wants: her mother's love. This is an enormous issue and quandary for unloved daughters whose religious faith encourages forgiveness in every circumstance.

So it might not be about whether you forgive your mother but when you do and your deepest motivation for doing so.

FORGIVENESS AFTER GOING NO-CONTACT

Forgiveness comes with healing, and healing begins with honesty and self-love. And by forgiveness, I don't mean saying, "It's okay what you did because I see you just made a mistake and you had no bad intentions." That's the "normal" kind of forgiveness that we exercise every day, because we as human are flawed and we do make mistakes. But this kind of forgiveness is different. This forgiveness is saying, "I see the truth of what you did, it was horrible and unacceptable, and has caused me irreparable harm; but I am moving on with my healing in life and letting you go." That is the forgiveness I am working towards as I heal from severe trauma. But again, forgiveness is not the goal; healing is the goal. Forgiveness comes as a result of healing.

~Amy

Many unloved daughters speak of forgiveness as a final step in letting go; from their descriptions, it's less about forgiving their mothers for their behavior than choosing no longer to focus on them as central to their lives. It's true enough that continuing to feel anger—feeling the active sting of how miserably your mother treated you, the ongoing appreciation of how terribly unfair it was that she was your mother in the first place—keeps you emotionally in the relationship even if you've abandoned it. In this scenario, forgiveness becomes the ultimate act of disengagement.

One daughter, though, was careful to draw a distinction between forgiveness and disengagement, a point of view worth considering: "Here's the thing. I'm not turning the other cheek and offering the olive branch (ever again). The closest I can get to forgiveness is 'let go of the story' in the Buddhist sense. Ruminating about 'it' builds a rut in the brain, so I stay in the moment. When I catch myself thinking about 'it,' I come back to the present moment, perhaps by focusing on my breath. Again and again and again. As many times as it takes. Depression is thinking about the past, and anxiety is thinking about the future. Mindfulness has been the answer. Compassion also stops the rut-building process in the brain, so I think about what must have happened to my mother. But I do that for the benefit of my brain. Forgiveness? No."

So, finally, the decision whether to forgive your mother is a complex one and one that depends on motivations and intentions perhaps more than not. I'm often asked if I've forgiven my mother, who is long gone from this earth, and the truth is that I haven't. I find intentional cruelty toward children an unforgivable act, and she certainly was guilty of that so no forgiveness there. But if one component of forgiveness is letting go, that's another matter. The truth is that I never, ever think about my mother unless I am writing about her or I do something really nice for my daughter and I remind her to "thank Rita Streep." Yes, that's both true and ironic because without her miserable example, I might not have been a dedicated parent.

That said, never thinking about your mother in the day-to-day as I do is the ultimate disengagement.

MOVING FORWARD: EARNED SECURITY

I'm not the same person I was ten years ago. Therapy has helped enormously and so has living mindfully. Checking my responses and reactions has become a habit of mind. Sure, there are lapses, but my life is so much better, happier, now.

-April, 47

While there's no magic eraser to wipe the chalkboard of childhood clean, your attachment style isn't set in stone, as many studies show; we can thank the brain, that ever-plastic piece of equipment lodged in our skull, for this gift. By making sense of your childhood experiences, you can actually begin to see the world of relationship as a securely attached person does. This is what psychologists call "earned security." All the work you have done and continue to do in terms of making the narrative of your childhood experiences coherent, bringing your unconscious patterns of behavior into consciousness and disarming them, and learning to change your behavior moves you in the direction of earned security.

But for earned security to become your new default setting, an attuned relationship—with a therapist, a mentor, a close friend, a spouse—appears to be necessary for the reset to happen fully. In an article called "The Verdict Is In," Alan Sroufe and Daniel Siegel write, "the brain continues to remodel itself in response to experience throughout our lives and emerging understanding of neuroplasticity is showing us how relationships can stimulate neuronal activity and even remove the synaptic legacy of early social experience." In other words, the unconscious mental representations formed in childhood can be overwritten and edited on a neural level by relationships in adulthood. The authors also point out that, even with a largely negative history, there are "islands" of positive relational history that can be cultivated and grown through therapy. That's precisely what two studies conducted by Maria Zaccagnino, Martina Cussino, Rachel Saunders, and others showed when they measured the effect of alternative caregiving figures on adult attachment styles. Yes, participants were able to move to earned-secure status.

An interesting perspective is offered by Judith R. Schore and Allan N. Schore, which may be of use as you move forward in recovery. They rightly point out that attachment theory is really a regulation theory since the child learns to self-regulate through dyadic interaction with her mother, which is largely communicated by and through bodily gestures such as eye contact, touching, and smiling; words are not the primary form of communication. The authors assert that this dynamic of the expressed but unspoken is also key to successful therapeutic treatment. I suspect it's equally true of any relationship that can make the daughter rewrite her emotional history.

Think about the "islands" both past and present in your life—those relationships that have made you feel cared about, listened to, and heard, and that allowed you to give voice to yourself—and use them as springboards into the future. These relationships could be ones you had with a cousin, an aunt, or grandparent; a teacher, a camp counselor, or spiritual guide; a close friend; a spouse; or anyone who has truly heard and seen you and "gotten" who you really are in the course of your life. Since your goal is to move away from the older attachment styles, spend some time thinking about how physically receptive you are to other people's gestures and eye contact so as to become more aware of how others perceive you. Do you look away when you're talking to someone or avoid eye contact? Pay attention to your body language: Do you look open to communication (smiling, arms and hands relaxed, making eye contact) or closed (arms tight again the body, fingers clenched, tense in the face, looking away)? Again, becoming consciously aware of how you appear to others can only move you in the direction of closer, more intimate connections.

BREAKING THE SILENCE

One of the best things you can do to support your recovery is to begin letting go of the shame of being unloved by breaking your silence and beginning to talk to people you trust about your experiences. This isn't easy; the cultural mythologies and taboos about motherhood make speaking honestly very difficult. Still, breaking your silence is another way of owning your story fully, of validating your experiences and feelings, and no longer participating in the papered-over public version preferred by polite society. Again, share your experiences carefully and judiciously, especially if you are still maintaining a relationship with your mother and other relatives.

MUSINGS ON RECOVERY

The process of healing from childhood isn't altogether different from the way you felt sitting in a car on a family road trip when you were little; the question that kept rising to the top was "Are we there yet?" You must keep in mind that your behaviors and reactions were formed in response to literally thousands of interactions, large and small, most of which are beyond conscious recall, and that it's going to take time, patience, and the repetition of new behaviors to replace those old ones. You're basically retraining your brain and your emotional responses.

Keep the image of *kintsugi* in your mind as you move forward so as to keep your expectations realistic without losing any of your hopefulness. The scars we bear can, in time, be seen as emblems of our victories, large and small, over the tyranny of the past.

Understandably enough, I'm often asked whether I consider myself "fully recovered." My answer is "pretty much" because the older woman I am today is nothing like the girl or young woman I once was. Certain things have eluded me, such as a sustaining life-partnership, but I'm not sure I can attribute that to my childhood. I know people who had lousy childhoods and who have marriages they've made work; I know people who had loving parents and great sibling relationships and who still struggle with maintaining close connection. The truth is that life is hard even if you had a loving mother or a good-enough one, and that setbacks, disappointments, failures, and real tragedies befall us all.

Whether we were loved in childhood or not, all of us are by definition works in progress. We continue to grow and change throughout the lifespan, marked and shaped by experiences good and bad. Be kind to yourself in times of stress because it's these moments that will test your newly found behaviors and responses the most.

In the last chapter, you'll find exercises to help you on the journey. In the meantime: Godspeed.

Chapter Ten
Engaged Detox

This very last chapter offers the opportunity to put what you've learned by reading into action through thinking and journaling exercises. These are meant to be provocative—to allow you to continue to make sense of your childhood experiences with your mother and family of origin, understand how they affect you in the present, identify the unconscious motivations that drive your behavior today, clarify your thinking, and build up your skill set of managing emotions. They will help you create a coherent narrative of your life and experiences.

While most of these exercises involve writing in your journal, they will work best if you spend some time thinking about the questions posed first, unless you're asked to jot down what comes to mind immediately. Reread the section about journaling in the Introduction (pages 13-14) and heed the admonition about cool processing.

A reminder: If you are in therapy, please discuss these exercises with your therapist before doing them. If any exercise triggers anxiety or other symptoms, stop immediately.

The exercises are organized by chapter and stage but since recovery isn't a linear process, you may want to return to earlier exercises if you find yourself stuck or stymied. You may also want to date your journal entries so that you can compare and contrast how your responses to certain questions have changed over time. Remember that taking baby steps is fine. They eventually become strides.

DISCOVERY STAGE: CHAPTER ONE

Please consider these questions and think about them rather than writing them down. This is an opportunity to begin to discover your feelings and situate your thoughts calmly.

THINKING EXERCISE ON ATTACHMENT

Which style best describes you? Remember that these distinctions aren't carved in stone and that you are trying to figure out how you relate and react most of the time.

Secure: Needs and wants intimacy, trusts that people will be responsive, in touch with and aware of her feelings and thoughts.

Able to self regulate in times of stress.

Anxious-preoccupied: Characterized by wanting intimacy but being consumed by worry about rejection and abandonment.

Prone to anger and jealousy and emotional flooding.

Avoidant-fearful: Shies away from connection because she believes people are untrustworthy and unreliable and doesn't want to feel vulnerable.

Has a low opinion of self.

Avoidant-dismissive: Has a high opinion of self and a low opinion of others.

Believes people are too needy and dependent and prides herself on her self-reliance and independence, and not needing intimacy.

THINKING EXERCISE ON MOTIVATION

Are you generally more motivated by approach or avoidance? Are you willing to risk failure if you see an opportunity, or do you back off from risking failure at all costs? If you're in a relationship that's going through a rough patch, are you more likely to initiate a discussion, no matter how difficult, that might fix the problems you're having, or are you more likely to avoid talking about them directly and let sleeping dogs lie? Focus on what drives your behavior most of the time.

THINKING EXERCISE ON EXPERIENCE

Begin to cool-process by recalling a specific incident either from your childhood or any other point in your life that involves your interacting with your mother. Again, do not relive the moment in a blow-by-blow way because that will just have you re-experience your feelings and won't do anything to increase your understanding. Recall the incident as though you are seeing it from a distance and as though it happened to someone else. Focus on *why* you felt as you did. What do you see now in the pattern of interaction that you might not have before? How would you describe your own demeanor? Were you frightened or defensive? Did you flood with feeling, or did you force yourself to go numb? How, if at all, did you defend yourself?

DISCOVERY STAGE: CHAPTER TWO

THINKING ABOUT AND WRITING ON MATERNAL PATTERNS

Of the eight toxic patterns—dismissive, controlling, unavailable, unreliable, self-involved, combative, enmeshed, role-reversed—which most accurately describes how your mother treated you most of the time in childhood and adolescence? Spend some time thinking, jot down the descriptions, and then write down whatever words and thoughts come to mind. Yes, it's meant to be spontaneous and not thought out or orchestrated, so please write off the top of your head! If it makes you anxious, stop. And take a break.

WRITING ON PAST INTERACTION

Go back to the "Thinking Exercise on Experience" (page 236). This time, prepare yourself to write about it in as much detail as possible, focusing on *why* you felt as you did. For example: "I got angry because it was clear that she wasn't listening and kept saying that she had better things to do." "She kept denying that she'd written me that email, even after I handed her a printed copy, and it made me feel as frustrated and crazy as I felt when I was ten." "I felt scared because she used her physical size to intimidate me all the time." Describe your reactions, homing in on why you acted and felt as you did.

THINKING EXERCISE ON BOUNDARIES

Understanding the balance between independence and interdependence is key to having successful and intimate relationships. Take some time to explore your own worries and concerns about boundaries; are you someone who needs her own space and feels encroached upon easily, or are you someone who feels shut out when a close friend or partner needs time and space alone? This is a thinking exercise, but you may also want to tackle the question in your journal as well.

WRITING ON SELF-IMAGE

This activity has three parts and is meant to be done over the course of several days, not all at once.

Part 1: Describe yourself as a close friend might, beginning with a physical description and then going on to detail your personality, your talents and gifts, your strengths and weaknesses. Make your description as detailed as possible.

Part 2: Wait a few days, and then go back to what you wrote and answer the following questions:

• How accurate or inaccurate is the description? Why?

• Did taking the perspective of a friend permit you to see things about yourself that you might not have if you had written the description from a first-person perspective?

• How would your first-person description be different?

Part 3: Choose ten words that you think describe you most accurately and explain in your journal why these words capture who you are as a person; feel free to include both strengths and weaknesses as long as you don't self-criticize. These words can describe character traits ("diligent," "careful"), personality traits ("outgoing," "reserved"), behaviors ("impulsive," "cautious"), talents and gifts ("musical," "artistic," "intelligent," "athletic"), or physical characteristics ("strong," "coordinated" "pretty," "clumsy").

DISCERNMENT STAGE: CHAPTER THREE

WRITING ON SIBLINGS

Describe as concretely as you can how your mother's treatment of you and your siblings was different or alike. Think about whether how she treated each of you was a function of the child's personality, maternal goodness of fit, or something else, and write down your thoughts, illustrating each with a cool recall of an incident that exemplifies the treatment.

CREATING A FAMILY POWER CHART

You can do this as a drawing, or you can use words to describe as accurately as you can how power worked in your family, beginning with your mother and including your father and siblings. You should include yourself as well. This is an important exercise, and you may want to do it over the course of several days or sittings. The point of the exercise is to be able to see the dynamics on the page objectively. This fictional example is done in words, but it could be visualized as a pyramid (with Mom at the top with Dad just above her, with arrows pointing to each of the children to indicate interaction among the children) or a series of overlapping circles.

DAD: King but largely absentee. Always on Ben's case but uninvolved with me and David. Very proud of how well he provided for us, especially proud of Mom, a trophy wife. Everyone, including Mom, tiptoed around him. Ben was the punching bag.

MOM: Vain, controlling, and really insecure at heart. Very worried about what people thought of her and terrified of somehow failing. Always worried that Dad would leave her. David, the middle kid, was her favorite. She picked on Ben in solidarity with Dad and ignored me.

BEN: The oldest. Angry young kid, even angrier adolescent and adult. A lousy student and athlete, the weak link in the family's public face. Bullied me but hated David.

DAVID: The ultimate obedient child. Did everything Mom asked and curried favor as he got older so he could get all the goodies, which he did: best room, went on trips, got a car, which Ben was denied. A mediocre student but popular, which counted a lot in my parents' eyes. He ignored me and tattled on Ben as much as he could.

ME: The afterthought. Not pretty enough to warrant Mom's attention or popular enough either. A good student, but neither parent cared much about that. Unheard and unseen except by Ben, the bully. I had no sense of myself as being part of the family.

WRITING ON EMOTIONAL INTELLIGENCE

Look at the list of words below and pick the ones that best describe 1) how you felt when you were alone with your mother, 2) how you felt when you were alone with your father, 3) how you felt when you were with your siblings, if you had them, and 4) how you felt when the family was all together. Write them down in your journal and expand on your perceptions of the family dynamic as you experienced it.

upset	*fractious*	*sad*	*happy*
disconnected	*tense*	*depressed*	*uncomfortable*
afraid	*on edge*	*relaxed*	*calm*
angry	*alone*	*empty*	*adrift*
tense	*isolated*	*unfeeling*	*hopeful*
bewildered	*belligerent*	*walled off*	*defensive*
anxious	*worried*	*armored*	*frustrated*

WRITING ON PAST INTERACTION

Describe an incident from your family life—it can be recent or drawn from childhood—that captures the dynamics and interactions of family members. Be as descriptive and objective as you can, especially when writing about yourself.

❖   ❖   ❖

DISCERNMENT STAGE: CHAPTER FOUR

WRITING ON LABELING EMOTIONS

Describe in as much detail as possible a situation that you found stressful; it could be an argument you had with someone, a situation in which you felt challenged, or anything else that acted as an emotional trigger. Reread what you wrote and then describe the emotions you experienced in words—trying hard to distinguish them with some precision—and explain why you felt as you did.

Here's a slightly fictionalized example to use as a guide:

We were all leaving an event and I handed my iPhone to my close friend so I could put my coat on. He put the phone on a side table instead of holding it as I thought he would and put his own phone next to it. Someone else knocked my phone down and it shattered. I was upset, and we got into a heated argument about whose fault it was. He defended himself—he thought the phones would be safe or he wouldn't have put his there—and the guy who knocked it off by accident said the phones shouldn't have been lying on a low table in a coat room.

Feelings: Anger. Upset and disappointment with my friend not taking responsibility. Embarrassed at losing my temper in a public place in front of colleagues. Worried about the unbudgeted cost of a new phone. Insecure and uncertain about how to deal with my friend now. Distressed at cost to friendship.

WRITING ON MATERNAL PATTERNS

Go back to the notes you jotted down in your journal on the eight toxic patterns of maternal behavior (exercise on pages 237). Please review those thoughts and words and then use those words and thoughts to write about a situation in which those behaviors were in evidence. Use as much detail as possible in your description, focusing on why you felt as you did in the moment. Make sure you are using cool processing; if the act of writing is making you relive the moment, *stop!*

WRITING ON REACTIVITY

Describe an argument or disagreement you had in the recent past with someone in your life—it could be an intimate, an acquaintance, or even a colleague. Describe it as fully as you can, including the dialogue. Read what you wrote, and now focus on the moments that, in hindsight, were clearly triggers for you. Write a list of those triggers—what the person said or did—and what you felt in the moment.

WRITING ON EMOTIONAL INTELLIGENCE

This activity has two parts and is an exploration of whether your emotional reactions are consistent in stressful situations, no matter what the specifics of the interactions are. Do you experience the same emotions again and again or in a familiar combination? Are you reacting to content or are you being driven by triggers?

Part 1: Write about three kinds of situations that will predictably stress you out; they could be moments when you feel threatened by someone, are in an argument with someone, are being dressed down in public or criticized, feel excluded, or any other situation you can identify as being highly stressful and predictive of reactivity on your part. Describe each of these situations as completely as you can.

Part 2: Reread what you have written, and then focus on how your reactivity connects to either your experiences in childhood or your mother's treatment of you. Identify the triggers as much as you can, and write about the specific emotions you feel in those moments and how they reflect the past more than the present.

DISTINGUISH STAGE: CHAPTER FIVE

WRITING ON SEEING PATTERNS

This activity is in two parts.

Part 1: Pick three important relationships you've had in your adult life, the ones that either mattered most to you or influenced you most; you can include relationships that taught you both positive and negative things since the goal here is to ferret out your patterns of behavior. Think about the personalities and qualities of each person, and write down words and phrases that describe him or her best, and focus on one or two specific memories of each relationship that seem to sum up what was both good and bad about the connection.

Part 2: Wait at least two days, and preferably as long as a week, and go back to your descriptions and study them. Then write down the patterns and similarities you see among them and answer the following questions:

- What insight do you have into your choices of partners and friends?
- Is there a common thread that links these relationships?
- Were your behaviors in each relationship consistent?

WRITING ON CONFLICT RESOLUTION

Describe the dynamic between you and another person in your own words, focusing on how the two of you deal with disagreements or differences. The person could be a friend or romantic partner, past or present. Focus on your own behaviors and reactions.

WRITING ON PERSPECTIVE

Adopt the point of view of a stranger who doesn't know you and write a description of how you and your partner's interactions might be seen from the stranger's perspective. Write about one positive interaction and one that involved some tension or disagreement, using dialogue and as much detail as possible. Answer this question: What do you see in your description of your own behaviors that you hadn't realized before?

WRITING ON REACTIVITY

The goal here is to see how your reactivity affects your relationship with someone close to you. This exercise has two parts, done days apart.

Part 1: Choose an interaction involving minor stress (you feel frustrated or misunderstood, your partner isn't listening to you) and one that pushes all your buttons (you think your partner is lying or waffling, you've had a knock-down, drag-out fight) and describe each objectively, using cool processing. Then look at your own responses as you've described them and tackle whether these are your typical responses, specifically focusing on your motivations. For example, are you primarily focused on dodging the conflict, or are you looking to find a way to resolve it? Do you immediately apologize to try to dissipate the tension, or do you get defensive and angry?

Part 2: After several days, review your descriptions and see if you see a pattern in your responses that connects to your mother's treatment of you in childhood or that of other family members. Write about how your responses in the present are connected to older patterns of behavior.

◈　◈　◈

DISARM STAGE: CHAPTER SIX
WRITING ON THE DANCE OF DENIAL

Using cool processing, spend some time thinking about how you have excused, denied, rationalized, or normalized your mother's behaviors. Think about it objectively, and don't indulge in judgment or self-blame. See it from a third-party perspective, and write in your journal about the ways in which you participated. Then answer the following questions:

◆ In hindsight, what motivated you to act as you did? What were your goals?

◆ To what degree do you still feel the tug of the core conflict?

◆ Are there specific moments or instances when you feel more conflicted? Make a list of them, and explore why they are triggers and what you feel.

WRITING ON CUES AND PRIMES

Pick a recent situation you found yourself in that made you very reactive and triggered intense emotions. Using a third-person perspective, describe your reactions and their source(s) as completely as you can. End the entry by reflecting on how you wish you had acted if your best self had shown up.

WRITING ON SENSITIVITY

How much influence do cues and primes have on how you think and feel? Does the weather affect you, for example, in a demonstrable way? Do you largely respond to sound and words in an environment and interchange, or are you more visual and attuned to how a place looks and someone's physical appearance, facial expressions, and body language? Explore your thoughts in writing, giving examples, and then answer the following questions as fully as you can:

♦ When you meet someone new, what types of cues do you tend to rely on?

♦ Are you more sensitive to negative or positive cues? Explain.

♦ In what ways can you improve your response to positive cues and primes?

WRITING ON REJECTION SENSITIVITY

As objectively as you can, spend time thinking about how sensitive you are to rejection or possible signs of rejection. Write about how your sensitivity has affected you in all areas of your life, including both friendship and romantic relationships, as well as your work. See whether or not there are areas that are more affected and others that are less affected, and explore why.

RECLAIM STAGE: CHAPTER SEVEN

WRITING ON COGNITIVE REAPPRAISAL

Describe a recent emotionally stressful situation such as an argument you had with someone close to you or a situation in which you felt emotionally threatened in some way; focus on why you felt as you did, using cool processing. Now rewrite your description of your behaviors and feelings as they might have been had you availed yourself of cognitive reappraisal. The closer you come to capturing the moment-by-moment escalation of your emotions, the better.

WRITING ON NAMING EMOTIONS

This exercise should be done over the course of at least a week or longer. Becoming conscious of your feelings in the moment can help you become more adept at naming emotions. Forcing yourself to take a time-out from the rush of daily life and giving yourself time to reflect on what you're feeling and why can help you make real progress. You'll need a pocket-size pad or notebook so that when you perceive a shift in your emotions or a change in mood, you can jot down your observations. At the end of each day, use these observations to write about what you felt and why, working hard to name emotions with specificity and to identify triggers with precision.

Making this a conscious exercise will make you more aware of your emotions, especially if you're used to pushing off from them, and improve your ability to know exactly what you're feeling. Let's say, for example, you had a stressful day at work and get home feeling wiped. Spend some time thinking about the interactions that made you feel stressed and specifically the emotions you felt. For example: "My colleague didn't do her part on time, which pissed me off, but I got increasingly anxious that I would get blamed" (anger morphing into anxiety) or "I was so frustrated that no one responded to my email blast, and then I started worrying that maybe I'd done something wrong" (frustration changing into self-criticism), etc.

WRITING ON SELF-COMPASSION

Combining goal setting with an effort at self-compassion in a journal entry can be very instructive and revealing. Write down five of your goals; they can be personal or professional, as well as short-term, intermediate, and long-view ones. Under each goal, describe your personal attributes and qualities that you believe will make this goal possibly attainable. Then imagine what you would say to yourself if you encountered a setback or failed to achieve any one of these goals. Explore what your self-compassionate voice sounds like.

REDIRECTING STAGE: CHAPTER EIGHT

WRITING ON DEALING WITH YOUR MOTHER

If you are still on the fence about how to manage your relationship to your mother, think about the following questions and then answer them as fully and honestly as you can in your journal.

• What are the primary obstacles to salvaging or repairing the relationship?

• Is it possible to discuss the issues with your mother? If not, why?

• What rules or boundaries would have to be in place and respected for the relationship to continue?

• Do you believe low or infrequent contact is an option? Why or why not?

◆ How do you feel about maternal divorce or going no-contact?

◆ What are your greatest fears and worries about the decision you will make?

WRITING ON RELATIONAL GOALS

Taking a survey of all your relationships can be a helpful step toward growth. Of course, seeing how your behaviors contribute to the shape these connections take continues to be paramount. There will be some relationships you may wish to change or dispense with entirely, as well as important ties to others that need to be strengthened. Spend time thinking and then writing about five relational goals you wish to set for the future. They can be general (expand my circle of friends, develop a support system) or highly specific (communicate my needs more clearly to my partner or spouse, deal with my emotions when I argue with my sister). For each goal, come up with plans and strategies to achieve it.

WRITING ON SELF-DEFINITION

This exercise has two parts and explores whether you define yourself in simple or complex ways. Complexity yields greater personal resilience when there's a setback in life. The self is defined by relational roles; interests, activities, and hobbies; and work or vocation.

Part 1: Spend time thinking about how you define yourself, and then write about it with as much detail as possible. In addition to listing the definitions, expand upon why or why not these definitions sustain you in both good and stressful times.

Part 2: Describe how you want to redefine yourself in the months and years ahead. This may include how you will think about yourself— "I want to define myself not by my childhood or my status as a daughter but as the woman I am today"—as well as activities and roles you will take on in the future. Once again, enumerate how you will achieve these goals.

WRITING ON MOTHERHOOD

Whether you are a parent, still considering the question, or have already decided against motherhood, it's important to explore and clarify this issue, which is so closely bound both to childhood experiences and your definition of self. Answer the following questions in as much detail as possible, plumbing your deepest thoughts:

- What primarily drives your thinking about motherhood?
- What, if any, are your greatest concerns about the choice that you are making?
- How does being a mother or choosing not to mother define you?
- How do your childhood experiences influence your thinking?

RECOVERY STAGE: CHAPTER NINE

WRITING AND REFLECTING ON HEALING

This exercise should be done in two steps, preferably several days apart. Give yourself time to explore your thoughts in depth.

Part 1: Spend time exploring what you believe healing from childhood experience entails and whether you think that healing fully is possible. Be as honest as you can be with yourself and then write about the degree to which you have begun healing and what stands in the way of coping with your childhood experiences. Detail the specific issues you still have trouble with.

Part 2: Set at least five goals for healing as you look forward; you can, of course, set more. Be as specific as possible as you write about them, and come up with ways that you will implement those goals. For example: "I will try to be more open to experiences with new people by letting down my guard and engaging in new activities." "I will work through the pain in the holiday season by making plans with friends and doing things for myself and the people I care about." "I will actively work on self-compassion by writing down small victories in my journal every day."

WRITING ON THE MOTHER YOU DESERVED

Visualizing and then mourning the mother you deserved and needed are important to recovery. Writing may help you with this exercise as you imagine this mother in all the detail that you can—describing her personality and her reactions—and then move on to describe the interactions you would have had with her. Writing about the mother you deserved helps to legitimatize the needs that weren't met in childhood, and your ability to summon up this mother in times of stress will be bolstered and solidified by the act of writing.

WRITING ON SEEING YOURSELF AS MOM DIDN'T

Shifting your perspective on the mother-daughter relationship by focusing on what your mother missed out on is one way of moving yourself out of the old role. Using cool processing, make a list of all the things your mother never noticed about you, appreciated, or paid attention to; moments and milestones she wasn't a part of; as well as the people in your life she never really got to know or enjoy. Expand on each item with lots of detail.

WRITING ON MOMENTUM

Charting your progress—baby steps turn into strides over time—can keep you encouraged and shifts the focus from your flaws and weaknesses to positive changes. Pick a skill you've been actively working on—it could be managing your emotions, dealing with rumination, veering away from the habit of self-criticism—and write a progress report on how your efforts have begun to pay off and what you'd like to be able to achieve in the near future. Date your entry, and go back to it in a month and update it. You can do this as often as you like so that you can keep being your own best cheerleader! You can chart as many skills as you wish.

REVISITING THE CORE CONFLICT

This isn't a single exercise but one you should go back to again and again as a way of mapping your recovery. Again, dating your entries will be of use to you over time. Examine how you've been dealing with the core conflict and building your ability to let go by writing about it in detail. Explore how letting go of the core conflict helps to redefine your sense of self. Then, finally, journal about where you hope to find yourself in six months' time, a year from now, and five years hence. Go back to this exercise as often as you need to, reflecting on your previous entries and continuing to write.

ACKNOWLEDGMENTS

I wouldn't have written this book if it hadn't been for my readers, and I wouldn't have known my readers had I not started blogging at *Psychology Today* in 2012 and then at *Psych Central* in 2016. I thought I was pretty much done with the subject after I wrote *Mean Mothers*, but when I returned to it, this time as more of a science writer than before, I realized I wasn't. And the more I posted, the more readers asked me questions I couldn't answer in a single post or even a series of them. My hope is that *Daughter Detox* supplies at least some of the answers they seek.

And of course, there wouldn't be any stories to share if it weren't for my readers. Thank you all for participating, whether by filling out the questionnaire for the book or answering callouts for posts that became part of the book, especially The Stalwart Crew who were on my Facebook page when it was tiny. Thanks to Kaja Perina, Lybi Ma, and Matt Huston at *Psychology Today* and John Grohol at *Psych Central* for giving me a perch.

My friend Claudia Karabaic Sargent has been a great cheerleader and did me the honor of designing the book you hold in your hand, which required more than a little finesse because of all of its moving parts, and a honey of a cover design. Many mercis! The Hedgehog Angel came through in the end. You are very wonderful, my dear, and who knew we'd go back into the book business together?

Thanks to my pal, fellow writer Leslie Garisto Pfaff, for both hand-holding and skillful copyediting. Lori Stein, she of the best omelets in New York, was both enthusiastic and helpful. My agent, Gillian Mackenzie, believed in the project despite what we both knew about how publishing operates, and I thank her for the initial support and the title. Thank you to Maria Fairchild for her eagle eye. Patti Pitcher, thank you for everything, and helping as always. Rich Kelley, your wisdom over drinks was much appreciated and taught me about the flywheel effect and more. To all of my friends who passed along my posts when I was just starting to garner an audience, thank you—and I mean Robyn Cooper Henning, Ann Keeler Evans, and Joanne Almvig, in particular. Thanks to Stephen Marmon for the deer.

I cannot be grateful enough to both Dr. Joseph Burgo and Dr.

Craig Malkin, whom I am listing alphabetically because, with two great guys, it's impossible to decide whom to put first. They are both terrific writers, happen to be experts in narcissism, and they read the manuscript with enthusiasm and dedication. I owe you big time! A special shout-out to Joe for unveiling the mysteries of self-publishing and for glittering and stimulating conversations.

Finally, last but not least, a *merci beaucoup* to the best daughter in the world. You know who you are. Thank you for changing my life.

INDEX OF KEY WORDS AND TOPICS

The page numbers in **bold** indicate a primary definition or discussion

◈   ◈   ◈

REFERENCES

Introduction

Kross, Ethan, Ozlem Ayduk, and Walter Mischel. When Asking "Why" Does Not Hurt: Distinguishing Rumination from Reflective Processing of Negative Emotions. *Psychological Science*, 2005, vol. 16(9), pp. 709-715.

Pennebaker, James W., and Janel D. Segal. Forming a Story: The Health Benefits of Narrative. *Journal of Clinical Psychology*, 1999, vol. 55(10), pp. 1243-1254.

1. The Truth About Maternal Power

Adamson, Lauren B., and Janet E. Frick. The Still Face: A History of a Shared Experimental Paradigm. *Infancy*, 2003, vol. 4(4), pp. 451-473.

Adolph, Karen E., and Kari S. Kretch. Infants on the Edge: Beyond the Visual Cliff, in *Developmental Psychology*, edited by Alan M. Slater and Paul C. Quinn, pp. 36-55. London: SAGE Publications, 2012.

Ainsworth, Mary D. Salter, Mary C. Blehar, Everett Walters, and Sally N. Wall. *Patterns of Attachment: A Psychological Study of the Strange Situation*. Hillsdale, N.J.: Lawrence Erlbaum Associates, 1978.

Bartholomew, Kim, and Leonard M. Horowitz. Attachment Styles Among Young Adults: A Test of a Four-Category Model. *Journal of Personality and Social Psychology*, 1991, vol. 61(2), pp. 226-244.

Baumeister, Roy F., Ellen Bratslavsky, Catrin Finkenauer, and Kathleen D. Vohs. Bad Is Stronger Than Good. *Review of General Psychology*, 2001, vol. 5(4), pp. 323-370.

Bowlby, John. *Attachment and Loss: Volume 1: Attachment*. New York: Basic Books, 1969.

Bowlby, John. *Attachment and Loss: Volume 2: Separation, Anxiety and Anger*. New York: Basic Books, 1973.

Cassidy, Julie, and Phillip R. Shaver, eds. *Handbook of Attachment: Theory, Research, and Clinical Applications*, (second edition). New York: Guilford Press, 2008.

Chang, Rosemarie Sokol, and Nicholas Thompson. Whines, Cries, and Motherese: Their Relative Power to Distract. *Journal of Social, Evolutionary, and Cultural Psychology*, 2011, vol. 5(2), pp. 10-20.

De Haan, Michelle, Jay Belsky, Vincent Reid, Agnes Volern, and Mark. H. Johnson. Maternal Personality and Infants' Neural and Visual Responsivity to Facial Expressions of Emotion. *Journal of Child Psychology and Psychiatry*, 2004, vol. 45(7), pp. 1209-1218.

Elliott, Andrew J., and Todd M. Thrash. Approach and Avoidance Temperament as Basic Dimensions of Personality. *Journal of Personality*, 2010, vol. 78(3), pp. 865-906.

Elliott, Andrew J., and Todd M. Thrash. The Intergenerational Transmission of Fear of Failure. *Personality and Social Psychology Bulletin*, 2004, vol. 30(8), pp. 957-971.

Gibson, E. J., and Walk, R. D. The "Visual Cliff." *Scientific American*, 1960, vol. 202, pp. 67-71.

Hazan, Cindy, and Phillip Shaver. Romantic Love Conceptualized as an Attachment Process. *Journal of Personality and Social Psychology*, 1987, vol. 42(3), pp. 511-524.

Holmes, Bjarne M., and Kimberly R. Johnson. Adult Attachment and Romantic Partner Preference: A Review. *Journal of Social and Personal Relationships*, 2009, vol. 26(6-7), pp. 833-852.

Kisilevsky, Barbara S., et al. Effects of Experience on Fetal Voice Recognition. *Psychological Science*, 2003, vol. 14(3), pp. 220-224.

Lench, Heather C., and Linda J. Levin. Goals and Responses to Failure: Knowing When to Hold Them and When to Fold Them. *Motivation and Emotion*, 2008, vol. 32(2), pp. 127-140.

Mesman, Judi, Marinus H. van IJzendoorn, and Marian J. Bakermans-Kranenburg. The Many Faces of the Still-Face Paradigm: A Review and Meta-Analysis. *Developmental Review*, 2009, vol. 29(2), pp. 120-162.

Nishitani, S., et al. The Calming Effect of a Maternal Breast Milk Odor on the Human Newborn Infant. *Neuroscience Research*, 2009, vol. 63(1), pp. 66-71.

Ochsner, Kevin N., and James J. Gross. The Cognitive Control of Emotion. *Trends in Cognitive Science*, 2005, vol. 9(5), pp. 242-249.

Parsons, C. E., K. S. Young, L. Murray, A. Stein, and M. L. Kringelbach. The Functional Neuroanatomy of the Parent-Infant Relationship. *Progress in Neurobiology*, 2010, vol. 91(3), pp. 220-241.

Parsons, Christine E., et al. Ready for Action: A Role for the Human Midbrain in Responding to Infant Vocalizations. *Social Cognitive and Affective Neuroscience*, 2014, vol. 9(7), pp. 977–984.

Polcari, Ann, Karen Rabi, Elizabeth Bolger, and Martin H. Teicher. Parental Verbal Affection and Verbal Aggression in Childhood Differentially Influence Psychiatric Symptoms and Wellbeing in Young Adulthood. *Child Abuse and Neglect*, 2014, vol. 38(1), pp. 91-102.

Schore, Allan N. Attachment and the Regulation of the Right Brain. *Attachment and Human Development*, 2002, vol. 2(1), pp. 23-47.

Schore, Allan N. Effects of a Secure Attachment Relationship on Right Brain Development, Affect Regulation, and Infant Mental Health. *Infant Mental Health*, 2001, vol. 22(1-2), pp. 7-66.

Sorce, James F., Robert Ende, Joseph J. Campos, and Mary D. Klinnert. Maternal Emotional Signaling: Its Effects on the Visual Cliff Behavior of One-Year-Olds. *Developmental Psychology*, 1985, vol. 21(1), pp. 195-200.

Striano, Tricia, Amrisha Vaish, and Joann P. Benigno. The Meaning of Infants' Looks: Information Seeking and Comfort Seeking. *British Journal of Developmental Psychology*, 2006, vol. 24, pp. 615-630.

Teicher, Martin H., et al. The Neurobiological Consequences of Early Stress and Childhood Maltreatment. *Neuroscience and Biobehavioral Reviews*, 2003, vol. 27, pp. 33-44.

Tomoda, Akemi, et al. Exposure to Parental Verbal Abuse Is Associated with Increased Gray Matter Volume in Superior Temporal Gyrus. *NeuroImage*, 2011, vol. 54, pp. 5280-5286.

Tronick, Edward Z. Emotions and Emotional Communication in Infants. *American Psychologist*, 1989, vol. 44(2), pp. 112-119.

Tronick, Edward, Heidelise Als, Lauren Adamson, Susan Wise, and T. Berry Brazelton. The Infant's Response to Entrapment Between Contradictory Messages in Face-to-Face Interaction. *Journal of the American Academy of Child and Adolescent Psychiatry*, 1978, vol. 17(1), pp. 1-13.

Weinberger, M. Katherine, and Edward Z. Tronick. Infant Affective Reactions to the Resumption of Maternal Interaction After the Still-Face. *Child Development*, 1996, vol. 67(3), pp. 905-914.

2. The Power She Had over You

Bassoff, Evelyn S. *Mothering Ourselves: Help and Healing for Adult Daughters*. New York: Dutton, 1991.

Bureau, Jean-François, et al. Perceived Dimensions of Parenting and Non-Suicidal Self-Injury in Young Adults. *Journal of Youth and Adolescence*, 2010, vol. 39(5), pp. 484-494.

Chernin, Kim. *The Hungry Self: Women, Eating, and Identity*. New York: Harper & Row, 1985.

Conterio, Karen, and Wendy Lader. *Bodily Harm: The Breakthrough Healing Program for Self-Injurers*. New York: Hyperion Books, 1998.

Edelman, Hope. *Motherless Daughters: The Legacy of Loss*. New York: Delta, 1994.

Elgin, Jenna, and Mary Pritchard. Adult Attachment and Disordered Eating in Undergraduate Men and Women. *Journal of College Student Psychotherapy*, 2006, vol. 21(2), pp. 25-40.

Finzi-Dottan, Ricky, and Toby Karu. From Emotional Abuse in Childhood to Psychopathology in Adulthood. *The Journal of Nervous and Mental Disease*, 2006, vol. 94(8), pp. 616-622.

Goldsmith, Rachel E., and Jennifer J. Freyd. Effects of Emotional Abuse in Family and Work Environments: Awareness for Emotional Abuse. *Journal of Emotional Abuse*, 2005, vol. 5(1), pp. 95-123.

Gornick, Vivian. *Fierce Attachments: A Memoir*. New York: Farrar, Straus & Giroux, 2005.

Mikulincer, Mario, and Phillip R. Shaver. Adult Attachment and Affect Regulation, in *Handbook of Attachment: Theory, Research, and Clinical Applications* (second edition), edited by Jude Cassidy and Phillip R. Shaver, pp. 503-531. New York and London: Guilford Press, 2008.

Roth, Geneen. *When Food Is Love: Exploring the Relationship Between Eating and Intimacy*. New York: Plume, 1992.

Sachs-Ericsson, Natalie, Edelyn Verona, Thomas Joiner, and Kristopher J. Preacher. Parental Verbal Abuse and the Mediating Role of Self-criticism in Adult Internalizing Disorders. *Journal of Affective Disorders*, 2006, vol. 93(1-3), pp. 71-78.

Schrodt, Paul, Paul L. Witt, and Jenna R. Shimkowski. A Meta-Analytical Review of the Demand/Withdraw Pattern of Interaction and its Associations with Individual, Relational, and Communicative Outcomes. *Communication Monographs*, 2014, vol. 81(1), pp. 28-58.

Tannen, Deborah. *You're Wearing That? Understanding Mothers and Daughters in Conversation*. New York: Ballantine Books, 2006.

3. All in the Family: Understanding Ripple Effects

Bank, Stephen, and Michael Kahn. *The Sibling Bond*. New York: Basic Books, 1997.

Berntsen, Dorthe, David C. Rubin, and Ilene C. Siegler. Two Versions of Life: Emotionally Negative and Positive Events Have Different Roles in the Organization of Life Story and Identity. *Emotion*, 2011, vol. 11(5), pp. 1190-1201.

Boer, Frits, Arnold Goedhart, and Philip Treffers. Siblings and Their Parents, in *Children's Sibling Relationships: Developmental and Clinical Issues*, edited by Frits Boer and Judy Dunn. Hillsdale, N.J.: Lawrence Erlbaum Associates, 1992, pp. 41-50.

Brys-Craven, Jennifer, Brandon J. Auer, Douglas A. Granger, and Amber R. Massey. The Father-Daughter Dance: The Relationship Between Father-Daughter Relationship Quality and Daughters' Stress Response. *Journal of Family Psychology*, 2012, vol. 26(1), pp. 87-94.

DeLuccie, Mary. Mothers: Influential Agents in Father-Child Relations. *Genetic, Social, and General Psychology Monographs*, 1996, vol. 122(3), pp. 285-307.

Dunn, Judy, and Robert Plomin. *Separate Lives: Why Siblings Are So Different*. New York: Basic Books, 1990.

Jensen, Alexander, Shawn Whiteman, Karen Fingerman, and Kira Birditt. "Life Still Isn't Fair": Parental Differential Treatment of Young Adult Siblings. *Journal of Marriage and Family*, 2013, vol. 75(2), pp. 438-452.

Lamb. Michael E., ed. *The Role of the Father in Child Development* (fourth edition). Hoboken, N.J.: John Wiley & Sons, 2004.

Leve, Ariel. *An Abbreviated Life: A Memoir*. New York: Harper, 2016.

Richmond, Melissa K., Clare M. Stocker, and Shauna L. Rienks. Longitudinal

Associations Between Sibling Relationship Quality, Parental Differential Treatment, and Children's Adjustment. *Journal of Family Psychology*, 2005, vol. 19(4), pp. 550-559.

Schoppe-Sullivan, Sarah. J., Lauren E. Altenburger, Meghan A. Lee, Daniel J. Bower, and Claire M. Kamp Dush. Who Are the Gatekeepers? Predictors of Maternal Gatekeeping. *Parenting: Science and Practice*, 2015, vol. 15(3), pp. 166-186.

Sroufe, Alan, and Daniel Siegel. The Verdict Is In: The Case for Attachment Theory. drdansiegel.com/uploads/1271-the-verdict-is-in.pdf.

Trent, Katherine, and Glenna D. Spitze. Growing Up Without Siblings and Adult Sociability Behaviors. *Journal of Family Issues*, 2011, vol. 32(9), pp. 1178-1204.

Whiteman, Shawn D., Susan M. McHale, and Anna Soli. Theoretical Perspectives on Sibling Relationships. *Journal of Family Theory and Review*, 2011, vol. 3(2), pp. 124-139.

4. Adaptation: How Her Behaviors Shaped Yours

Barrett, Lisa Feldman, James Gross, Tamlin Conner Christensen, and Michael Benvenuto. Knowing What You're Feeling and Knowing What to Do About It: Mapping the Relation Between Emotion Differentiation and Emotion Regulation. *Cognition and Emotion*, 2001, vol. 15(6), pp. 713-724.

Bartholomew, Kim, and Leonard M. Horowitz. Attachment Styles Among Young Adults: A Test of a Four-Category Model. *Journal of Personality and Social Psychology*, 1991, vol. 61(2), pp. 226-244.

Baumeister, Roy E., Ellen Bratslavsky, Mark Muraven, and Dianne M. Tice. Ego Depletion: Is the Active Self a Limited Resource? *Journal of Personality and Social Psychology*, 1998, vol. 74(5), pp. 1252-1265.

Bernier, Annie, Stephanie M. Carlson, Marie Deschênes, and Célia Matte-Gagné. Social Factors in the Development of Early Executive Functioning: A Closer Look at the Caregiving Environment. *Developmental Science*, 2012, vol. 15(1), pp. 12–24.

Bernier, Annie, Stephanie M. Carlson, and Natasha Whipple. From External Regulation to Self-Regulation: Early Parenting Precursors of Young Children's Executive Functioning. *Child Development*, 2010, vol. 81(1), pp. 326-339.

Birnbaum, Gurit E., Harry T. Reis, Mario Mikulincer, Omri Gillath, and Ayala Orpaz. When Sex Is More than Just Sex: Attachment Orientations, Sexual Experience, and Relationship Quality. *Journal of Personality and Social Psychology*, 2006, vol. 91(5), pp. 929-943.

Brackett, Marc A., Nicole Lerner, Susan E. Rivers, Peter Salovey, and Sara Schiffman. Relating Emotional Abilities to Social Functioning: A Comparison of Self-Report and Performance Measures of Emotional Intelligence. *Journal of Personality and Social Psychology*, 2006, vol. 91(4), pp. 780-795.

DeWall, C. Nathan, et al. So Far Away from One's Partner, Yet So Close to Romantic Alternatives: Avoidant Attachment, Interest in Alternatives, and Infidelity. *Journal of Personality and Social Psychology*, 2011, vol. 101(6), pp. 1302-1316.

Ein-Dor, Tsachi, Mario Mikulincer, Guy Doron, and Phillip R. Shaver. The Attachment Paradox: How Can So Many of Us (the Insecure Ones) Have No Adaptive Advantages? *Perspectives on Psychological Science*, 2010, vol. 5(2), pp. 123-141.

Gyurak, Anett, James J. Gross, and Amit Etkin. Explicit and Implicit Emotion Regulation: A Dual-Process Framework. *Cognition and Emotion*, 2011, vol. 25(3), pp. 400-412.

Kidd, Celeste, Holly Palmeri, and Richard N. Aslin. Rational Snacking: Young Children's Decision-Making on the Marshmallow Task Is Moderated by Beliefs About Environmental Reliability. *Cognition*, 2013, vol. 126(1), pp. 109-114.

Lewis, Thomas, Fari Amini, and Richard Lannon. *A General Theory of Love*. New York: Vintage Books, 2001.

Lyubomirsky, Sonja, Kennon M. Sheldon, and David Schkade. Pursuing Happiness: The Architecture of Sustainable Change. *Review of General Psychology*, 2005, vol. 9(2), pp. 111-131.

Mayer, John D., and Peter Salovey, What is Emotional Intelligence?, in *Emotional Development and Emotional Intelligence: Educational Implications*, edited by Peter Salovey and David J. Sluyter. New York: Basic Books, 1997.

Mischel, Walter. *The Marshmallow Test: Why Self-Control Is the Engine of Success*. New York: Little, Brown and Company, 2015.

Shoda, Yuichi, Walter Mischel, and Philip K. Peake. Predicting Adolescent

Cognitive and Self-Regulatory Competencies from Preschool Delay of Gratification: Identifying Diagnostic Conditions. *Developmental Psychology*, 1990, vol. 26(6), pp. 978-986.

5. Flashes of Recognition: Patterns and Partners

Amato, Paul R., and Denise Previti. People's Reasons for Divorcing. *Journal of Family Issues*, 2003, vol. 24(5), pp. 602-626.

Barry, Robin A., and Erika Lawrence. "Don't Stand So Close to Me": An Attachment Perspective of Disengagement and Avoidance in Marriage. *Journal of Family Psychology*, 2013, vol. 27(3), pp. 484-494.

Birnbaum, Gurit E., Harry T. Reis, Mario Mikulincer, Omri Gillath, and Agala Orpaz. When Sex Is More than Just Sex: Attachment Orientations, Sexual Experience, and Relationship Quality. *Journal of Personality and Social Psychology*, 2006, vol. 91(5), pp. 929-943.

Bradbury, Thomas N., Frank D. Fincham, and Steven R. H. Beach. Research on the Nature and Determinants of Marital Satisfaction: A Decade in Review. *Journal of Marriage and Family*, 2000, vol. 62(4), pp. 964-680.

Brumbaugh, C. C., and R. C. Fraley. Adult Attachment and Dating Strategies: How Do Insecure People Attract Mates? *Personal Relationships*, 2010, vol. 17, pp. 599–614.

Buote, Vanessa M., et al. The Importance of Friends: Friendship and Adjustment Among 1st-Year University Students. *Journal of Adolescent Research*, 2007, vol. 22(6), pp. 665-689.

Burgo, Joseph. *The Narcissist You Know: Defending Yourself Against Extreme Narcissism in an All-About-Me Age.* New York: Touchstone, 2016.

Campbell, Lorne, Jeffry A. Simpson, Jennifer Boldry, and Deborah A. Kashy. Perceptions of Conflict and Support in Romantic Relationships: The Role of Attachment Anxiety. *Journal of Personality and Social Psychology*, 2005, vol. 88(3), pp. 510-531.

Downey, Geraldine, and Scott I. Feldman. Implications of Rejection Sensitivity for Intimate Relationships. *Journal of Personality and Social Psychology*, 1996, vol. 70(6), pp. 1327-1343.

Downey, Geraldine, Antonio L. Freitas, Benjamin Michaelis, and Hala Khouri. The Self-Fulfilling Prophecy in Close Relationships: Rejection Sensitivity and Rejection by Romantic Partners. *Journal of Personality and*

Social Psychology, 1998, vol. 75(2), pp. 545-560.

Ein-dor, Tsachi, Mario Mikulincer, Guy Duron, and Phillip R. Shaver. The Attachment Paradox: How Can So Many of Us (the Insecure Ones) Have No Adaptive Advantages? *Perspectives on Psychological Science*, vol. 5(2), pp. 123-141.

Feeney, Brooke C. The Dependency Paradox in Close Relationships: Accepting Dependence Promotes Independence. *Journal of Personality and Social Psychology*, 2007, vol. 92(2), pp. 268-285.

Geher, Glenn. Perceived and Actual Characteristics of Parents and Partners: A Test of a Freudian Model of Mate Selection. *Current Psychology*, 2000, vol. 19(3), pp. 194-214.

Gottman, John. *Why Marriages Succeed or Fail: And How You Can Make Yours Last*. New York: Fireside, 1994.

Jang, Su Ahn, Sandi W. Smith, and Timothy R. Levine. To Stay or to Leave? The Role of Attachment Styles in Communication Patterns and Potential Termination of Romantic Relationships Following Discovery of Deception, *Communication Monographs*, 2002, vol. 69(3), pp. 236-252.

Luke, Michelle Anne, Constantine Sedikides, and Kathy Carnelley. Your Love Lifts Me Higher!: The Energizing Quality of Secure Relationships. *Personality and Social Psychology Bulletin*, 2012, vol. 38(6), pp. 721-733.

Malkin, Craig. *Rethinking Narcissism: The Secret to Recognizing and Coping with Narcissists*. New York: Harper Perennial, 2016.

Noftle, Erik E., and Phillip R. Shaver. Attachment Dimensions and the Big Five Personality Traits: Associations and Comparative Ability to Predict Relationship Quality. *Journal of Research in Personality*, 2006, vol. 40, pp. 179-208.

Papp, Lauren M., Chrystyna D. Kouros, and E. Mark Cummings. Demand-Withdraw Patterns in Marital Conflict in the Home. *Personal Relationships*, 2009, vol. 16(2), pp. 285-300.

Schachner, Dory A., and Phillip R. Shaver. Attachment Dimensions and Sexual Motives. *Personal Relationships*, 2004, vol. 11(2), pp. 135-265.

Schrodt, Paul, Paul L. Witt, and Jenna R. Shimkowski. A Meta-Analytical Review of the Demand/Withdraw Pattern of Interaction and Its Association with Individual, Relational, and Communicative Outcomes. *Communication Monographs*, 2014, vol. 81(1), pp. 28-58.

Simpson, Jeffry A., and W. Steven Rholes. Adult Attachment, Stress, and Romantic Relationships. *Current Opinion in Psychology*, 2017, vol. 13, pp. 19-24.

Simpson, Jeffry A., W. Steven Rholes, and Heike A. Winterheld. Attachment Working Models Twist Memories of Relationship Events. *Psychological Science*, 2010, vol. 21(2), pp. 252-259.

Wegner, Daniel, Toni Guiliani, and Paula Hertel. Cognitive Interdependence in Close Relationships, in *Compatible and Incompatible Relationships*, edited by William Ickes, pp. 253-276. New York: Springer Verlag, 1985.

6. Making the Unconscious Conscious

Bargh, John A., and Tanya L. Chartrand. The Unbearable Automaticity of Being. *American Psychologist*, 1999, vol. 54(7), pp. 462-479.

Bargh, John A., Mark Chen, and Lara Burrows. Automaticity of Social Behavior: Direct Effects of Trait Construct and Stereotype-Activation on Action. *Journal of Personality and Social Psychology*, 1996, vol. 71(2), pp. 230-244.

Barrett, Lisa Feldman, James Gross, Tamlin Conner Christensen, and Michael Benvenuto. Knowing What You're Feeling and Knowing What to Do About It: Mapping the Relation Between Emotion Differentiation and Emotional Regulation. *Cognition and Emotion*, 2001, vol. 15(6), pp. 713-724.

Baumann, Nicola, and Julius Kuhl. Intuition, Affect, and Personality: Unconscious Coherence Judgments and Self-Regulation of Negative Affect. *Journal of Personality and Social Psychology*, 2002, vol. 83(5), pp. 1213-1223.

Boden, Matthew Tyler, Renee J. Thompson. Mûgé Dizén, Howard Berenbaum, and John P. Baker. Are Emotional Clarity and Emotion Differentiation Related? *Cognition and Emotion*, 2013, vol. 27(6), pp. 961-978.

Carnelley, Katherine B., and Angela C. Rowe. Repeated Priming of Attachment Security Influences Later Views of Self and Relationships. *Personal Relationships*, 2007, vol. 14(2), pp. 307-320.

Chabris, Christopher, and Daniel Simons. *The Invisible Gorilla: How Our Intuitions Deceive Us*. New York: Broadway Paperbacks, 2011.

Chartrand, Tanya L., and John A. Bargh. The Chameleon Effect: The Perception-Behavior Link and Social Interaction. Journal of Personality and Social Psychology 1999, vol. 76(6), pp. 893-910.

Erbas, Yasemin, Eva Ceulemans, Madeline Lee Pe, Peter Koval, and Peter Kuppens. Negative Emotion Differentiation: Its Personality and Well-being Correlates and a Comparison of Different Assessment Methods. *Cognition and Emotion*, 2014, vol. 28(7), pp. 1196-1213.

Kahneman, Daniel. *Thinking, Fast and Slow*. New York: Farrar, Straus & Giroux, 2011.

Kahneman, Daniel, and Amos Tversky. Prospect Theory: An Analysis of Decision Under Risk. *Econometrica*, 1979, vol. 47(2), pp. 263-292.

Kay, Aaron C., S. Christian Wheeler, John A. Bargh, and Lee Ross. Material Priming: The Influence of Mundane Physical Objects on Situational Construal and Competitive Behavior Choice. *Organizational Behavior and Human Decision Processes*, 2004, vol. 95(1), pp. 83-96.

Koole, Sander L., and Daniel A. Fockenberg. Implicit Emotion Regulation Under Demanding Conditions: The Moderating Role of Action Versus State Orientation. *Cognition and Emotion*, 2011, vol. 25(3), pp. 440-452.

Koole, Sander L., and Nils B. Jostmann. Getting a Grip on Your Feelings: Effects of Action Orientation and External Demands on Intuitive Affect Regulation. *Journal of Personality and Social Psychology*, 2004, vol. 87(6), pp. 974-990.

Lieberman, Matthew D., et al. Putting Feelings into Words. *Psychological Science*, 2007, vol. 18(5), pp. 421-428.

Lyubomirsky, Sonja, Kennon M. Sheldon, and David Schkade. Pursuing Happiness: The Architecture of Sustainable Change. *Review of General Psychology*, 2005, vol. 9(2), 111-131.

Pazda, Adam, Pavol Prokop, and Andrew J. Elliot. Red and Romantic Rivalry: Viewing Another Woman in Red Increases Perceptions of Sexual Receptivity, Derogation, and Intentions to Mate-Guard. *Personality and Social Psychology Bulletin*, 2014, vol. 40(10), pp. 1260-1269.

Simons, Daniel J., and Christopher F. Chabris. Gorillas in Our Midst: Sustained Inattentional Blindness for Dynamic Events. *Perception*, 1999, vol. 28, pp. 1059-1074.

Wegner, Daniel M. Ironic Processes of Mental Control. *Psychological Review*, 1994, vol. 101(1), pp. 34-52.

Wegner, Daniel M. Setting Free the Bears: Escape from Thought Suppression.

American Psychologist, 2011, vol. 66(8), pp. 671-679.

Wegner, Daniel M. *White Bears and Other Unwanted Thoughts: Suppression, Obsession, and the Psychology of Mental Control.* New York and London: Guilford Press, 1994.

Wilson, Timothy D., and Daniel T. Gilbert. Affective Forecasting. *Advances in Experimental Social Psychology,* 2003, vol. 35, pp. 345-411.

7. Reclaiming Your Power

Achtziger, Anya, Thorsten Fehr, Gabriele Oettingen, Peter M. Gollwitzer, and Brigitte Rockstroh. Strategies of Intention Formation Are Reflected in Continuous MEG Activity. *Social Neuroscience,* 2009, vol. 4(1), pp. 11-27.

Alloy, Lauren B., and Lyn Y. Abramson. Judgment of Contingency in Depressed and Non-Depressed Students: Sadder But Wiser? *Journal of Experimental Psychology: General,* 1979, vol. 108(4), pp. 441-485.

Ayduk, Ozlem, et al. Regulating the Interpersonal Self: Strategic Self-Regulation for Coping With Rejection Sensitivity. *Journal of Personality and Social Psychology,* 2000, vol. 79(5), pp. 776-792.

Breines, Juliana G., and Serena Chen. Self-Compassion Increases Self-Improvement Motivation. *Personality and Social Psychology Bulletin,* 2012, vol. 38(9), pp. 1133-1143.

Brockman, Robert, Joseph Ciarrochi, Philip Parker, and Todd Kashdan. Emotion Regulation Strategies in Daily Life: Mindfulness, Cognitive Reappraisal and Emotion Suppression. *Cognitive Behaviour Therapy,* 2017, vol. 46(2), pp. 1-23.

Caldwell, Jon G., and Phillip R. Shaver. Mediators of the Link Between Adult Attachment and Mindfulness. *Interpersona,* 2013, vol. 7(2), pp. 299-310.

Caldwell, Jon G., and Phillip R. Shaver. Promoting Attachment-Related Mindfulness and Compassion: A Wait-List-Controlled Study of Women Who Were Mistreated During Childhood. *Mindfulness,* 2015, vol. 6(3), pp. 624-636.

Chambers, Richard, Eleonora Gullone, and Nicholas B. Allen. Mindful Emotion Regulation: An Integrative Review. *Clinical Psychology Review,* 2009, vol. 29(6), pp. 560-572.

Cullen, Margaret. Mindfulness-Based Interventions: An Emerging

Phenomenon. *Mindfulness*, 2011, vol. 2(3), pp. 186-193.

Davis, Daphne M., and Jeffrey A. Hays. What Are the Benefits of Mindfulness? A Practice Review of Psychotherapy-Related Research. *Psychotherapy*, 2011, vol. 48(2), pp. 198-208.

Dweck, Carol S. Can Personality Be Changed? The Role of Beliefs in Personality and Change. *Current Directions in Psychological Science*, 2008, vol. 17(6), pp. 391-394.

Elliott, Andrew J., and Todd M. Thrash. The Intergenerational Transmission of Fear of Failure. *Personality and Social Psychology Bulletin*, 2004, vol. 30(8), pp. 957-971.

Gross, James J. Emotion Regulation: Affective, Cognitive, and Social Consequences. *Psychophysiology*, 2002, vol. 39(3), pp. 281-291.

Harris, Adam J. L., and Ulrike Hahn. Unrealistic Optimism About Future Life Events: A Cautionary Note. *Psychological Review*, 2011, vol. 118(1), pp. 135-154.

Howe, Lauren C., and Carol S. Dweck. Changes in Self-Definition Impede Recovery from Rejection. *Personality and Social Psychology Bulletin*, 2015, vol. 42(1), pp. 54-71.

Kircanski, Katharina, Matthew D. Lieberman, and Michelle G. Craske. Feelings into Words: Contributions of Language to Exposure Therapy. *Psychological Science*, 2012, vol. 23(10), pp. 1086-1091.

Koo, Minkyung, Sara B. Algoe, Timothy D. Wilson, and Daniel T. Gilbert. It's a Wonderful Life: Mentally Subtracting Positive Events Improves People's Affective States, Contrary to Their Affective Forecasts. *Journal of Personality and Social Psychology*, 2008, vol. 95(5), pp. 1217-1224.

Legare, Christine H., and André L. Souza. Searching for Control: Priming Randomness Increases the Evaluation of Ritual Efficacy. *Cognitive Science*, 2014, vol. 38, pp. 152-161.

Lieberman, Matthew D., Naomi I. Eisenberger, Molly J. Crockett, Sabrina M. Tom, Jennifer H. Pfeifer, and Baldwin M. Way. Putting Feelings into Words: Affect Labeling Disrupts Amygdala Activity in Response to Affective Stimuli. *Psychological Science*, 2007, vol. 18(5), pp. 421-428.

Neff, Kristin. *Self-Compassion: The Proven Power of Being Kind to Yourself.* New York: William Morrow, 2011.

Neff, Kristin D., et al. The Development and Validation of a Scale to Measure Self-Compassion. *Self and Identity*, 2003, vol. 2, pp. 223-250.

Neff, Kristin D., Ya-Ping Hsieh, and Kullaya Dejitterat. Self-Compassion, Achievement Goals, and Coping with Academic Failure. *Self and Identity*, 2005, vol. 4, pp. 263-287.

Oettingen, Gabriele, and Peter M. Gollwitzer, Strategies of Setting and Implementing Goals: Mental Contrasting and Implementation Intentions, in *Social Psychological Foundations of Clinical Psychology*, edited by James E. Maddux and June Price Tangney, pp. 114-135. New York: Guilford Press, 2010.

Oettingen, Gabriele, Doris Mayer, Jennifer S. Thorpe, Hanna Janetzke, and Solvig Lorenz. Turning Fantasies About Positive and Negative Futures into Self-Improvement Goals. *Motivation and Emotion*, 2005, vol. 29(4), pp. 237-267.

Opitz, Philipp C., Sarah R. Cavanagh, and Heather L. Urry. Uninstructed Emotion Regulation Choice in Four Studies of Cognitive Reappraisal. *Personality and Individual Differences*, 2015, vol. 86, pp. 455-464.

Raes, Filip, Elizabeth Pommier, Kristin D. Neff, and Dinska Van Gucht. Construction and Factorial Validation of a Short Form of the Self-Compassion Scale. *Clinical Psychology & Psychotherapy*, 2011, vol. 18(3), pp. 250-255.

Roisman, Glenn, Elena Padrōn, Alan Sroufe, and Byron Egeland. Earned-Secure Attachment Status in Retrospect and Prospect. *Child Development*, 2002, vol. 73(4), pp. 1204-1219.

Senay, Ibrahim, Dolores Albarracín, and Kenji Noguchi. Motivating Goal-Directed Behavior Through Introspective Self-Talk: The Role of the Interrogative Form of Simple Future Tense. *Psychological Science*, 2010, vol. 21(4), pp. 499-504.

Sharot, Tali, Ryota Kanai, David Marston, Christopher W. Korn, Geraint Rees, and Raymond J. Dolan. Selectively Altering Belief Formation in the Human Brain. *Proceedings of the National Academy of Sciences*, 2012, vol. 109(42), pp. 17058-17062.

Streep, Peg, and Alan Bernstein. *Quitting: Why We Fear It—and Why We Shouldn't—in Life, Love, and Work*. New York: Da Capo, 2015.

Weinstein, Neil D. Unrealistic Optimism About Future Life Events. *Journal of Personality and Social Psychology*, 1980, vol. 39(5), pp. 806-820.

8. Redirecting Your Life: Making Choices

Bowen, Murray. *Family Therapy in Clinical Practice*. London and New York: Rowman & Littlefield Publishers, 2004.

Carver, Charles S., and Michael F. Scheier, *On the Self-Regulation of Behavior*. Cambridge and London: Cambridge University Press, 1998.

Friedman, Richard A. When Parents Are Too Toxic to Tolerate. *The New York Times*, October 19, 2009.

Linville, Patricia W. Self-Complexity and Affective Extremity: Don't Put All of Your Eggs in One Cognitive Basket. *Social Cognition*, 1985, vol. 3(1), pp. 94-120.

Linville, Patricia W. Self-Complexity As a Cognitive Buffer Against Stress-Related Illness and Depression. *Journal of Personality and Social Psychology*, 1987, vol. 52(4), pp. 663-676.

Siegel, Daniel J., and Mary Hartzell, *Parenting from the Inside Out: How a Deeper Understanding Can Help You Raise Children Who Thrive*. New York: Jeremy A. Tarcher/Penguin, 2004.

9. Recovery and Works in Progress

Burnette, Jeni L., et al. Self-Control and Forgiveness: A Meta-Analytic Review. *Social Psychological and Personality Science*, 2013, vol. 5(4), pp. 443-450.

Burnette, Jeni L., Michael E. McCullough, Daryl R. van Tongeren, and Don E. Davis. Forgiveness Results from Integrating Information About Relationship Value and Exploitation Risk. *Personality and Social Psychology Bulletin*, 2012, vol. 38(3), pp. 345-356.

Fincham, Frank. The Kiss of the Porcupines: From Attributing Responsibility to Forgiving. *Personal Relationships*, 2000, vol. 7(1), pp. 1-23.

Fincham, Frank D., Julie Hall, and Steven R. H. Beach. Forgiveness in Marriage: Current Status and Future Directions. *Family Relations*, 2006, vol. 55(4), pp. 415-427.

Kübler-Ross, Elisabeth, and David Kessler. *On Grief and Grieving: Finding the Meaning of Grief Through the Five Stages of Loss*. New York: Scribner, 2005.

Luchies, Laura B., Eli J. Finkel, James K. McNulty, and Madoka Kumashiro. The Doormat Effect: When Forgiveness Erodes Self-Respect and Self-Concept

Clarity. *Journal of Personality and Social Psychology*, 2010, vol. 98(5), pp. 734-749.

McCullough, Michael E. Forgiveness: Who Does It and How Do They Do It? *Current Directions in Psychological Science*, 2001, vol. 10(6), pp. 194-197.

Norton, Michael I., and Francesca Gino. Rituals Alleviate Grieving for Loved Ones, Lovers, and Lotteries. *Journal of Experimental Psychology*, 2014, vol. 143(1), pp. 266-272.

Schore, Judith R., and Allan N. Schore. Regulation Theory and Affect Regulation Psychotherapy: A Clinical Primer. *Smith College Studies in Social Work*, 2014, vol. 84(2-3), pp. 178-195.

Sroufe, Alan, and Daniel Siegel. The Verdict is In: The Case for Attachment Theory. drdansiegel.com/uploads/1271-the-verdict-is-in.pdf.

Zaccagnino, Maria, Martina Cussino, Rachel Saunders, Deborah Jacobvitz, and Fabio Veglia. Alternative Caregiving Figures and their Role on Adult Attachment Representations. *Clinical Psychology and Psychotherapy*, 2014, vol. 21(3), pp. 276-287.

ABOUT THE AUTHOR

Since my bio is on the back of the book and available elsewhere, I figure you don't need to hear about how I trained in literature, was elected to Phi Beta Kappa, and worked in publishing, right? Or that this is my 12th book—if you don't count my anthologies—and that I've been researching and writing about mothers and daughters for just short of twenty years? Okay, here's what a Google search won't tell you.

I'm a first-generation American who never felt she totally belonged or was quite American enough, especially since Dutch was spoken at home and I spent my first 15 summers in Europe. I didn't celebrate the Fourth of July until I was 16! Since I also had an unloving mother who made me feel as though I didn't belong in my own family, my sense of not belonging was pretty intense. The death of my father when I was 15 only made me feel more singled out. But interestingly, that feeling of being outside, looking in, has been a boon to me as a writer, and fuels my passion for this subject and real empathy for the daughters and sons who also share that sense of not belonging.

I am committed to getting a fruitful dialogue going about mothering, and an admission from the culture that maybe thinking of all mothers as loving isn't helpful. And that verbal and emotional abuse are every bit as harmful and damaging as a slap, punch, or worse. I happen to believe that the silence that surrounds these subjects hobbles mothers who are really trying their best and know they're falling short but are too ashamed to ask for help, while isolating daughters who have a story to tell and who deserve to be heard. In truth, mothers can be cruel, heartless, and punitive, and it's about time we collectively acknowledge that fact. I am also given to rants, as you may already have noticed.

Other random things about me you won't find out from a Google search:

♦ I'm someone who loves a cityscape more than a mountain view, but I love gardening.

- I wish I had been married fewer times and had been more successful at it.
- I am a collector of beautiful objects, plants, art, and jewelry.
- I do love to write, and I find people and their stories endlessly interesting.
- I love research and libraries.
- I read lots of poetry, both to relax and to stir up my thinking.
- I love Lifetime movies and chick flicks, as well as serious cinema. There are movies I have seen so often that, hearing just the music, I can recite whole stretches of dialogue.
- I dream of living in Paris or, alternatively, La Jolla, California. That shows a soul in conflict. The likelihood is that I will stay on my granite island where I was born, bounded by the Hudson and an estuary of the Atlantic Ocean, for the foreseeable future.

You can find me on Facebook
(www.Facebook.com/PegStreepAuthor)
and at www.pegstreep.com.